FEDERAL CRIMINAL PRACTICE

■ ■ ■

C.J. Williams
United States Magistrate Judge
U.S. District Court Northern District of Iowa
Adjunct Professor, University of Iowa College of Law

Sean R. Berry
Assistant United States Attorney
Adjunct Professor, University of Iowa College of Law

AMERICAN CASEBOOK SERIES®

WEST
ACADEMIC
PUBLISHING

American Casebook Series is a trademark registered in the U.S. Patent and Trademark Office.

© 2016 LEG, Inc. d/b/a West Academic
    444 Cedar Street, Suite 700
    St. Paul, MN 55101
    1-877-888-1330

West, West Academic Publishing, and West Academic are trademarks of West Publishing Corporation, used under license.

Printed in the United States of America

ISBN: 978-1-63460-356-0

DISCLAIMER

The authors of this text are acting in their private capacities and not as employees of the United States government. All statements made herein reflect only the authors' own positions and statements and not those of the United States of America, the United States Courts, or the United States Department of Justice.

The mock case problem used in conjunction with this text is entirely fictitious. It was not based on any real case, the names and locations are fictionalized, and the United States District Court for the Eastern District of Iowa does not exist.

SUMMARY OF CONTENTS

TABLE OF CONTENTS

TABLE OF CASES

The principal cases are in bold type.

FEDERAL CRIMINAL PRACTICE

CHAPTER 1

INTRODUCTION TO FEDERAL CRIMINAL PRACTICE

■ ■ ■

This course addresses the practice of law in federal criminal cases. The practice of federal criminal law is, in some ways, similar to the practice of criminal law in state courts. There are, however, many significant differences. Certainly, many aspects of federal criminal procedure are unlike state criminal procedure, most notably with regard to the role and use of grand juries in the investigative and charging process. Likewise, the Federal Rules of Evidence contain provisions with unique application in federal criminal cases, the like of which lawyers seldom encounter in state practice. A much more fundamental difference between federal criminal practice and state criminal practice is the nature, length and complexity of the cases.

Generally, federal criminal cases involve matters that affect a national interest. Accordingly, local crimes against individuals or businesses (such as burglary, assault, rape, and the like) seldom become the subject of federal criminal prosecution. Only when otherwise local crimes are tied to a national interest, and there is a basis for federal jurisdiction, does the federal government get involved. For example, armed robbery of a convenience store would typically constitute a local crime, investigated by the local police department and prosecuted by the local county attorney. When, however, that robbery is one in a series of robberies orchestrated by a criminal organization, it may then become the focus of a federal investigation, and federal criminal charges. Federal jurisdiction would be premised on the crime involving interstate commerce. The federal government may take the case because of the impact the robberies have on the national economy or because the size or geographic reach of the criminal organization is beyond the scope of local law enforcement authorities.

This seemingly clear delineation between a state and federal interests, however, is blurry in practice. In response to constituents' demands for more effective law enforcement, Congress has made federal crimes out of acts traditionally prosecuted by the states and which, some argue, should remain within the realm of local prosecution. This sometimes calls upon prosecutors to use their discretion in determining when a case should "go federal" or stay in the state system.

Federal cases also differ from state and local criminal prosecutions because of the length and complexity of the investigations. Most state and local prosecutions are "reactive"; in other words, law enforcement officers react to a crime after it has been committed. Police initiate an investigation of the crime after it occurred, and if successful in procuring evidence, present the case to the district attorney for prosecution. The local prosecutor typically has little or no involvement in the investigation until after the local police officer has completed the investigation and, in many cases, arrested the suspect. Moreover, police officers often make the charging decisions without input from county attorneys, and the county attorneys are then required to either prosecute the case or decline prosecution.

In contrast, federal cases are typically long-term investigations, and are quite often "proactive," meaning that the investigation is focused on continuing or imminent criminal activity, rather than completed crimes. Federal cases are often more complex than typical state or local prosecutions, often involving multiple jurisdictions, multiple defendants, and sophisticated criminal activity. Furthermore, unlike their state counterparts, Assistant United States Attorneys are usually involved in investigations at the earliest stages, sometimes even initiating investigations on their own volition. Federal prosecutors normally work hand-in-hand with federal agents in making tactical and strategic decisions regarding the direction, scope, and nature of the criminal investigation. Similarly, criminal defense attorneys are sometimes involved in defending their clients in federal criminal cases long before indictments are returned by federal grand juries. It is not uncommon, for example, that a white collar defendant discovers he is the subject of federal criminal investigation as a result of the issuance of a grand jury subpoena *duces tecum* (a subpoena requiring production of documents to the grand jury) to the targeted defendant or the defendant's company. Defense attorneys, therefore, often become involved in federal criminal cases during the investigative stages, which opens up possibilities, and reveal pitfalls, for defense attorneys not shared by their state counterparts who typically meet their clients in the jail after the defendants have been arrested.

In order to understand federal criminal practice, one must first have some grounding in the basis for federal jurisdiction in criminal cases. The origin and nature of federal jurisdiction explain, in many ways, how and why federal criminal cases differ from state criminal cases. In this Chapter we will provide some background on the basis for federal criminal jurisdiction. We will also discuss some of the primary federal investigative agencies and the delineation and overlap in their respective areas of control.

Just as it is necessary to understand the origin of federal criminal jurisdiction in order to comprehend the essentials of federal criminal practice, it is likewise necessary to master some basics of federal criminal procedure. This is not a course on Federal Criminal Procedure, but we will explore in this Chapter some of the Federal Rules of Criminal Procedure, their application in a federal criminal investigation and prosecution, and how they sometimes differ from state rules. We will discuss in this Chapter the use of grand juries, the charging process, and the essentials of the discovery process in federal criminal cases.

Also, in this Chapter we will review certain evidentiary rules important in federal criminal practice. Again, this is not an evidence course and it is not our intention here to teach the nuances and niceties of the Federal Rules of Evidence. To play a game of chess, (and federal criminal cases can be said to resemble chess games), a player must have some familiarity with the rules of the game in order to know what moves are possible and which moves are best. This course is designed to teach the fundamentals of "playing the game" of a federal criminal case, so to that end you will become passingly familiar with some basic rules of evidence.

Finally, the last part of this Chapter explains the relationships among investigative agencies and with prosecutors, describes federal criminal prosecutors and the Department of Justice, identifies members of the federal criminal defense bar, and provides an overview of the structure of the federal judiciary. For you fully to appreciate the role of a lawyer in the practice of federal criminal law, it is helpful to have some understanding of how cases are investigated, who investigates the cases, how the cases come to the attention of federal prosecutors, and how the investigators and prosecutors work together. Understanding these relationships is equally important for those students who may be interested in criminal defense work because such knowledge may provide insight valuable in such areas as plea negotiation and cross examination. Likewise, it is helpful to understand the structure of the Department of Justice, the defense bar, and the judiciary in order to understand the players in the drama of federal criminal practice.

A. FEDERAL CRIMINAL JURISDICTION

One of the primary reasons federal criminal practice differs from state criminal practice has to do with the basis for federal jurisdiction. As mentioned in the preface to this book, federal criminal law enforcement is of relatively recent origin. The Constitution did not explicitly provide a basis for federal criminal jurisdiction. Nor was there a tradition in America of participation by the national government in criminal law enforcement. Rather, criminal law enforcement was traditionally the responsibility of state and local governments.

Most cultures have a history of laws and morals enforced by family or village groups. English law enforcement, from which the United States derives many of its legal traditions, shares a similar origin. The enforcement of English laws originated with family units and communities imposing punishment on their own members for violations of accepted norms of behavior. Over time, however, the power to and responsibility for enforcing criminal laws expanded beyond the family unit and village. Law enforcement authority gradually became vested in third-parties, such as local constables and other officials, who owed fealty to the sovereign. As advances were made in communication, transportation and industrialization, the need for and ability of the national government to enforce criminal laws grew.

Similarly, in America, responsibility for criminal law enforcement was historically based in local authorities. Before the American Revolution, colonial governments exercised little power in the enforcement of criminal laws, save that which was necessary for the collection of taxes. Immediately after the Revolution, the newly formed national government lacked the authority under the Articles of Confederation to implement or enforce criminal laws. There was little need for the national government to enter into the field of criminal law enforcement in those days, in any event. Unless a crime affected the national government, such as treason, local law enforcement authorities were better able to discern the local morals and rules of appropriate human behavior and to enforce them at the local level.

The new national government under the United States Constitution created a federal system. Instead of the central government operating as a confederation of sovereign states, the central government became the body politic of a new sovereign nation. The separate states retained their sovereignty within their geographic area, but subordinate to the central government. Under this dual sovereign system, the central government, or federal government, was granted only those powers specifically enumerate in the Constitution, with all other powers retained by the separate states.

The adoption of the Constitution did not alter the tradition of local criminal law enforcement. The Constitution was expressly silent regarding law enforcement except for the limited offenses of counterfeiting,[1] piracy,[2] and treason.[3] The Fourth, Fifth, and Sixth Amendments contemplated enactment of federal criminal laws to the extent they addressed the federal government's power to search and seize

---

[1]   U.S. Const. Art. I, § 8 (granting Congress the power "[t]o provide for the Punishment of counterfeiting the Securities and current Coin of the United States.").

[2]   U.S. Const. Art. I, § 8 (granting Congress the power "[t]o define and punish Piracies and Felonies committed on the high Seas, and Offenses against the Law of Nations.").

[3]   U.S. Const. Art. III, § 3 (defining "Treason against the United States.").

evidence and people, use of a grand jury to charge federal offenses or subject citizens to double jeopardy, and the right to a jury trial, respectfully. But no provision was made in the Constitution or its amendments to expressly identify the power of the federal government to enact criminal laws or to define the scope or jurisdiction of such laws. Moreover, no provision was expressly made in the Constitution for creation of a federal criminal law enforcement apparatus—rather, Congress was granted the broad power to "make all Laws which shall be necessary and proper for carrying into Execution" powers granted it by the Constitution[4] and the executive branch was charged with the responsibility to "take Care that the Laws be faithfully executed."[5]

Federal criminal law essentially began with the enactment of the Crimes Act of 1790, which established some narrowly tailored criminal laws limited to crimes affecting the federal government. The year before, in 1789, Congress created the first federal police agency when it authorized 25 detectives for the Revenue Cutter Service to prevent evasion of import duties by smuggling. The early expansion of federal criminal law arose, however, as crime began affecting the orderly operation of the federal government. The first significant federal criminal laws dealt with crimes affecting the United States Mail. Jurisdiction for the federal government to step into the role of enacting and enforcing criminal laws in these early stages was premised upon a showing that the crime had a direct impact on the federal government. During the civil war, for example, federal criminal jurisdiction expanded to cover counterfeiting when the federal government issued paper money in significant amounts for the first time. Federal criminal jurisdiction remained tied to a showing that the crime directly affected federal property or a federal agency. As federal programs expanded, of course, so too did the scope of federal criminal law.

As the nation developed and industrialized, and transportation and communication between the states increased, there arose a greater need for law enforcement at a national level. As travel and business dealings became more common between states and across state lines, the possibility for crime to have implications beyond the local level also grew. Crimes against individuals, particularly violent crimes, remained the responsibility and primary interest of local authorities. In many case, however, criminal activity was no longer just a local matter. Criminals were increasingly able to conduct fraudulent schemes, moving from one state to another, making it difficult for any single state or local jurisdiction effectively to investigate and prosecute the entirety of the criminal conduct. These crimes, which crossed state boundaries, did not

---

[4]   U.S. Const. Art. I, § 8.
[5]   U.S. Const. Art. II, § 3.

necessarily have a direct impact on federal property or a federal agency, so the traditional basis for federal intervention was not implicated.

In order to address the problem of criminal conduct with interstate impact, therefore, Congress began to wield the federal government's power to tax, and ultimately relied on the Commerce Clause,[6] as grounds for exercising federal jurisdiction over these interstate crimes. The first period of expansion in federal criminal law enforcement coincided with the so-called Progressive Era shortly after the turn of the century and came about as the result of a changing public attitude toward the responsibility of the federal government to effect positive change in society. Responding to public demand, Congress passed a great number of laws using its authority under the Commerce Clause. This fundamentally changed the role of the federal government, and consequently, the role of federal criminal law enforcement. In 1910, two years after its formation, the Federal Bureau of Investigation ("FBI") expanded from eight agents to nearly 300 agents in response to the passage of the White Slave Traffic Act (Mann Act), which prohibited the interstate transportation of women for immoral purposes. Then in 1914, Congress passed the Harrison Act which was designed to regulate the importation and distribution of drugs, the responsibility for which Congress gave to the Bureau of Internal Revenue within the Treasury Department. In response, the Treasury Department created a Narcotics Section within the Department, a precursor to the Drug Enforcement Agency. In 1919, Congress enacted the Dyer Act, prohibiting the interstate transportation of stolen motor vehicles, foisting on the FBI additional responsibilities. Then Congress passed the Narcotic Drug Import and Export Act of 1922, causing Treasury's Narcotics "section" to grow into a "division."

The next significant period of growth occurred as a result of the Great Depression and Prohibition. When the Depression hit the nation in 1929, it added new strains to an already stressed social fabric. A Congressional review concluded that crime was running rampant and was beyond the ability of the state and local governments to control. Congress responded to this national crisis by enacting a host of laws that made it federal offenses to commit crimes against individuals and businesses which had any national impact, however marginal. Thus, for example, during this era it became a federal offense to rob a bank, extort money, or commit a robbery if it affected interstate commerce. In 1934, Congress made it a federal offense to rob a federally-insured bank, flee across state lines to avoid prosecution, engage in interstate racketeering, or transport stolen property across state lines. Congress also made it a federal offense to violate firearm regulations enacted under the National Firearms Act. In addition, President Franklin D. Roosevelt gave the FBI increased responsibilities in the area of counterespionage, domestic

---

[6]   U.S. Const. Art. I, § 8.

espionage, and sabotage. In response, the Federal Bureau of Investigation grew steadily during the Roosevelt administration.

Federal law enforcement continued to grow after World War II, for a number of reasons, such as organized crime, drug abuse, and increased interstate travel and communication. Thus, from 1950 through the 1980s, Congress expanded the scope of federal criminal law. For example, during the 1950s, Congress enacted federal criminal laws related to gambling and the embezzlement of labor union funds, both believed to be areas under the influence of organized crime. In the 1960s, Congress enacted the Travel Act, which prohibits interstate travel in connection with the violation of certain crimes, such as gambling, narcotics, prostitution and bribery, all crimes traditionally prosecuted at the state and local level. Congress also enacted laws making federal offenses out of such acts as the embezzlement of employee benefit plan funds, engaging in riots, and the abuse of guns, explosives, and switchblade knives. The 1970s saw substantive federal criminal legislation relating to racketeering, gambling (again), drugs (again), and the exploitation of children. Finally, in the 1980s and early 1990s, Congress enacted new federal criminal laws relating to such areas as robbery or burglary of pharmacies, hostage taking, counterfeiting securities issued by states, and drive-by shootings, to name a few.

The expansion of federal criminal law enforcement continues today. Whenever criminal conduct has an impact beyond the local level, or for that matter whenever a crime garners national attention in the press, Congress often reacts by enacting new federal criminal laws. Thus, after the terrorist attacks of September 11, 2001, Congress passed legislation, for example, making it a federal crime to help finance terrorist organizations or possess weapons of mass destruction. When it was perceived that criminal schemes involving mortgage financing brought on the Great Recession in 2009, Congress reacted by passing bills which created federal offenses for criminal conduct tied to fraudulent mortgage financial transactions.

Thus, federal criminal law enforcement has expanded greatly during the last 100 years. Its jurisdiction is premised primarily on three grounds: federal property or programs, federal taxing power, and the commerce clause. Thus, some federal criminal statutes rely on the fact that federal property or funds are involved in order to establish federal jurisdiction over the criminal conduct. Examples of this are statutes making it a federal offense to damage federal property, or statutes which make it a crime to commit a fraud involving Medicare funds. Congress premises other federal criminal statutes on the constitutional provision authorizing Congress to enact taxation laws. Examples of these statutes include, of course, the crimes related to the filing of false tax returns, but also include crimes such as possession of a sawed-off shotgun which constitutes a federal offense only if the person fails to register the shotgun and pay a tax on it. Primarily, however, Congress premises most federal criminal statutes upon the commerce clause such that the statute requires the crossing of state lines or some effect on or involvement in interstate commerce for the conduct to constitute a federal offense. The scope of federal criminal law enforcement is likely to continue to expand as people find new ways to commit criminal acts which have a national impact.

B. FEDERAL CRIMINAL PROCEDURE

Criminal procedure involves rules governing the operation of criminal cases through the court system. In many respects, federal criminal procedural rules are similar to most state criminal procedural rules. There are, of course, many nuances and minor differences between federal and state criminal procedures. In the end, however, there are several procedures fairly unique to federal criminal practice, the comprehension of which is essential for a student in this course.

1. DISCOVERY

In most states, there is fairly broad discovery permitted by both sides in criminal cases. Thus, just as in civil cases, in state criminal cases defendants may conduct depositions of government witnesses in order to discover what the witnesses know and what they are likely to say should the case proceed to trial. As a result, in state cases, criminal defense attorneys have a fairly good idea of exactly what evidence the government has in its possession that implicates the defendant, and can reasonably predict what the evidence will look like at trial. In the federal system, in contrast, the discovery process is very different and generally very limited. There is no constitutional right to discovery in federal criminal cases. Rather, a criminal defendant's right to discover the government's evidence is limited to what the government must disclose pursuant to some federal rules and statues. These include Federal Rules of Criminal Procedure 16 and the Jencks Act.

Rule 16 of the Federal Rules of Criminal Procedure generally sets forth the basic discovery rights of both the defendant and the government. Rule 16 requires that the government provide to a defendant any relevant written or recorded statements made by the defendant, in particular any statements made by the defendant to a person then known to him to be a law enforcement officer. Fed. R. Crim. P. 16(a)(1)(A). This includes statements made by a representative of a corporation if that statement could legally bind the corporation. In addition, the government must provide a defendant with a copy of his prior criminal record (Rule 16(a)(1)(B)) and papers, photographs and similar documents "which are material to the preparation of the defendant's defense or are intended for use by the government as evidence in chief at the trial, or were obtained from or belonged to the defendant." Fed. R. Crim. P. 16(a)(1)(C). Rule 16 also requires disclosure of test results (such as drug laboratory reports and fingerprint reports) and expert information. Fed. R. Crim. P. 16(a)(1)(D) & (E).

A quick perusal of Rule 16 demonstrates that strict adherence to that rule would result in defendants receiving very little evidence indeed. For example, federal cases are driven by agent reports (regarding surveillance, interviews agents conduct of witnesses, collection of evidence, and the like), and of grand jury testimony. Rule 16 (a)(2) specifically excludes these key documents from being subject to discovery. In other words, there is nothing in Rule 16 that would typically require the government to produce in discovery the very core documents reflecting the government's investigation.

The Jencks Act (18 U.S.C. § 3500 et seq.), requires the government to provide to a criminal defendant copies of statements made by a government witness on the subject matter upon which that witness is anticipated to testify. The contours of the Jencks Act are addressed in a later chapter. Although the Jencks Act does not require the government to produce these statements until after the witness has testified, that is not a practical or realistic arrangement. Were the government to delay producing Jencks Act statements until after the witness testified, it would necessitate a delay in the proceedings so as to allow the defense attorney time to review the prior statements by the witness in order to conduct an effective cross examination. Federal district courts resolve this unrealistic time table by adopting local rules which require the government to produce Jencks Act statements a few days in advance of trial.

The government also has an obligation to disclose to the defense exculpatory evidence, or information that could impeach a government witness. This is not a discovery obligation, but, rather, a constitutional obligation. The United States must provide defendants with any evidence which would tend to exonerate the defendant as a matter of due process. *Brady v. Maryland*, 373 U.S. 8 (1963). In addition, the United States must provide to the defendant any evidence which would tend to impeach the credibility of a government witness. *Giglio v. United States*, 405 U.S. 150 (1972).

The federal government, then, is in a position to control and severely limit the information it is obliged to provide to a criminal defendant in advance of trial. Should the government err in its judgment of determining what it must disclose to a defendant under Rule 16, the Jencks Act, or pursuant to *Brady* and *Giglio*, however, it risks suppression of evidence, a mistrial, or possibly even dismissal of charges. It can be particularly difficult for a prosecutor to determine what information in its possession is exculpatory or impeaching. Of course, some information can be clearly exculpatory, but more often information is exculpatory only if one knows of the theory of defense. A piece of information may have no apparent value to a prosecutor, but may fit perfectly into a defendant's theory of defense. Because a failure to comply with discovery requirements and with *Brady* and *Giglio* has such dire consequences, many United States Attorney's offices have adopted discovery procedures whereby the entire government discovery file is generally provided to the defense for review. Under this practice, the defense attorney has as much access to the material as the government, and is equally capable of determining whether there is exonerating or impeaching evidence, thus negating the government's responsibility to make those determinations. *See, e.g., United States v. Newton*, 259 F.3d 964 (8th Cir. 2001) (finding that there was no Jencks Act violation when materials were available to defense in the government's open file discovery); *United States v. Johnson*, 751 F.2d 291, 295 (8th Cir. 1984) (open file discovery makes discovery motions unnecessary because defense has access to as much information as the government). The government will often keep out of the open discovery file, however, material that is purely rebuttal evidence and is not part of the case-in-chief. Likewise, in cases involving national security or risks to witnesses or others, a United States Attorney's office may decide, in a particular case, to maintain a closed file and provide the defendant only what is required under the Federal Rules of Criminal Procedure, the Jencks Act, or the Constitution.

Although the government has an obligation to, and in practice does, provide defendants with a fair amount of discovery, defendants, in turn, have very little obligation to provide the government with reciprocal discovery. Rule 16(b) of the Federal Rules of Criminal Procedure outlines a defendant's reciprocal discovery obligations. Generally speaking, a defendant need only provide the government with expert information and the results of tests or examinations. Rule 16(b)(1)(B) & (C). Although a defendant is obligated to provide the government with copies of papers, photographs, and other documents, it need do so only to the extent the defendant intends to introduce those items into evidence in his or her case. Rule 16(b)(1)(A). There is no time frame attached to this category of reciprocal discovery. Thus, some defense attorneys wait until the government presents its entire case before deciding what documents, photographs or other documents he or she intends to introduce in the defense case. Obviously, discovery of those items at that late date is of minimal value to the government. Defendants also have an obligation to produce statements of witnesses the defendant intends to call as witnesses. This is sometimes referred to as "reverse Jencks Act material." Again, this obligation is triggered only when the defendant decides who he is going to call as a witness at trial. So, a defendant can delay disclosure of this reciprocal discovery to the government by delaying the decision of whom to call as witnesses at trial.

2.   DEFENSES UNDER THE FEDERAL RULES OF CRIMINAL PROCEDURE

Rule 12 of the Federal Rules of Criminal Procedure require that certain defenses must be raised before trial. In particular, Rule 12(b) mandates that, unless raised by motion before trial, a defendant waives any defense based on an allegation that the "institution of the prosecution" was defective, or if it is based on an assertion that the indictment or information is defective. Fed. R. Crim. P. 12(b)(1) & (2). Likewise, a defendant must raise pretrial any motion to suppress evidence. Rule 12(b)(3). Further, upon written demand by the government, a defendant must also provide notice of any alibi defense to the government. Fed. R. Crim. P. 12.1. Similarly, a defendant must give notice to the government before trial if he or she intends to rely upon an insanity or diminished capacity defense. Fed. R. Crim. P. 12.2. Finally, if a defendant intends to assert a defense that he was authorized by a legal authority to commit the act for which he has been charged, the defendant must give timely written notice to the government of that defense before the trial. Fed. R. Crim. P. 12.3. We discuss these and other defenses in greater detail in Chapter 8.

C. FEDERAL RULES OF EVIDENCE

This is not an evidence course, yet to learn the skills involved in trying federal criminal cases, it will be necessary for the student of this course to have a basic understanding of the rules of evidence most frequently encountered in trying federal criminal cases. Although many rules of evidence are implicated in both civil and criminal cases, such as the rules governing hearsay evidence, some rules of evidence are particular to federal criminal cases, while other rules, though not limited to federal criminal cases, are more often used in that context than in the civil arena. Accordingly, we will review below some of the rules of evidence of most importance in a federal criminal trial.

1.   CHARACTER EVIDENCE

Rule 404 generally prohibits the admission of character evidence for the purpose of proving "action in conformity therewith on a particular occasion." Fed. R. Evid. 404(a). In other words, the government cannot introduce evidence the defendant committed similar acts for the sole purpose of showing the defendant has the propensity to commit such acts. For example, in the prosecution of a defendant for shooting a teller during a bank robbery, the government cannot introduce evidence that the defendant previously robbed a bank to show that it is more likely that he robbed the bank at issue in the current case. There are exceptions to that rule, however. Rule 404(a)(1) provides that "evidence of a pertinent trait of character" may be "offered by an accused, or by the prosecution to rebut the same." This also applies, with some nuances, to the character of a victim of a crime. Fed. R. Evid. 404(a)(2). Note that this rule applies to a defendant regardless of whether he takes the stand to testify. Rules 608, and 609 (discussed below) address the admission of character traits of witnesses.

Of particular note in federal criminal cases is Rule 404(b) of the Federal Rules of Evidence. That rule provides that evidence of other crimes, wrongs, or acts (which occurred before or after the alleged criminal act) may be admitted if done so for purpose other than propensity, such as a "proof of motive, opportunity, intent, preparation, plan, knowledge, identity, or absence of mistake or accident." Fed. R. Evid. 404(b). Thus, evidence of other wrongful conduct, whether itself criminal or not, may be admitted into evidence, using a preponderance of the evidence standard, to show that the person committed the act, if the evidence of the act is probative of a material issue at trial other than the person's character. *Huddleston v. United States*, 485 U.S. 681 (1988). Although Rule 404(b) is not specifically limited in application to criminal cases, it is seldom used outside that context.

Rule 404(b) evidence can be particularly devastating to a defendant in a criminal case. Returning to the bank robber, for example; although the government cannot introduce evidence the defendant previously robbed another bank to show propensity, it could introduce that evidence to show the defendant knew the security measures at a bank, or to show how he planned or prepared for the instant robbery, or to show intent or motive. In other words, the government can introduce such evidence for any reason, so long as it is not solely for the purpose to show propensity. Because this evidence can be misused by a jury for propensity, courts will often provide a limiting instruction to the jury to ensure the jury uses the evidence only for the intended, permitted purpose.

Rule 404(b) also contains a quasi-discovery requirement. If requested by the defense, the government must "provide reasonable notice in advance of trial, or during trial if the court excuses pretrial notice on good cause shown, of the general nature of any such evidence it intends to introduce at trial."

With respect to a witness's character, Rule 608 provides that "the credibility of a witness may be attacked or supported by evidence in the form of opinion or reputation" subject to certain limitations. Fed. R. Evid. 608(a). First, the evidence must relate to the witnesses' character for truthfulness, and second, it may only be introduced after the witnesses' truthfulness has been attacked. Fed. R. Evid. 608(a). To avoid the possibility of delays during trial, or jurors becoming confused or misled by testimony concerning specific instances of truthful or untruthful conduct, evidence of specific instances is inadmissible except with respect to prior convictions. Fed. R. Evid. 608(b).

2. PRIOR CONVICTIONS

Rule 609 governs the admissibility of prior convictions—evidence of specific conduct that goes to the character trait of honesty. Rule 609 is quite often applied in federal criminal cases for obvious reasons. There are two components to Rule 609: the nature of the crime and the age of the conviction. Within the first component, there are two additional subcomponents: whether the conviction is for a felony or whether it is a conviction involving dishonesty or false statement. Finally, within the felony component, there are again two sub components: whether the evidence is being offered against the criminal defendant, or whether it is being offered against a witness other than the criminal defendant.

If the prior conviction was a felony offense (and not, at the same time, a crime involving a false statement or dishonesty), the evidence may be used against a witness *other than the criminal defendant* if it passes the Rule 403 test (*i.e.*, danger of unfair prejudice does not substantially outweigh probative value). Fed. R. Evid. 609(a)(1). If the prior conviction is for a felony offense and the witness *is the criminal defendant*, then it may be admitted if the probative value outweighs the danger of unfair prejudice (sort of the opposite of Rule 403). If the prior conviction involved a crime of dishonesty or a false statement, then it is admissible regardless of whether it was a felony offense and regardless of whether the witness is also the defendant. Fed. R. Evid. 609(a)(2).

The time component is covered in Rule 609(b). Rule 609 generally permits the use of such prior convictions to impeach witnesses, so long as the conviction or release from custody occurred within the prior ten years, though older convictions may be admitted into evidence by the court if the proponent of the evidence gives advance notice to the other side and the court finds good cause. Fed. R. Evid. Rule 609(b). There are additional nuances to the rule, addressing such matters as pardons (Rule 609(c)), juvenile convictions (Rule 609(d)), and convictions on appeal (Rule 609(e)), but they are more rarely encountered and better addressed in an evidence class.

3. HEARSAY IN FEDERAL CRIMINAL CASES

By this subheading we do not mean to suggest that there are hearsay rules applicable to federal criminal cases which are different from those applicable to civil cases: they are all the same. Rather, there are a few of the hearsay rules which are more commonly confronted in federal criminal trials with which you should be familiar.

Hearsay is defined as "a statement, other than one made by the declarant while testifying at the trial or hearing, offered in evidence to prove the truth of the matter asserted." Fed. R. Evid. 801(c). It is important to recognize that in federal criminal cases that there are statements which, though they may fit this definition, are nonetheless deemed not to constitute hearsay. First, certain prior statements by the witness are not hearsay. Fed. R. Evid 801(d)(1). There are two main categories of prior statements which are not hearsay: 1) prior statements by the witness who is testifying at trial, and; 2) prior statements by one of the parties.

There are three categories of prior statements by a witness which are not considered hearsay. The first is prior statements made under oath (such as grand jury testimony) which are *inconsistent* with the testimony offered during the trial. Fed. R. Evid. 801(d)(1)(A). The second is prior *consistent* statements which are introduced to prove that the witness's testimony at trial was not recently fabricated. Fed. R. Evid. 801(d)(1)(B). Note that this second category of prior statement need not be under oath, so a prior consistent statement to a police officer may, for example, be introduced under these circumstances. Finally, a prior statement which constituted an identification of a person is not hearsay. Fed. R. Evid. 801(d)(1)(C). So, for example, it is not hearsay for a bank teller to testify during trial that after the bank robbery she was shown a photo array and stated to the FBI agent: "The guy in the third picture is the robber."

The other category of prior statements which are not considered hearsay is those made by one of the parties. Fed. R. Evid. 801(d)(2). These include a defendant's own statements, a statement by someone authorized to speak for a defendant, and statements made by a defendant's agent. These last two categories are encountered often when the defendant is a company or corporation.

It is also important to know that statements by co-conspirators are not hearsay. Fed. R. Evid. 801(d)(2)(E). In other words, if two people are involved in a conspiracy to commit an offense, and in the process one of them makes a statement during the course of the conspiracy, and the statement was made in some way in furtherance of the conspiracy, then it is deemed an admission by all the conspirators and admissible against any of them. Note that the statements must be made during the existence of the conspiracy, *United States v. Perez*, 989 F.2d 1574 (10th Cir. 1993), and must be made in furtherance of the conspiracy. *United States v. Santiago*, 837 F.2d 1545 (11th Cir. 1988). A prosecutor must be careful, however, when introducing evidence under this Rule, for if a trial judge determines that the statement was not made by a member of the conspiracy, or not made during the conspiracy or in furtherance of the conspiracy, the court may have to declare a mistrial. *Bourjaily v. United States*, 483 U.S. 171, 176–77 (1987).

4. EXCEPTIONS TO THE HEARSAY RULE

There are many exceptions to the hearsay rule, but we are not going to review them all here. Rather, we will simply note some of the exceptions most commonly encountered in federal criminal trials. These include business records, public records, criminal convictions, and prior sworn testimony. The reason that these out-of-court statements are exceptions to the rule excluding hearsay is because they are deemed reliable due to the manner in which the statements were made or recorded.

The so-called business records exception to the hearsay rule applies regardless of whether the witness is available to testify. Under Rule 803(6), any record or report generated and maintained in the regular course of business is an exception to the hearsay rule. Thus, for example, a bank record indicating that a defendant made a deposit of money on a given day is not hearsay, even though it is a prior statement by the clerk making that entry and it is being introduced to prove that the defendant did make that deposit. Of course, a party still must lay a foundation for the document (*i.e.*, it is, in fact, a true record of the defendant's account from the bank). Along the same lines, the absence of a record which would normally be made in the regular course of business is also an exception to the hearsay rule. Fed. R. Evid. 803(7). For example, the absence of a record of the defendant entering his safe deposit box is not hearsay if, had he done so as claimed, there would, in the normal course of business, have been a record of it.

Public records and reports are also excluded from the rule barring hearsay. Fed. R. Evid. 803(8). This includes records of public agencies setting forth the activities of the agency and matters observed pursuant to official duty. Importantly, police reports and other reports by law enforcement officers are specifically excluded from this exception. Fed. R. Evid. 803(8)(B). Further, reports containing factual findings from an investigation are admissible only against the government in criminal cases. Fed. R. Evid. 803(8)(C). Just as with business records, the absence of a public document is also considered an exception to the hearsay rule. Fed. R. Evid. 803(10).

Records showing a prior criminal conviction do not constitute hearsay. Fed. R. Evid. 803(22). Of course, since such records are always public records, this specific exception is largely redundant of Rule 803(8). Interestingly, however, this rule applies only to felony convictions and excludes such records except for purposes of impeachment against any witness other than a criminal defendant.

If the person who made the prior statement is not available (as defined in Fed. R. Evid. 804(a)), prior sworn testimony is considered an exception to the hearsay rule if the party against whom it is offered had the same or similar motive to develop the testimony as the person who previously asked the questions. Fed. R. Evid. 804(b)(1). This rule is often most often used against the government in federal criminal cases because often the only prior sworn testimony is grand jury testimony. The government, in contrast, cannot use prior grand jury testimony as evidence because no defense attorney was present during the grand jury examination.

A prior statement made by a witness who is unavailable at the time of trial is not considered hearsay if the statement was made against the person's interest or tended to subject the person to criminal liability. Fed. R. Evid. 804(b)(3). In federal criminal cases, this rule most often arises when one criminal has made a prior statement implicating himself and the defendant in a crime, and the other criminal is unavailable because of his Fifth Amendment right against self-incrimination. Under these circumstances, the parties must also grapple with the implications of a criminal defendant's right under the Sixth Amendment to confront witnesses against him. We will not delve into the morass of case law dealing with this issue other than to make you aware that these statements, although they fall into an exception to the hearsay rule, are generally not admissible because they violate a defendant's rights under the Sixth Amendment. *Bruton v. United States*, 391 U.S. 123 (1968). There are ways around this problem, however, such as redacting the prior statement to exclude a specific reference to the defendant. *See, e.g., United States v. Logan*, 210 F.3d 820, 821–23 (8th Cir. 2000).

Of course, there is nothing more important or fundamental in trying any case, including a federal criminal case, than to know how to lay a foundation and authenticate tangible evidence, such as papers, photographs, handwriting samples, and the like. Rule 901 of the Federal Rules of Evidence sets forth the basis for authenticating evidence. The fundamental task is to demonstrate that an item is what you claim it is. Logic will, in many cases, dictate how you prove this. With handwriting for example, you prove that certain handwriting belongs to the defendant by having people familiar with the handwriting say so, or have an expert say so. You should be aware that certain documents are self-authenticating (such as certified public documents), meaning that because of the way they are generated and kept, it is clear on their face that they are what you claim them to be. Fed. R. Evid. 902.

As stated above, this is not a course on the Federal Rules of Criminal Procedure or the Federal Rules of Evidence. Rather, we have reviewed some of the primary rules so that you have a sufficient basis in order to better understand how to play the game of trying a federal criminal case.

D. INVESTIGATORS, PROSECUTORS, AND DEFENSE ATTORNEYS

Federal cases arise from a variety of sources, and are investigated by a variety of agencies. A significant number of federal criminal cases start as investigations by state or local law enforcement officers, or as a result of a cooperative effort between state or local law enforcement agencies with federal law enforcement agencies. Although we discussed the sources of federal jurisdiction above, the goal of this section is to explain more the mechanics of how a case gets started in the federal pipe line. We will also briefly describe federal prosecutors and defense attorneys in federal criminal cases. Finally, we will outline the federal judicial positions and the roles played by the various judges in the federal criminal justice system.

1. INVESTIGATORS

There are a large number of federal agencies that have law enforcement authority. Most people are familiar with, or have at least heard of, the Federal Bureau of Investigation (FBI), the Drug Enforcement Administration (DEA), and the Bureau of Alcohol, Tobacco, Firearms, and Explosives (ATF), as federal law enforcement agencies. Few people are aware, however, that the United States Department of Agriculture, the Environmental Protection Agency, the Department of Transportation, the Veterans Administration, and even the Federal Railroad Retirement Board, to name just a few examples, each have federal agents who are responsible for law enforcement in their own special areas. There are more than fifty major federal law enforcement agencies in existence today. The FBI has more than 13,000 agents, the DEA more than 4,500 agents, and the ATF has more than 1,600 agents. The federal law enforcement community has grown significantly in pace with the growth of the number of federal criminal statutes enacted by Congress. This has required agencies to stake out areas of primary jurisdiction so that law enforcement efforts are not duplicated.

Federal law enforcement agencies often work in close association with state and local law enforcement agencies. Depending on the crime, it is often the state or local agency that arrives first on the scene of a crime and conducts the majority (if not all) of the investigation. For example, in bank robbery cases, the local police are the primary investigative authorities and the FBI often assumes a coordinating and assisting role.

On the other hand, other cases, such as those involving international espionage, will rarely involve any state or local law enforcement except in a supporting role. Within the last several decades, a major development in federal law enforcement has been the establishment of joint state and federal task forces. Their purpose has been to combine the resources of all levels of government and to increase the cooperation and communication between them in order more effectively to enforce the criminal laws. In these circumstances, when a case is investigated by one of these task forces and the crime (say, drug distribution) could be prosecuted by either the state or federal government, the agents and prosecutors must decide which jurisdiction is the most effective place to prosecute the defendant.

2. PROSECUTORS

Federal attorneys prosecute the defendants arrested by all these federal law enforcement agencies. The number of federal prosecutors has increased to keep pace with the increased demands Congress has placed upon the executive branch to conduct criminal law enforcement. As previously noted, the Judiciary Act of 1789 created the office of Attorney General of the United States and fourteen United States Attorneys. Today, federal prosecutors, in the Criminal Division of the United States Department of Justice and in each of the 94 United States Attorneys offices across the country, number more than 8,000, a substantial increase from the original fourteen spots created by the Judiciary Act of 1789.

The United States Department of Justice is comprised of the offices in Washington, D.C. (so-called "Main Justice"), and 94 United States Attorney's' Offices located in each of the federal judicial districts throughout the United States and its territories (Puerto Rico, Guam, the Northern Mariana Islands, and the U.S. Virgin Islands). The United States Department of Justice in Washington consists of several divisions, including the Criminal Division, Civil Division, and National Security Division. Based in Washington, D.C., the Criminal Division includes litigation components engaged in active criminal prosecutions. There are numerous components or units, each of which focuses on a particular area of federal criminal conduct. Thus, the sections or units include: Narcotics and Dangerous Drugs Section, Capital Case Section, Fraud Section, Environmental Crimes Section, Organized Crime Unit, Gang Unit, Criminal Tax Unit, and the Public Integrity Section, to name a few. These components are sometimes solely responsible for the prosecution of crimes within their specialty, and on other occasions, team up with Assistant United States Attorneys in the district where the crime occurred. So, for example, a prosecutor from the Environmental Crimes Section of the Criminal Division may have sole responsibility for prosecuting the violation of an environmental crime statute in the Northern District of

Florida. On the other hand, a prosecutor from the Capital Case Section of the Criminal Division may second-chair an Assistant United States Attorney prosecuting a death penalty case in same Northern District of Florida.

United States Attorneys' Offices can be thought of as "field offices" of "Main Justice." They are part of the Department of Justice headed by the Attorney General of the United States. Each United States Attorney's Office, however, is headed by the United States Attorney for that district. The United States Attorney is appointed by the President of the United States and confirmed by the Senate. Each United States Attorney's Office is comprised of a number of Assistant United States Attorneys, some of whom will work on civil matters, but the majority of whom will be federal prosecutors. Although the management structure may be unique to each United States Attorney's Office, there is often a First Assistant United States Attorney (who is second in command), a Criminal Chief (in charge of all of the prosecutors in the office), and a Senior Litigation Counsel (who handles or oversees complex criminal cases, and provides assistance and training to all of the other prosecutors in the office). Depending on the size of the United States Attorney's Office, there are sometimes further sections or units within a criminal division, such as a White Collar Crime Section, Violent Crimes Section, General Crimes Section, or Narcotics Crimes Section. The sizes of United States Attorneys' Offices vary significantly from district to district with some in the larger cities like Los Angles, Chicago, and New York employing hundreds of Assistant United States Attorneys, while other districts like the Northern District of Iowa may count only 25 to 35 Assistant United States Attorneys.

As discussed above, federal prosecutors generally take a very active role in federal criminal cases, even during the early investigative stages of cases. In some instances, federal prosecutors may even initiate an investigation by asking a federal agency to look into a matter which has come to the prosecutor's attention through another case, the press, or some other source. In most cases, however, the prosecutor is brought into the case after some initial investigation by a state or federal law enforcement agency. Often a case is presented to the prosecutor at the point in time when the agent has developed a reasonable suspicion, or possibly probable cause to believe, that a specific person has committed a crime.

Agents contact the federal prosecutor at early stages of an investigation to obtain the assistance of the Assistant United States Attorney in furthering the investigation. Prosecutors may be of assistance in evaluating a criminal case, determining areas of investigation, or by identifying crimes that may have been committed. It is also often necessary that agents consult an Assistant United States Attorney in order to access investigation tools available only through a prosecutor and not otherwise available to an agent. The primary example of this is the power of a grand jury subpoena. This subpoena power permits the federal government to subpoena documents and/or people in order to further investigate the leads developed by the agent. Federal grand jury subpoena power is national in scope. In other words, a federal prosecutor in Iowa can compel the appearance of any witness, or the production of any document or tangible thing, before an Iowa federal grand jury from any state in the Union, or from any territory over seas controlled by the United States. Witnesses cannot "opt out" or choose not to comply with the subpoena because of inconvenience. Failure to comply with a federal grand jury subpoena may constitute contempt of court and a recalcitrant witness may find himself escorted to Iowa in handcuffs in the company of United States Marshals.

Another principal tool available through an Assistant United States Attorney is the ability to conduct search warrants. Although not technically necessary, most (if not all) federal courts have adopted rules requiring an Assistant United States Attorney to be involved with the preparation and presentation of a federal search warrant application to a federal judicial officer. This is quite different from most states where police officers usually apply directly to a local judges for search warrants without ever notifying the local prosecutor. In practice, Assistant United States Attorneys are integrally involved with federal agents in assessing whether to search locations, what locations should be searched, what items should be searched for in the location, whether probable cause exists to search for those items in those locations. Assistant United States Attorneys are also involved in the actual drafting of search warrant applications and the critical agents' affidavits setting forth the facts establishing probable cause for the search warrants.

There are other investigative tools available to federal agents only through the auspices of the United States Attorney's Office. These include such things as wire taps (recording people's telephone conversations or electronic communications), pen registers (recording data about telephone calls, but not the conversation), and obtaining tax returns, to name a few. A discussion of these and other investigative methods are discussed in more detail in the next chapter.

From the point in time that the agent comes to the Assistant United States Attorney, the prosecutor often becomes an active member of the investigative team. The prosecutor must focus not only on the determination of whether a crime was committed and who committed it, but more important, how to prove in court that the suspect committed the crime. Ultimately, it is the prosecutor's decision whether to present the investigation to a grand jury for purposes of seeking an indictment.

To bring a federal criminal charge against a person is an exercise of awesome power. A federal prosecutor must take great care to wield that power responsibly.

> The United States Attorney is the representative not of an ordinary party to a controversy, but of a sovereignty whose obligation to govern impartially is as compelling as its obligation to govern at all; and whose interest, therefore, in a criminal prosecution is not that it shall win a case, but that justice shall be done. As such, he is in a peculiar and very definite sense a servant of the law, the twofold aim of which is that guilt shall not escape or innocence suffer. He may prosecute with earnestness and vigor—indeed, he should do so. But, while he may strike hard blows, he is not at liberty to strike foul ones. It is as much his duty to refrain from improper methods calculated to produce a wrongful convictions as it is to use every legitimate means to bring about a just one.

Berger v. United States, 295 U.S. 78, 88 (1935).

3. DEFENSE ATTORNEYS

The federal criminal justice system is incomplete and inequitable without counsel to represent the accused. Just as prosecuting federal criminal cases carries awesome responsibilities, so too does defending those accused of often complex federal crimes which often carry very harsh penalties. There are three sources for federal defense counsel: Federal Public Defenders, Criminal Justice Act attorneys, and privately retained counsel. Each is discussed briefly below.

Federal Public Defenders are employees of the judicial branch—the United States Courts—and are appointed to represent defendants who cannot afford counsel. They are paid by salary, so their compensation remains the same regardless of the hours devoted to their cases. Generally speaking, Federal Public Defenders are some of the most highly trained, well-educated, and experienced defense attorneys in the federal criminal justice system. Their positions are highly coveted among defense attorneys, and they carry great respect with federal prosecutors and federal judges.

There are not enough Federal Public Defenders to represent all those accused of federal offenses, however, and conflicts of interest also sometimes prevent Federal Public Defenders from representing some indigent defendants. The Criminal Justice Act, Title 18, United States Code, Section 3006A, was enacted to provide a means for the federal courts to appoint attorneys to represent indigent defendants who are not represented by Federal Public Defenders. These "CJA attorneys" consequently represent the vast majority of federal criminal defendants.

To become a CJA attorney, a criminal defense lawyer must have a certain level of experience and demonstrated competence in the federal court room. The district court judges, together with the Federal Public Defender's Office, evaluate applications by attorneys to serve as CJA attorneys, and continue to review performance of the attorneys to ensure competence. Unless an attorney is approved, a federal court will not appoint the attorney to represent a federal criminal defendant. CJA panel attorneys are paid an hourly rate; at the time this book was published, it was set by statute at $127.00 an hour in noncapital cases, and $181.00 an hour in capital cases, with waivable maximum payments in non-capital cases.

The final source for representation is privately retained counsel. A defendant generally has the right to representation of choice, so he or she may hire who they wish to represent them, regardless of experience level. That said, the attorney must either be licensed to appear in federal court, or have permission from the judge to appear on the particular case. Federal courts do not oversee this type of representation, or supervise fee arrangements. As one can imagine, the quality of representation provided by privately retained defense attorneys varies greatly.

4.   JUDICIAL POSITIONS

The structure of the federal judiciary applicable to federal criminal practice is a product of Article III of the United States Constitution and the Federal Magistrate's Act of 1968.[7] The structure includes lower-level judges who handle the initial criminal procedures short of trial, trial judges, and appellate judges. We will briefly identify each of the judges, how they are selected, the scope of their authority, and the nature of their role in federal criminal practice.

The first echelon of the judiciary a criminal defendant encounters in the federal criminal justice system is Federal Magistrate Judges. These judges are chosen by the district court judges based on candidate identified through a merit selection process, and serve eight-year renewable terms. Their authority is limited by statute and they cannot exercise powers granted to judges under Article III of the United States Constitution. Without delving in great detail into the precise authority granted Federal Magistrate Judges, suffice it to say that in federal criminal cases these judges can handle almost everything short of trial and sentencing. So, agents and prosecutors often see federal magistrate judges to obtain search warrants and arrest warrants, or in many other instances when judicial approval is necessary for investigative procedures. It is a federal magistrate judge who presides over the initial pretrial proceedings involved in federal criminal cases, such as initial

---

[7]   H.R. Rep. No. 1629, 90th Cong., 2d Sess., 11 (1968).

appearances and arraignments, discovery motions, and the like. A federal magistrate judge does not have statutory authority to rule on dispositive motions, such as motions to suppress evidence or dismiss a case, but federal trial judges often delegate to federal magistrate judges the responsibility to preside over hearings on these motions and to then issue a Report and Recommendation (commonly referred to as an "R&R") to the trial judge. In the R&R, a federal magistrate judge will set out the court's factual findings, legal analysis, and conclusion and then recommend to the trial judge how the trial judge should rule on the dispositive motion. The parties can object to the federal magistrate judge's R&R, and review is *de novo* by the trial judge. Likewise, many trial judges also delegate to federal magistrate judges the responsibility to preside over change of plea hearings where criminal defendants enter guilty pleas. Because this is obviously dispositive regarding the charges, the federal magistrate judge cannot formally accept a guilty plea. Rather, the magistrate judge will issue an R&R, and the trial judge makes the formal acceptance of the guilty plea. Finally, federal magistrate judges cannot preside over a federal criminal felony trial, but can preside over misdemeanor trials. Trial judges will often ask magistrate judges to preside over the jury selection portion of federal felony trials, which is permissible so long as both parties consent.

Federal trial judges are known as District Court Judges whose authority is found in Article III of the United States Constitution. Article III authorizes Congress to appoint a Supreme Court and "such inferior courts as the Congress may from time to time ordain and establish." All Article III judges are nominated by the President of the United States and confirmed by the Senate. They serve for life, during which time their compensation cannot be decreased. U.S. Const. Art. III, § 1. Article III judges have judicial power over all cases in law and equity under the Constitution or the law of the United States. U.S. Const. Art. III, § 2. With regard to District Court Judges, in particular, this means that they can preside over and decide any matter properly brought in federal court. In federal criminal cases, therefore, District Court Judges can rule on dispositive motions, preside over felony trials, and sentence criminal defendants. District Court Judges have authority on cases arising in their federal judicial district. As mentioned, there are 94 such districts. Some states have a single district (such as Minnesota) while other states have two or more districts within the state (Iowa, for example, has two judicial districts, geographically divided into the Northern and Southern Districts of Iowa).

Above United States District Courts are appellate courts and the United States Supreme Court. There are twelve United States Courts of

Appeal, which are referred to as Circuit Courts of Appeal.[8] Each is comprised of a number of districts. The Eighth Circuit Court of Appeals, for example, is comprised of all the United States District Courts in North and South Dakota, Nebraska, Minnesota, Iowa, Missouri, and Arkansas. The appellate courts determine whether the law was applied properly by the district courts. So, in a federal criminal case, the parties may appeal decisions by the district court to the court of appeals. In some circumstances, parties can seek review of a district court's pretrial rulings. This is called an interlocutory appeal. In federal criminal cases, a criminal defendant has the right to appeal his or her case to the court of appeals, and the government can sometimes appeal district court rulings when the defendant is convicted of an offense. Appellate cases are typically heard and decided by a panel of three United States Circuit Judges randomly drawn from all the appellate judges in the circuit. On occasion, all of the judges will hear and decide a case, sitting *en banc*, meaning the entire court is present.

Finally, the United States Supreme Court reviews decisions made by the United States Courts of Appeal. A criminal defendant does not have a right to review by the Supreme Court in federal criminal cases. Rather, a criminal defendant can petition the Supreme Court to review his or her case by filing a Petition for a Writ of Certiorari. The United States Supreme Court reviews very few of the total number of federal criminal cases handled by district courts each year. So, when the Supreme Court does issue an opinion in a federal criminal case, it often has dramatic impact on federal criminal practice.

---

[8]   There is a thirteenth appellate court, called the Court of Appeals for the Federal Circuit, which has nationwide jurisdiction to hear appeals in specialized areas, such as patent cases, but that court does not pertain to federal criminal practice.

CHAPTER 2

INVESTIGATION OF FEDERAL OFFENSES

■ ■ ■

It is important for attorneys, representing both the government and criminal defendants, to understand how the government investigates federal offenses. As indicated in the preceding chapter, attorneys on both sides of the courtroom must understand the investigative process because in federal criminal cases, unlike most state cases, the attorneys are often intimately involved in a federal criminal case during the investigation stage. Thus, effective representation of the government and potential defendants requires a working knowledge of the investigative methods used by federal agents.

Federal prosecutors often work hand-in-hand with federal agents in determining the direction, scope and nature of federal criminal investigations. Assistant United States Attorneys will often make fundamental decisions concerning the investigation, such as whom to question, what locations can and should be searched, what documents should be subpoenaed, and the timing of each step of the investigation. Unlike most state prosecutors, federal prosecutors work with agents in drafting affidavits in support of search warrants and in determining whether there is probable cause to conduct a search. Federal prosecutors are often involved determining which investigation tool can and should be used by the agents. When evidence is collected as a result of the investigation, federal prosecutors will not leave to the agents the job of sifting through the evidence. Rather, the prosecutors will often roll up their sleeves and plow through the evidence alongside the agents, particularly in white collar cases where the evidence consists primarily of documents.

Likewise, in many federal criminal cases, particularly in white collar cases, defense attorneys become aware that their clients are under investigation before charges have even been filed. When this occurs, defense attorneys often undertake an active role investigating the cases on behalf of their clients at the same time the federal government is conducting its investigations. Criminal defense attorneys will sometimes hire their own private investigators to conduct interviews, obtain records, conduct surveillance, and take other investigative steps similar to those performed by federal law enforcement agents. Indeed, not infrequently the private investigator hired by the defense attorney is a retired or former federal, state, or local law enforcement agent or officer. Defense attorneys will, like their prosecutor counterparts, work with their private investigators to determine the nature and scope of the defense investigation. Defense attorneys will also slog through boxes of documents, either those produced by their clients or their clients' companies in response to grand jury subpoenas, or documents which their clients produce or to the attorneys, but may not have been produced to the government.

This chapter will explore some of the investigative techniques used in federal criminal investigations. The primary focus will be on investigative tools and techniques used by the federal government. Although there is a short section regarding investigative techniques used by defense attorneys, you should bear in mind that opposite many government investigative efforts, an active defense attorney will be probing where possible.

A. GOVERNMENT CRIMINAL INVESTIGATIONS

This section will briefly address some of the more common criminal investigative methods and techniques allowed by law which are utilized by the federal government. The focus will primarily be on those methods which call upon input from and participation by federal prosecutors. This section will not attempt to mention every investigative technique, nor will it delve into detail regarding the mechanics or technical aspects of some of the methods. Likewise, this section does not attempt to summarize the many judicial opinions which address the scope and limitations of these investigative methods under the Constitution. The purpose of this section is only to alert students to some basic investigative techniques so that they can understand how federal criminal cases can be investigated and, more important, how federal prosecutors and defense attorneys are involved in the investigation stage of a federal criminal case.

Criminal investigation methods fall into two broad categories: covert investigations and overt investigations. Within the category of covert, or secret, investigations, common investigative techniques include: 1) use of the grand jury to subpoena certain types of records; 2) monitoring of communication; 3) undercover operations; 4) surveillance; and 5) covert evidence collection. Within the category of overt, or open, investigations, there are such investigative methods as: 1) use of the grand jury to subpoena certain types of documents or question witnesses; 2) search warrants; 3) witness interviews; 4) document and record collection; and 5) overt evidence collection. These are not, by any means, all of the methods available to federal law enforcement officers. Further, in discussing some of these methods, we will only briefly mention the nature of the investigative method and address some legal issues. The student should be aware that there is a large body of statutory and case law which addresses each of the investigative methods mentioned.

A criminal investigation should almost always exploit and use all covert methods of investigation first before going overt. This ensures that the evidence can be collected without the target of the investigation knowing about the investigation and doing anything to destroy or alter evidence. It also increases the possibility of obtaining incriminating evidence from the target through undercover operations and the like. Prosecutors work with agents to weigh the benefits of covert investigation techniques against other considerations, such as whether the defendant may pose a danger to the public, or whether evidence may be lost if an overt method is not used. For example, the government may judge it necessary to execute a search warrant at the defendant's house to seize a shipment of cocaine to prevent the loss of the evidence or the danger to the public posed by the controlled substance, even though by doing so there will be no more chance of conducting a covert investigation.

1. COVERT INVESTIGATIONS

As a category, covert investigations encompass some of what people typically consider to be traditional law enforcement investigative techniques. For a number of reasons, law enforcement officers attempt to conduct as much of an investigation in secret as possible. These reasons include a desire to prevent the destruction of evidence by targets, to prevent the suspect from fleeing the jurisdiction, and to prevent witness intimidation or elimination.

a. Grand Jury Investigations

The use of the grand jury as an investigative tool is more fully discussed in the following chapter. Suffice it to say here that the investigative power of the grand jury is its power to issue subpoenas. Grand jury subpoenas can be used to secure the testimony of witnesses and the production of documents or objects. Grand jury subpoenas can be used to obtain almost any kind of record, including medical files, bank records, credit reports, and the like. A federal grand jury subpoena is nationwide in scope; in other words, a grand jury in Iowa can subpoena any person or any document located anywhere in the United States or its territories.

Grand jury proceedings are conducted in secret. Under Rule 6(e) of the Federal Rules of Criminal Procedure, generally only the prosecutor, the court reporter, the witness, the grand jurors, and, when necessary, interpreters are permitted to be in the grand jury room while testimony is obtained. Witnesses who appear before grand juries may divulge to others the questions asked and the answers given during the grand jury session, but all other parties who are present are sworn to secrecy. Fed. R. Crim.

P. Rule 6(e). Further, documents produced pursuant to the grand jury subpoena are similarly held in confidence by the grand jury and the government. Except with respect to certain types of documents in certain types of criminal investigations, however, a person or entity can reveal to others the fact of the subpoena and disclose what was produced to the grand jury. So, for example, federal law prohibits a financial institution from disclosing anything about a grand jury subpoena if the investigation involves potential money laundering charges.[1] The financial institution could, however, reveal the existence of the grand jury subpoena for the same documents if the investigation involved a different crime, like kidnapping.

Grand jury investigations, therefore, are sometimes covert and sometimes overt. If the witness or entity subpoenaed keeps the information confidential, either because they are bound to do so or chose to do so, then the grand jury investigation could occur and remain covert. In other circumstances, a criminal suspect may know that he or she is the subject of a grand jury investigation because friends, family, or an entity disclose the existence of the subpoena to the target. Absent witnesses divulging the information about their own appearance before the grand jury, a criminal suspect and his or her attorney would not know what occurred before the grand jury. If a witness or entity reveals to a criminal suspect the existence of the subpoena and the information disclosed to the grand jury, then, of course, the grand jury investigation is no longer covert.

There are other times when the grand jury investigation is overt because it directly involves the prospective defendant or his or her corporation. For example, a prosecutor may extend an invitation to a prospective defendant to testify before the grand jury, although it is the policy of the United States Department of Justice generally not to subpoena a target of the investigation to testify before the grand jury. United States Attorney's Manual 9–11.150. A prosecutor may constitutionally subpoena a target before the grand jury, but Department of Justice policy requires prior approval of the United States Attorney for the district or the responsible Assistant Attorney General. Grand jury subpoenas may also be used to obtain handwriting or voice exemplars from the defendant, or the defendant's fingerprints or blood samples. This type of evidence is discussed in greater detail in the next section dealing with overt investigations, but just be aware that the grand jury power is sometimes used to obtain the evidence directly from the target.

---

[1]   *See* 18 U.S.C. § 1510(b).

b. Monitoring Communication

There are a number of ways for law enforcement agents to monitor communication by or between criminal suspects, with which some are familiar to the general public, while others are less well known. One method of covert monitoring communication is called a "mail cover." This is a method by which the post office will, at the request of law enforcement agents, maintain a record of all mail going to and coming from a suspect's home or business. The post office does not open the mail or read the mail, but rather, simply documents the information which is publically available on the outside of the envelope or package. Because this information is open to the public, the recipient does not have a reasonable expectation of privacy with respect to that information. Accordingly, the recording of such information does not violate a person's constitutional rights or constitute a "search" under the Fourth Amendment to the Constitution. Nevertheless, a postal employee must obtain authorization of the Chief Postal Inspector to conduct a mail cover. *See, e.g., United States v. Hinton*, 222 F.3d 664, 674 (9th Cir. 2000); *United States v. Krauth*, 769 F.2d 473, 475 (8th Cir. 1985). Mail covers are especially useful in cases where law enforcement officers are attempting to determine the identity of other members of a criminal organization, the location of assets or accounts, or the scope and nature of a fraudulent scheme which uses the mails.

Pen registers and "trap and trace" devices are other methods utilized by law enforcement agents to covertly obtain information concerning wire communication. Like the mail cover, the only information obtained in a pen register is the number called from a subject telephone. Pen registers do not record or give access to the actual communication occurring during a telephone call, however. A "trap and trace" device serves essentially the same function as a pen register, with the additional benefit that it provides information about both incoming and outgoing calls. In either case, law enforcement can receive information about the calls made, whether long distance or local, at essentially the same instant the call is being made. Court approval is necessary to obtain a pen register or trap and trace, which requires a showing that it is being requested by a law enforcement officer or agent that "the information likely to be obtained is relevant to an ongoing criminal investigation." Title 18, United States Code, Section 3122. Because the information recorded is otherwise exposed to the public, in the sense that the telephone company must necessarily know the numbers called, the use of pen registers or trap and trace devices does not constitute a search under the Fourth Amendment. *Smith v. Maryland*, 442 U.S. 735, 743–44 (1979). It should be noted that in conjunction with pen registers, it is necessary to subpoena subscriber information from the telephone company to learn the identity of the callers, as a pen register only provides an agent with the numbers called.

Toll records (which are simply records similar to telephone bills which list numbers called, duration of calls, and similar data), are also sources of information regarding telephone calls. Unlike pen registers or trap and trace devices, which provide current information, toll records provide historical data regarding telephone calls made by or to a criminal suspect. Agents can obtain this information through administrative subpoenas, or a prosecutor can obtain the same information using a grand jury subpoena. This is typically a covert method of evidence collection because telecommunication companies historically have not provided notice of the disclosure to the target. Recently, however, some telecommunication companies have adopted policies of disclosing to their customers the fact they have been subpoenaed and produced records to federal law enforcement agencies. Accordingly, whether this method of evidence collection is overt or covert depends on the company and its policy.

Finally, wire taps are another covert method of monitoring communication. Wire taps permit the monitoring and recording of verbal or written communication. We are here using the term wiretap broadly, to include not only the traditional taping of a telephone line, but also the secreting of listening devices used to pick up conversations. The term includes, further, not just the interception of oral communication, but also real time electronic communication through emails, texts, tweets, and other forms of electronic communication through social media.

Wire taps clearly invade privacy, so the government must demonstrate probable cause to believe that the phone, location, or device which it seeks to monitor is being used to conduct, or will produce evidence of, criminal conduct. The specific requirements for obtaining permission to wiretap are numerous and strict (*See* Title 18, United States Code, Section 2510 *et seq.*), because wiretaps are, by their very nature, so invasive of privacy. Although the regulations and requirements are set up so that wiretaps are not used as a routine method of investigation, it also does not mean that the government must exhaust every other method available before resorting to a wiretap. *See United States v. Macklin*, 902 F.2d 1320, 1326 (8th Cir. 1990).

Wire taps are extremely labor intensive, requiring many, many hours of tedious monitoring of phone calls or other communication. The government must minimize the invasion of privacy by attempting to determine, as the communication is occurring, whether it is nonprivileged communication and whether it references criminal activity. If it does, the government may listen and record. If it does not, the agents must stop monitoring the communication for a few minutes, check again, determine if they can monitor, and if not stop monitoring for a few minutes, and repeat. This is called "minimization." Furthermore, wiretaps often involve interception of communication in foreign languages or in the form of coded communication of varying sophistication. This, obviously, requires interpretation and decoding, a further tax on limited government resources. While a wiretap is in place, the government must make frequent disclosures to the court *in camera* (meaning to the court only and not publicly filed) and *ex parte* (meaning no disclosure is made to an opposing party) so that the court can ensure that the wiretap is still appropriate and supported by probable cause, and that the agents are engaging in proper minimization. Despite all these hurdles, in the appropriate case wiretap evidence may be necessary and can be extremely valuable. Prosecutors help determine when a wiretap is appropriate and are responsible to ensure that it complies with federal law.

c.   Undercover Operations

Anyone who has watched popular television shows and movies involving the police and detective genre have been exposed to the situation where police officers "go undercover" to investigate a crime. This often involves an officer posing as a criminal in order to gain access to information that other criminals would impart only to another member of their criminal world. Undercover agents are usually "wired," meaning that they are wearing recording devices so that the conversations they have with the criminals are recorded and monitored at the same time by other officers hidden in the immediate vicinity. The use of undercover officers is most common in the enforcement of federal narcotics' laws, though organized crime is another notable area where undercover officers have gained significant results. Undercover operations are less common, though not unheard of, in white collar crime investigations.

Although Hollywood typically presents a scene where an officer is undercover, it is not always the case that the person acting undercover on behalf of the government is a law enforcement officer. Just as often, the person who is undercover is a cooperating witness. The typical situation is where a lower-level criminal has been caught and is given an opportunity to reduce his charges or sentence by cooperating with law enforcement authorities. This cooperation sometimes encompasses engaging in proactive investigations, which may call upon him to "go undercover." There is a risk in using cooperators in an undercover capacity because cooperators can never to be fully trusted. They could attempt to plant evidence on a suspect in a misguided and improper effort to gain favor with the government. On the other hand, cooperators could attempt to warn a suspect about the investigation. Law enforcement officers must be very careful when using cooperators in an undercover capacity to guard against these and other conduct which could jeopardize a suspect's rights or the investigation. Unfortunately, it is sometimes necessary to use cooperators in an undercover capacity simply because criminal suspects are too wary to trust an unknown person and the only way to gain entry into a criminal organization is to use a former member of the organization who is now cooperating with law enforcement officers. Agents usually try to have the cooperator introduce an undercover agent into the organization, however, as soon as possible so as to avoid the pitfalls with using the cooperator.

The use of undercover operations is not available, appropriate or necessary in every federal case. In some cases, the criminal conduct is complete. In other cases, there may be little likelihood of successfully introducing an undercover agent or little likelihood of gaining much evidence even if it could be done. Although the decision whether to use undercover agents in a given case ultimately belongs to the investigative agency, federal prosecutors may need to weigh in to determine whether it is appropriate, legally, in a given situation. This is particularly true when agents contemplate using a cooperator facing federal charges in an undercover capacity. A significant concern for federal prosecutors is the possibility that an undercover operation may invade a suspect's Sixth Amendment rights, or may run afoul of ethical rules, when the suspect may be represented by an attorney. A full discussion of the scope of the Sixth Amendment rights and the ethical rules with regard to contact with represented parties is beyond the scope of this chapter and this course. For the purposes of this class, it is merely important to point out that it can become an issue in an investigation.

d. Surveillance

One of the staples of law enforcement is surveillance of criminals and criminal activity. When thinking of surveillance, of course, most people immediately conjure up the image of a couple of plain clothes detectives sitting in an unmarked police car, sipping bad coffee, and peering through binoculars at the bad guys across the street. This type of surveillance certainly does take place, but there are many nuances to modern surveillance techniques. For instance, agents may now utilize high-powered binoculars and cameras when conducting this traditional type of surveillance, allowing them to occupy more hidden and comfortable settings. Further, agents sometimes establish surveillance through the use of hidden cameras trained on the suspect's house or place of business. There are pinhole cameras, for example, that can be fixed on the peephole in the door of a hotel room, so that officers may record anyone entering the room across the hall. Cameras can be clandestinely mounted on telephone poles (referred to as "pole cameras") or other objects or buildings, or law enforcement officers can feed off of pre-existing surveillance cameras that many businesses already have installed. Some surveillance is conducted from the air, as well, such as from airplanes, helicopters, and drones.

Attorneys engaged in the practice of federal criminal law need to be aware of the case law dealing with the scope of Fourth Amendment protections. Generally, anything open to the public view has no Fourth Amendment protection because one does not have a reasonable expectation of privacy with regard to matters visible to the public. It is well settled that visual observation alone does not constitute an invasion of privacy, necessitating a search warrant, even if the object of the surveillance, such as a house, is itself protected by the Fourth Amendment. *Dow Chemical Co. v. United States*, 476 U.S. 227, 234–25 (1986). With regard to aerial surveillance, the law is generally that there is no Fourth Amendment violation so long as the surveillance is conducted from airspace normally open to aircraft. *See, e.g., Florida v. Riley*, 488 U.S. 445, 457 (1989); *California v. Ciraolo*, 476 U.S. 207, 213 (1986). With the advent of drones, however, this area of the law may be ripe for re-evaluation and revision to ensure that the law keeps pace with new technology.

Some surveillance can invade a person's rights under the Fourth Amendment. When technology permits law enforcement officers to see more than is reasonably exposed to the public, a warrant establishing probable cause is required before the government may use that technique. Thermal imaging is a method utilizing technology to monitor the amount and location of heat emanating from a given source, such as a house. Thermal imaging is very useful, for example, to detect clandestine marijuana growing operations because such operations utilize a tremendous amount of heat from heat lamps. In *Kyllo v. United States*, 533 U.S. 27 (2001), however, the Supreme Court held that thermal imaging devices provide law enforcement with information that is not readily open to the public. Accordingly, in order for law enforcement agents to use a thermal imaging device, they must first obtain a warrant by demonstrating probable cause to believe that the subject location is being used for criminal activity and that the thermal imaging device is likely to produce evidence of that criminal activity. Similarly, agents use tracking devices clandestinely attached to vehicles or other means of transportation to monitor the movements of suspects. The Supreme Court has determined that this, too, provides the government with more information than is reasonably exposed to the public. Accordingly, the government must generally obtain a warrant before clandestinely attaching a tracking device on a vehicle. *See United States v. Jones*, ___ U.S. ___, 132 S. Ct. 945 (2012) (finding that attaching a tracking device to a vehicle and monitoring its movements constituted a search under the Fourth Amendment).

e. Covert Evidence Collection

Another staple of American law enforcement is the clandestine collection of information about a suspect. This means obtaining information from or about a suspect in any manner which is designed not to alert the suspect that he or she is under investigation. Covert evidence collection includes accessing public records, such as driving records, criminal records, and the like, the procurement of which would not typically be reported to the suspect. There is a vast amount of information available today about people through public records, the internet, and social media. The government may covertly gather most of this information exposed to the public without the target of the investigation becoming aware. When carefully analyzed, this type of information can provide a significant amount of information about the target and the target's criminal activities. It can disclose a pattern of past conduct, identify associates and other ties, and even produce photographs or statements on social media of the target engaged in or talking about criminal activity.

Another form of covert evidence collection is an investigative technique known euphemistically as "trash pulls" or "trash rips." A "trash rip" occurs when a law enforcement officer visits the suspect's house on trash day and takes the suspect's trash off of the curb. So long as the trash is outside the curtilage of the property, it is deemed by the law to be abandoned property in which the former owner no longer retains a reasonable expectation of privacy. *California v. Greenwood*, 846 U.S. 35, 41 (1988). A trained agent can learn a lot about a suspect by going through the suspect's trash. Further, sometimes items found in the trash constitute evidence of the crime itself, or can provide the basis for establishing probable cause to search the location. For example, discovery of marijuana seeds or the like in a person's trash can be enough to support probable cause to search the residence. *See United States v. Timley*, 443 F.3d 615, 624 (8th Cir. 2006) (court found probable cause to support search warrant when trash pull yielded forty marijuana seeds and twenty-five marijuana stems). The very clever criminals, of course, know of this technique so they personally take their trash to the landfill.

2. OVERT INVESTIGATIONS

As a category, overt investigations refer to those investigative techniques where the agents fully expect that the suspect will become aware of the investigation. Overt investigative methods typically are used either after the suspect is in custody, or when there is little real concern that the suspect will seek to flee or endanger witnesses or others if he or she learns of the investigation and after all covert methods have been exhausted. There are many overt investigative methods, only a few of which will be touched upon here.

a. Search Warrants

Search warrants are, of course, a frequently used method of investigating criminal cases. By its very nature (the invasion of the suspect's personal privacy), the execution of a search warrant clearly notifies the suspect that he or she is the subject of a criminal investigation. Rule 41(f)(3) of the Federal Rules of Criminal Procedure does permit a judge to authorized delayed notification of a search when cause is established as part of the search warrant application. In these circumstances, the government may sometimes execute a search warrant in such a way that the target may not immediately know of the search, assuming the government can do so without leaving signs of the search. Courts seldom permit the delay in notification to stretch beyond a week or so. Accordingly, even delayed notification warrants are covert for only a limited period of time.

The standard for obtaining a search warrant is probable cause to believe that there is evidence of criminal activity likely to be located in the premises searched. Probable cause for a search exists if "there is a fair probability that contraband or evidence of a crime will be found in a particular place." *Illinois v. Gates*, 462 U.S. 213, 238 (1983). When reviewing the sufficiency of an affidavit to support probable cause, a court is to consider the "totality of the circumstances." *United States v. Wright*, 145 F.3d 972, 975 (8th Cir. 1998). Probable cause may be established by the observations of trained law enforcement officers and/or by circumstantial evidence. *See, e.g., Walden v. Carmack*, 156 F.3d 861, 870 (8th Cir. 1998) (probable cause can be based on observations of trained law enforcement officers); *United States v. Edmiston*, 46 F.3d 786, 789 (8th Cir. 1995) (probable cause can be based on circumstantial evidence); *United States v. McGlynn*, 671 F.2d 1140, 1146 (8th Cir. 1982) (magistrate may rely on normal inferences drawn from surrounding circumstances and the allegations of fact contained in the application for the search warrant). The requirements for, and limitations on, the execution of a search warrant are generally found in Rule 41 of the Federal Rules of Criminal Procedure. You should also be aware that in *United States v. Leon*, 468 U.S. 897 (1984), the United States Supreme Court recognized a good faith exception to the exclusionary rule, finding that the intent to deter improper police conduct is not furthered when officers act in good faith reliance upon a warrant.

b. Witness Interviews

Not all witness interviews necessarily will alert the suspect of the investigation, and therefore inclusion of witness interviews in the "overt investigations" section may be questioned. For example, many interviews may be conducted of victims and witnesses far removed from, or adverse to, the suspect without the suspect ever becoming aware of the interviews. However, witness interviews often take place at the witnesses' residences or businesses, are not subject to any of the rules of secrecy protecting the grand jury proceedings, and carry the risk, however slight that risk may be in some cases, of becoming known to the suspect. Accordingly, witness interviews should be conducted with the anticipation that the suspect will learn of the interview and will become aware of the information imparted to the government during the interview.

Witness interviews are the bread and butter of any law enforcement investigation. There is no substitute for an agent to get out in the field and interview people with knowledge of the crime. Beyond the obvious witnesses, however, a federal prosecutor must be actively engaged in the investigation to make sure that other people necessary to prove elements of the crime are also interviewed. For example, if the government has to prove an interstate nexus element in order for the federal government to have jurisdiction over a crime, then the agent needs to interview witnesses necessary to prove this element.

c.   Document and Record Collection

Although a lot of document and record collection activities in federal criminal investigations are conducted by means of grand jury or trial subpoenas, there are times that public documents are obtained without the use of a subpoena. For example, an investigation may call for agents to obtain documentation regarding a suspect's ownership of vehicles or real property, which may be obtained from a local courthouse. It is unlikely, in most cases, that such document and record collection would become known to the target of the criminal investigation. It is possible that word may get back to the target, however, depending on the type of document sought, and the customer notification policy or practice of the business or entity in possession of the document. Discovery by the target of this type of evidence collection is particularly likely in small towns where the grapevine is short, yet covers the entire city.

d.   Overt Evidence Collection

Finally, some investigations require obtaining evidence directly from the suspect him or herself. For example, there may be a need to obtain fingerprints, handwriting exemplars, voice exemplars, a live line-up, or blood from a suspect in order to compare it to evidence obtained during an investigation. Generally, a defendant does not have Fifth Amendment protection when it comes to obtaining evidence which is open to the public, such as the suspect's appearance, voice, handwriting or even fingerprints. *See, e.g., United States v. Wade*, 388 U.S. 218 (1967) (no Fifth Amendment protection with regard to giving voice exemplar); *Gilbert v. California*, 388 U.S. 263 (1967) (no Fifth Amendment protection with respect to giving handwriting exemplar); *Schmerber v. California*,

384 U.S. 757 (1966) (no Fifth Amendment protection with regard to giving blood sample); *Holt v. United States*, 218 U.S. 245 (1910) (no Fifth Amendment protection against appearing in line-up).

Again, the various investigation methods outlined above, both covert and overt, do not constitute a complete list. Rather, our objective here was to introduce the student to the most commonly used methods in order to demonstrate how and why lawyers, both prosecutors and defense attorneys, are involved in federal criminal investigations. A large number of the investigation methods require the involvement of federal prosecutors in order to get court authorization to conduct the activity. Even with regard to those methods which do not require active participation by a federal prosecutor, they may involve questions of constitutional magnitude upon which the prosecutor may need to provide advice to the agents.

B. DEFENSE INVESTIGATIONS

As mentioned above, defense attorneys sometimes mount their own, independent investigations, especially in white collar cases where the targets of the federal investigation are more likely to become aware of the investigation and are more likely to have the funds necessary to conduct such an investigation. This course is not intended to provide detailed information about defense investigation techniques, let alone defense investigation tactics or strategy. Nevertheless, we will give a short overview of defense investigations and some issues that arise during defense investigations.

There are two primary types of investigations conducted by defendants. First, there are internal corporate investigations that arise from an ongoing program of self-policing by a company. The second consists of investigations that are initiated only as a result of a suspect (company or individual) learning that he (or it) is the subject of a federal criminal investigation.

1. CORPORATE INTERNAL INVESTIGATIONS

Many of the larger corporations in America have internal corporate compliance departments. These departments are often tasked with conducting internal investigations of such matters as internal fraud, theft of company property, and employment discrimination, to protect the corporation from harm committed by its own employees. Corporate compliance departments are often staffed by former federal or state law enforcement agents. Corporate directors, officers, and employees may, of course, commit federal criminal offenses that give rise to individual criminal liability. These crimes may directly harm the corporation (such as embezzlement) or may harm others or society at large (such as bribing officials so the corporation can secure a contract). Directors, officers, and employees may thus expose the corporation itself to possible criminal charges when the director, officer, or employee engages in criminal conduct while acting in the scope of their employment and with the intent to benefit the corporation.

In the 1990s, two developments made it advantageous for corporations to create and maintain effective corporate compliance departments to ensure that their employees were complying with the law and the corporation was being a good and responsible corporate citizen. First, the Department of Justice adopted policy guidelines for prosecutors to consider in determining whether to prosecute corporations for violations of federal criminal law. If a corporation has an effective corporate compliance program, it is one of the factors contained in those guidelines that militate against bringing criminal charges against the corporation. *See* http://www.justice.gov/usam/usam-9-28000-principles-federal-prosecution-business-organizations#9-28.300. Second, the United States Sentencing Commission adopted a federal sentencing guideline that provides for a reduced sentence for corporations which have effective compliance programs. *See* United States Sentencing Guidelines § 8C2.5(f). Accordingly, it is in the shareholders' best interest that corporations have effective compliance programs and departments which are capable of effectively policing the corporation to ensure that directors, officers, and employees comply with federal criminal laws.

Increasingly, therefore, corporate investigators are discovering criminal conduct through their own internal investigations before any federal or state authorities become aware of the criminal activity. For example, a defense contractor may discover, through its own internal investigation, that one of its executives is receiving kickbacks to award subcontract work to a certain company. Once this criminal activity is discovered, and presuming that the corporation acts responsibly and wants to disclose this discovery to the authorities, a criminal defense attorney is often contacted. Once hired, the criminal defense attorney may direct a further investigation into the criminal conduct. This could take the form of further interviews and retrieving and reviewing additional documents relevant to the criminal conduct.

Ultimately, the defense attorney must make decisions regarding whether, when, and how disclosure of information from the internal investigation is made to the government. Disclosure by the corporation of information from its own internal investigation is another factor the Department of Justice guidelines direct prosecutors to consider in determining whether to charge a corporation. It may be in the corporation's best interest to disclose an internal criminal investigation, but not in the best interest of a corporate officer. Similarly, it may be in the corporation's best interest to waive any attorney/client privilege necessary to disclose the internal investigation, but not in the officer's best interest. Defense attorneys must be careful to make sure they represent the best interest of their clients, be they corporations or individuals. This becomes especially difficult when corporate officers, who themselves may be individual targets of the criminal investigation, hire attorneys to represent the corporation.

2. REACTIVE DEFENSE INVESTIGATIONS

Criminal defense attorneys also become involved in defense investigations when targets of a federal criminal investigation become aware of the federal investigation and reach out to a criminal defense attorney for help. A target may become aware of the federal criminal investigation because some part of the investigation became overt, perhaps because the existence of a grand jury subpoena has been disclosed to the target, or a close associate of the target was interviewed by the FBI and reported this back to the target. On other occasions, a criminal defense attorney is hired only after federal criminal charges have been brought against the target.

A criminal defense attorney will likely launch a defense investigation into the alleged criminal conduct as soon as the attorney is hired. A defense attorney may undertake some of the investigative tasks him or herself, such as researching public documents and the like. In other cases, however, it may be appropriate for a defense attorney to hire a private investigator to interview witnesses, research records, or even conduct surveillance. These private investigators are often former police officers or federal agents. These investigators may use many of the same investigation techniques discussed above in relation to the government investigation, except, of course, those that require government authority. So, for example, a private investigator may conduct surveillance, interview witnesses, and collect relevant documents, but cannot conduct a mail cover, intercept phone calls, or compel witnesses to testify under oath before a grand jury.

A defense attorney who becomes aware that his or her client is the subject of a grand jury investigation may take steps to monitor the federal investigation for purposes of developing leads or monitoring the strength of the government's case. Defense attorneys will sometimes interview witnesses both before and after they testify before the grand jury, for example. This is especially the case when the target of an investigation is a company and the witnesses called before the grand jury consists of employees of the company. Of course, attorneys must always be cautious to make sure that in conducting such interviews witnesses are advised that they must always tell the truth before the grand jury. Attorneys should also make sure that witnesses understand that, absent a subpoena, they have the right to talk or not talk with an attorney for either side.

In some cases, especially where the target has sufficient funds, criminal defense attorneys conduct investigations that very much mirror the government's investigation efforts. In some respects, criminal defense attorneys are at an advantage in conducting these investigations because they have access to the target who committed the crime. The target knows better than anyone what he or she did, how it was done, and what evidence that might exist of the crime. This can arm the criminal defense attorney with significant information and place the defense attorney at a distinct advantage over his or her government counterpart who is trying to discover what happened from the outside. A criminal defense attorney, of course, has no obligation to disclose to the government any incriminating information that may be discovered during such an investigation. A criminal defense attorney can use this information to determine whether and when to approach the government to work out a plea agreement, and whether as part of that process to disclose the information to the government, or whether to retain the information and prepare for trial.

CHAPTER 3

THE FEDERAL GRAND JURY

■ ■ ■

A federal grand juries is an essential tool and required step in the investigation and prosecution of federal criminal cases. Federal grand juries constitute a critical means of investigating federal offenses, allowing the government to obtain documents and other evidence by subpoena, and to question witnesses under oath prior to making a charging decision. Moreover, absent a waiver of indictment by a defendant, the government must have a grand jury return an indictment against a defendant before the government may try a defendant on a felony offense. Thus, unlike in the state system, the grand jury is an integral part of federal criminal practice. A grand jury proceeding is different from almost anything else in the practice of law. It is a one-sided presentation of some evidence to a group of citizens where the presentation is not bound by rules of evidence or overseen by a judicial officer, and the jury's decision is not an ultimate determination of guilt.

An understanding of the grand jury's origin, power, composition, mechanics and secrecy requirements are important for both federal prosecutors and defense attorneys. Federal prosecutors must also appreciate and develop skills in grand jury advocacy. This chapter will address all those issues.

A. ORIGINS AND PURPOSE OF THE FEDERAL GRAND JURY

The history of grand juries reaches far back into the early struggles between the King of England and his noblemen. Brought over to North America by the colonists, the grand jury developed here as a means of protecting the people against the unbridled power of the government. *See Branzburg v. Hayes*, 408 U.S. 665, 686–87 (1972) (purpose of Grand Jury Clause of Fifth Amendment is to protect citizens "against unfounded criminal prosecutions."). The Fifth Amendment to the United States Constitution provides, in pertinent part: "No person shall be held to answer for a capital, or otherwise infamous crime, unless on a presentment or indictment of a Grand Jury. . . ." U.S. Const., Amend. V. The Fifth Amendment grand jury requirement has been interpreted to mean that the federal government may not try a person on a felony charge without having first presented the case to a federal grand jury and having the grand jury vote to indict the person on the felony charges.

This right to a grand jury under the Fifth Amendment has not, however, been extended to apply to states. A state may, therefore, charge someone with a felony offense without ever having presented the matter to a grand jury. Even though state prosecutors do not have to present a felony case to a grand jury, they sometimes use a grand jury to investigate and evaluate criminal cases. These cases, however, are the exception to the rule. State grand juries are often used only in high-profile cases where the local county attorney desires the protection of having an independent body decide whether criminal charges are appropriate, such as in the case of alleged police brutality.

Because every felony case must be presented to a grand jury under federal law, the role of the grand jury in federal criminal cases is completely different from that in state courts. A federal grand jury serves two basic functions. First, it is an investigatory body with the power to call witnesses and subpoena documents and other things in an effort to investigate the underlying criminal activity. Second, it must decide, in conjunction with the federal prosecutor, whether there is probable cause to believe that the target of the investigation committed the federal offense under investigation. *See* Wright, *Federal Practice and Procedure*, Criminal Section 110. Thus, federal prosecutors work with a grand jury, using its subpoena power as a tool to investigate the underlying criminal activity. Further, Assistant United States Attorneys work with grand juries to determine whether and against whom to bring criminal charges. Although a federal grand jury has significant independent power, it cannot bring charges against a person without the agreement of an Assistant United States Attorney (or other Department of Justice Attorney), just as a federal prosecutor cannot bring felony charges against a person without the agreement of a federal grand jury. *Fields v. Soloff*, 920 F.2d 1114, 1118 (2d Cir. 1990); *United Sates v. Cox*, 342 F.2d 167, 171 (5th Cir. 1965).

B. GRAND JURY'S POWER

A federal prosecutor may use a federal grand jury to investigate any federal criminal offense. There are no rules on how the government may conduct the investigation. In other words, a federal prosecutor has wide discretion to determine what documents or things or people to subpoena to appear before the grand jury. A grand jury investigation can be completed in an hour, or may continue for years so long as the prosecutor is in good faith investigating the possible violation of federal criminal law. The scope of a grand jury's power is limited by the job it is tasked to perform—determining whether there is probable cause to believe a crime has been committed. Thus, a federal prosecutor cannot use a federal grand jury to investigate a defendant after he has been indicted unless the purpose is to pursue additional charges or defendants in a superseding indictment. *See, e.g., Costello v. United States*, 350 U.S. 359, 362 (1956); *In re Grand Jury Subpoena Duces Tecum, Dated January 2, 1985*, 767 F.2d 26, 29–30 (2d Cir. 1985).

One of the most powerful aspects of a grand jury's ability to investigate criminal conduct is its ability to compel the production of documents or witnesses to the grand jury. Rule 17 of the Federal Rules of Criminal Procedure governs subpoenas issued under the authority of the grand jury. Rule 17 permits the issuance of grand juries subpoenas to secure testimony or to require the production of documents, or both. The United States has the power to subpoena a person anywhere in the United States or its territories. So, for example, a prosecutor investigating a fraud scheme in Iowa can issue a subpoena to a company in Puerto Rico to produce documents, or can issue a subpoena to a witness in Alaska to appear before a grand jury in Iowa, if there is a good faith belief that doing so could produce evidence that would further the criminal investigation.

The power to subpoena a person to appear before the grand jury includes the power to subpoena a target of a grand jury investigation. *See United States v. Wong*, 431 U.S. 174, 179 n.8 (1977). The United States Department of Justice has a policy, however, against issuing subpoenas to have targets appear before the grand jury. United States Attorney's Manual 9–11.150. A prosecutor may constitutionally subpoena a target before the grand jury, but Department of Justice policy requires prior approval of the United States Attorney for the district or the responsible Assistant Attorney General. Nevertheless, targets sometimes volunteer to appear before the grand jury in white collar cases. There are advantages and disadvantages of having a target appear before the grand jury investigating him or her. For example, a target may be able to persuade a grand jury not to indict by eliciting sympathy from the grand jury. On the other hand, a target may further incriminate himself or herself by testifying in a grand jury, or may commit perjury in an attempt to evade an indictment. If a target lies before the grand jury and a prosecutor can prove it, not only is it a federal offense in itself, it also serves as strong evidence of consciousness of guilt for the underlying crime under investigation.

C. COMPOSITION OF A GRAND JURY

A federal grand jury is composed of twenty-three jurors who are randomly selected from the citizenry much like jurors are selected for petit or trial juries. *See* 18 U.S.C. § 3321 ("Every grand jury impaneled before any district court shall consist of not less than sixteen nor more than twenty-three persons."); Fed. R. Crim. P. 6(a)(1) ("A grand jury must have 16 to 23 members. . . ."). A district court judge presides over the selection of citizens to serve as grand jurors. Although a United States Attorney is present during the grand jury selection process, the government does not actively participate in the selection process. Indeed, the judge does not engage in the typical voir dire practice conducted in selecting a petite or trial jury. Rather, the judge will typically conduct limited questioning to make sure that the citizens are qualified and able to serve. The judge will then swear in the first twenty-three citizens out of the venire who are qualified and able to serve as grand jurors. The court will choose one of the grand jurors to serve as foreperson and one or more others to serve as deputy forepersons. The judge will then administer an oath to the grand jurors and charge them, that is instruct the grand jurors, as to their duty to decide cases based on the evidence and the law as instructed to them by the prosecutors.

There must be a quorum of sixteen grand jurors present to conduct business before a grand jury. *See United States v. Leverage Funding Systems*, 637 F.2d 645, 648 (9th Cir. 1980) (noting that, though Rule 6 does not explicitly impose a quorum requirement, courts have read in such a requirement). Further, no indictment can be returned absent the concurrence of twelve or more jurors. Fed. R. Crim. P. 6(f).

Federal grand juries are usually empaneled for periods of eighteen months' service, which can be extended by the court. A grand jury will typically meet once per month, and will convene for as long as the United States Attorney's Office has the need. In practice, grand juries usually convene for two or three days each month. A federal district may, and often does, have more than one grand jury meeting each month. For example, a district may have a grand jury convene in one city the second week of each month, a different grand jury convene the third week of each month in a second city, and then have yet a third grand jury meet on the fourth week in the first city.

In some very large districts, like Los Angeles, New York, or Chicago, special "accusatory" grand juries may be empaneled separate from "investigatory" grand juries. In other words, in very busy districts where scores of defendants are charged each month, the district may empanel an accusatory grand jury whose job it is to listen to evidence in reactive cases, such as bank robberies or drug offenses, where the evidence consists of a single agent testifying before the grand jury to summarize the evidence, after which the prosecutor asks the grand jury to deliberate on the indictment. Such an accusatory grand jury would not typically investigate lengthy cases with many witnesses in investigations lasting for months. Rather, that type of grand jury investigation would take place before the investigatory grand jury. In smaller districts both types of cases are presented to the same grand jury.

When the grand jury is in session, no one else is allowed in the grand jury room other than the grand jurors, a court reporter, the prosecutor and the witness. There is no judicial officer present to preside over the grand jury session. The prosecutor is responsible for conducting the grand jury proceeding, although the foreperson supervises deliberations. The court reporter must be present and record anything that is said in the grand jury when a prosecutor is present. This includes any time the prosecutor speaks to the grand jury, including when introducing the case or instructing on the law, regardless of whether a witness is present in the grand jury room. When the grand jury deliberates, however, only the grand jurors may be in the room and its deliberations are not recorded.

D. MECHANICS OF PRESENTING A CASE BEFORE A FEDERAL GRAND JURY

Presentation of a case before a grand jury will usually begin with the prosecutor introducing the case to the grand jurors without a witness being present. This presentation usually takes the form of a short summary statement about the nature of the case, as opposed to an opening statement. So, for example, the prosecutor may tell the jury that they will be hearing evidence about a methamphetamine trafficking case, that the target of the investigation is John Doe, that the grand jury will hear from two witnesses and the case agent, and that at the end of the presentation the government will ask the grand jury to deliberate on an indictment charging John Doe with the certain offenses. It is also common practice to identify the anticipated witnesses to ensure that the grand jurors are not familiar with the witnesses such that they cannot fairly and impartially decide the case. It is permissible for the government to make a more lengthy opening statement about what the prosecutor anticipates the evidence will show, but this is seldom done primarily because the case is still in the investigatory stage at the grand jury and it may not be clear what the evidence will ultimately show. It is important that the grand jury is reminded that what the prosecutor says to them about the case is not evidence the grand jury is to consider in voting on the indictment.

Following the introduction, the prosecutor will then call witnesses before the grand jury. Again, depending on the nature of the investigation, and whether the case is a reactionary or proactive one, this may involve one or many witnesses, and it may require many grand jury sessions to present all of the witnesses in a case. Which witnesses are called before the grand jury, and in what order, is the prosecutor's decision to make, although occasionally the grand jury may indicate a preference to hear from a particular witness. After the witness is sworn in by the foreperson, the prosecutor will advise the witness of certain rights and obligations the witness has before the grand jury. This is not constitutionally required, but is standard practice. This will include a warning that the witness could be prosecuted for perjury if the witness lies during testimony before the grand jury, that the witness can refuse to answer a question if it may incriminate the witness, and that the witness has the right to consult with an attorney in connection with the witness's appearance before the grand jury. As noted above, though, a witness's attorney may not be present in the grand jury room during questioning. Thus, if the witness has an attorney and wishes to consult with the attorney during questioning, then the prosecutor may take a recess and allow the witness to consult with the attorney outside the grand jury room.

Once the witness has been advised of his or her rights and obligations before the grand jury, the prosecutor will then question the witness. When the prosecutor has completed questioning, the prosecutor will permit the grand jurors to ask questions. The manner in which this is done varies from district to district and is within the control of the prosecutor to ensure that the questions are appropriate and relevant to the investigation. So, in some districts, prosecutors simply open it up to the grand jurors to ask questions, calling on grand jurors who raise their hands indicating they have a question. If the prosecutor determines the question is inappropriate (for example, it would invade a privilege) or irrelevant, then the prosecutor may instruct the witness that the witness does not have to answer the question. In other districts, the practice may be for the grand jurors to submit written questions to the prosecutor and then the prosecutor reviews those questions and asks the ones that are deemed appropriate and relevant.

The Federal Rules of Evidence do not apply in a proceeding before a federal grand jury. Thus, hearsay evidence is admissible before a grand jury. *See United States v. Calandra*, 414 U.S. 338 (1974). A fundamental reason that the evidence rules do not apply is because a grand jury proceeding takes place at the investigatory stage of the case. A grand jury is investigating leads to evidence that would prove a criminal case, just like a police office may rely on hearsay statements to pursue leads that result in the discovery of admissible evidence. Prosecutors should take care, however, to make it clear to the grand jury when hearsay testimony is presented so that a grand jury is not misled into thinking that a witness has direct evidence when the testimony is actually hearsay. *See United States v. Leibowitz*, 420 F.2d 39 (2d Cir. 1969). In addition, there is no legal requirement that the United States present exculpatory evidence to a grand jury, *United States v. Williams*, 504 U.S. 36 (1992), though the policy of the United States Department of Justice is that a prosecutor present to a grand jury any substantial evidence that directly negates the guilt of a subject of the grand jury investigation. U.S. Attorney's Manual, 9–11.241.

Because the evidence rules do not apply in grand jury proceedings, it is possible for the government to present through a single case agent all the evidence necessary to show probable cause to believe the target committed a criminal offense. In other words, there is no requirement that the government present any or all the witnesses with actual knowledge of a case before a grand jury. In some cases, the government relies on a case agent to summarize all the evidence. For example, imagine a case where a drug trafficker is pulled over in a traffic stop and the officer finds a hidden stash of 30 pounds of methamphetamine. Perhaps the trafficker makes incriminating statements, or other incriminating evidence is found in the car, but there is nothing else really known about the target or his criminal conduct. In such a case, the prosecutor may simply have the case agent, like the DEA agent who submitted the case to the office for prosecution, testify before the grand jury by summarizing the evidence from the traffic stop. The agent can do this even where the agent was not present at the traffic stop and has no personal knowledge of the events. Other than in cases like this, where the government is reacting to a completed crime, federal prosecutors are more likely to use the power of the grand jury to secure the testimony of key witnesses under oath.

When the prosecutor is seeking an indictment, the prosecutor will present the draft indictment to the grand jury after the questioning of all the witnesses has been completed. In presenting the indictment, the government will generally describe the indictment, such as who is named in the indictment as defendants and the number and nature of counts. The prosecutor will also instruct the jury as to the elements of any crimes charged in indictment. If the grand jury is experienced by reason of sitting as a grand jury for months, then the prosecutor may dispense with instructing the grand jury as to the elements of a crime with which the grand jury is already familiar. Then the prosecutor will hand the indictment and ballot (a document which records the grand jury's vote) to the foreperson and ask the grand jury to deliberate on the indictment. Although it is permissible for the prosecutor to present a closing argument to the grand jury, summarizing what the prosecutor believes the evidence has shown, this is rarely done because the standard of proof is low—probable cause—and the government typically will not seek indictment unless the prosecutor is convinced that the evidence presented to the grand jury proves the defendant's guilt beyond a reasonable doubt.

Once the prosecutor has provided the indictment to the foreperson, the prosecutor and court reporter leave the grand jury room and permit the grand jury to deliberate. Once the grand jury has reached a verdict, the foreperson will open the door to the grand jury room and let the government know that a verdict has been reached. The prosecutor and court reporter will then re-enter the grand jury room and the prosecutor will make a record of the grand jury's verdict. In other words, the prosecutor will review the indictment and ballot and state whether the indictment and ballot has been signed. If the grand jury finds probable cause, then it is called a "true bill" and the prosecutor will also sign the indictment, making it a valid charging document. An indictment must bear the signature of both the prosecutor and the foreperson for it to be a valid charging document. If less than twelve of the grand jurors present voted in favor of the indictment, then the foreperson records that result on the ballot and does not sign the indictment. This is called a "no true bill." If this happens, the government may present the case again to another grand jury, but only with permission from the Attorney General and upon a showing of exceptional circumstances, such as an indication that the grand jurors voted against an indictment for improper reasons (sympathy for the defendant, for example), grand jury misconduct, or new evidence.

E. SECRECY REQUIREMENTS GOVERNING A GRAND JURY PROCEEDING

Federal grand jury proceedings are conducted in secret. Thus, during the presentation of evidence before the grand jury, again, only the witness, government attorneys, the court reporter and interpreters (when necessary), may be present with the grand jury. Fed. R. Crim. P. 6 (d). No one but the grand jurors may be present during deliberations. *Id*. Rule 6(e) of the Federal Rules of Criminal Procedure generally prohibits disclosure of any matters occurring before a federal grand jury, though a witness is generally free to discuss his or her testimony with anyone afterwards. The secrecy requirement is intended to encourage witnesses freely to divulge their information to the grand jury, to prevent those under investigation from fleeing from or influencing the investigation, and to protect those who are investigated but not charged by the grand jury to prevent those subjects from suffering prejudice by the mere fact that they were under investigation. *See Douglas Oil v. Petrol Stops Northwest*, 441 U.S. 211, 218 (1979).

Everything that happens before the grand jury, except deliberations of course, is recorded by the court reporter. After the grand jury session, the court reporter will generate a transcript of what each witness said before the grand jury, although the court reporter will not create a transcript of the government's discussion of the case, instructions on the law, or other matters occurring before the grand jury outside the presence of a witness. If there is an allegation of grand jury misconduct at some point in the future, the court reporter can always access this other record. The witness transcripts are provided to the government to be included in discovery provided to the defendant, should an indictment be returned.

F. GRAND JURY ADVOCACY

Questioning witnesses before a grand jury is in some ways similar and in some ways dissimilar to other advocacy skills. It is similar in the sense that there is a jury to whom the prosecutor presents a case. It is different because a grand jury is not a trial jury which the government must persuade beyond a reasonable doubt; rather, the government must prove only probable cause. Because it is ungoverned by the rules of evidence and not supervised by a judge, questioning witnesses before a grand jury can assume aspects of both direct and cross examination. Because it is such a unique area of federal criminal practice, we will devote some space here to discuss various issues involved with grand jury advocacy.

1. WHO TO CALL AS WITNESSES BEFORE THE GRAND JURY

One of the first decisions a federal prosecutor must make is who to call as witnesses before a federal grand jury. To make this decision, the prosecutor must first consider why one would want to call any witness before the grand jury. There are several reasons.

First, a prosecutor may decide to call a witness for the obvious purpose of discovering information unknown to the investigators and the grand jury. These witnesses would include people who may know about offense because of who they are or where they were on a given day. For example, in a bank fraud case this category of witnesses may include bank employees. In a money laundering case, it may be family members, employers, or other regarding the defendant's source for legal funds. In a bank robbery case, it could be the teller or a customer. A prosecutor may have reports of interviews of these witnesses, so may have at least some idea of what the witnesses know relevant to the investigation. Nevertheless, a prosecutor may and usually does have additional or different questions that may lead to the discovery of information that is not contained in the agent's report of interview that can be asked during a grand jury appearance.

Second, a prosecutor may call a witness not to discover new information, but to lock the witness into information previously provided in an interview with law enforcement officers. This is done, for example, with cooperators, associates of targets, or other potentially unfriendly witnesses who may have a motive to change their story later, when the case goes to trial. Although the government can rely on the statement previously provided to the agent, such statements are not made under oath, and usually are not verbatim. By having the witness testify before the grand jury, the government can obtain a sworn statement that more fully locks the witness into the statement they previously provided to the police. In certain circumstances, statements made before a grand jury can be used not only to impeach a witness who later testifies differently at trial, but also as substantive evidence if the witness appears at trial but then refuses to testify or feigns lack of memory.

Third, a prosecutor may call a reluctant or recalcitrant witness before the grand jury to obtain information that witness has previously been unwilling to provide to law enforcement officers. Witnesses sometimes do not want to cooperate with a criminal investigation, may be intimidated by the prospect of talking to federal agents, or may be afraid of retaliation from the target if he or she provides information to the police. Officers cannot make witnesses to talk to them. The grand jury, however, can require a witness to appear and testify by means of a grand jury subpoena. If the witness still refuses to testify in front of the grand jury, a prosecutor has several options to persuade or compel the witness to testify, including granting testimonial immunity or using contempt proceedings, if necessary.

Fourth, a prosecutor may call a witness before the grand jury simply to lay foundation for documents or other pieces of evidence. Although this may not be strictly necessary in many cases, since the Federal Rules of Evidence do not apply before grand juries, sometimes it is helpful for the grand jury to better understand a complex case by having someone with knowledge of the subject introduce a piece of evidence (say, a computer forensic report) and explain its meaning and importance to the grand jury. This may also be used when a witness has received a grand jury subpoena to produce documents to the grand jury and there is some question about whether the witness has fully complied with the subpoena. A prosecutor can question such a witness about what they did, where they looked, and similar questions relevant to responding to the subpoena in order for the prosecutor to ensure complete and honest compliance with the grand jury subpoena.

Fifth, a prosecutor sometimes call witnesses simply to establish evidence necessary to establish an essential element of the offense in order to allow the grand jury to return an indictment. So, for example, in a case charging a defendant with being a felon in possession of a firearm, the government may call a witness to establish that a review of the target's criminal history shows a prior conviction, or may call an ATF agent to testify to the interstate nexus element (*i.e.*, that the firearm was manufactured outside of the state).

Sixth, sometimes prosecutors call witnesses just to see how they will perform as a witness. This may be used, for example, with child victims of exploitation, or with elderly witnesses, or with expert witnesses. Not only is the witness testifying about matters relevant to the investigation, but it provides the prosecutor an opportunity to observe how he or she performs in front of an audience. This can be valuable in assessing the credibility of witnesses and the strength of the government's case, and can serve as a starting point for working with a witness to improve their appearance and performance.

2. WHEN TO CALL WITNESSES BEFORE THE GRAND JURY

Once a prosecutor determines who to call as witnesses before the grand jury, the prosecutor must determine when to call those people to testify before the grand jury. In part, it depends on why the prosecutor is calling the witness. For example, a prosecutor looking to uncover facts might call a witness that serves this purpose before she calls a witness simply to determine how the witness performs. Mostly, however, timing depends on how the grand jury investigation fits into the overall covert and overt status and nature of the criminal investigation. Unless a prosecutor is calling a law enforcement officer or someone in a similar position before the grand jury, there is always a risk that the witness may reveal the existence of the investigation to the target. After all, a witness before the grand jury may lawfully tell anyone about appearing before the grand jury and what he or she said to the grand jury. If there are other covert law enforcement procedures contemplated as part of the investigation, then the prosecutor will probably want to delay calling witnesses before the grand jury until all other covert operations have been completed.

Ultimately, it must be remembered that the prosecutor must call witnesses before the grand jury returns the indictment. Once an indictment is returned, it is improper to use the grand jury power to gather evidence, conduct pretrial discovery, or otherwise engage in preparation for trial. *See, e.g., United States v. Sasso*, 59 F.3d 341, 351–52 (2d Cir. 1995); *Resolution Trust Corp. v. Thornton*, 41 F.3d 1539, 1546–47 (D.C. Cir. 1994) (collecting cases). Thus, the grand jury process is abused if it is used "for the primary purpose of strengthening the government's case on a pending indictment or as a substitute for discovery." *United States v. Jenkins*, 904 F.3d 549, 559–60 (10th Cir. 1990). Even after an indictment is returned, however, the grand jury may still be used to pursue additional charges or additional defendants in an ongoing investigation, even if the effect is to aid in the prosecution of the original defendant on the original charge. *See, e.g., Sasso*, 59 F.3d at 352; *United States v. Phibbs*, 999 F.2d 1053, 1077 (6th Cir. 1993).

3. HOW TO QUESTION GRAND JURY WITNESSES

Recognizing that the Federal Rules of Evidence do not apply in proceedings before the grand jury, a prosecutor has the ability to question witnesses in whatever method is deemed most effective, whether through open-ended questions, leading questions, or some combination thereof. How a prosecutor questions a witness before the grand jury depends, in large measure, on the purpose of calling the witness. For example, if the purpose is to discover new evidence, open-ended questions will be more effective than leading questions. On the other hand, if the purpose is to lock the witness down to a prior statement, leading questions may be the most effective. In some cases, such as with a cooperator, a prosecutor may want to use a combination of questioning techniques, locking down the witness, for instance, on the key facts, then asking more exploratory questions of the witness to test the cooperator's veracity. Likewise, a prosecutor may shift methods depending on the performance of the witness. For example, if the witness becomes hostile during questioning, the prosecutor may wish to shift to a cross-examination method of examination.

Likewise, because the Federal Rules of Evidence do not apply in the grand jury, a prosecutor may solicit hearsay and opinion evidence. Remember that one principal purpose of the grand jury is to investigate criminal activity. This means grand jury examinations can be used to develop leads to admissible evidence, even if the lead itself would not be admissible at trial. A prosecutor should be careful, however, to ensure the grand jury understands and the record reflects when a witness is testifying based on hearsay so that there is no potential for misleading anyone that the witness is basing the testimony on personal knowledge. Thus, a prosecutor must be sure when soliciting hearsay testimony that attribution to the source is clearly established.

In addition to considering the method of questioning grand jury witnesses, a prosecutor should also evaluate the manner of questioning. With hostile witnesses or cooperators, a prosecutor may want to use a formal, no-nonsense tone. On the other hand, if the witness is someone who may have valuable information if they chose to be cooperative, a more conciliatory manner may be more effective. Again, the manner of questioning may change depending on the performance of the witness. A prosecutor should not be overly concerned with the impression that the manner of questioning has on the grand jury. In a jury trial lawyers should ask questions in a manner best designed to persuade the fact finder that the lawyer's position is the correct one. So, sometimes the lawyer has to be careful not to appear overbearing or offensive to a trial juror. Before a grand jury, prosecutors should not be so concerned with this. Rather, the prosecutor should be most concerned with asking questions in such a way as to most effectively uncover evidence. Because the standard of proof before the grand jury is low—probable cause— persuasion is less important than disclosure.

It should be recognized that questioning witnesses before the grand jury is not like questioning witnesses at trial. Questions are not always open-ended or leading, hearsay is admissible, and manner and tone may change as needed. Most important, although at trial a lawyer should almost never ask a question on cross examination to which they do not know the answer, the opposite is true in the grand jury. A prosecutor should never hesitate to ask hard questions, or questions that may reveal evidence unfavorable to the government. A prosecutor should never hesitate to ask a question in the grand jury on the ground that the answer may hurt the government's case. The grand jury is precisely the place to discover this information. If there are problems with the evidence, the grand jury investigation is the place to find out, while there is still time to use the grand jury to overcome those problems, or to determine that charges should not be brought.

4. PREPARING FOR QUESTIONING GRAND JURY WITNESSES

Prosecutors should prepare for questioning grand jury witnesses as much as they prepare for questioning witnesses at trial. Although it is not so important to use methods designed to persuade juries, such as looping or sequencing (which will be discussed later in relation to direct examinations), it is important to make sure questions are clearly articulated to eliminate ambiguities. A grand jury transcript is of little use for impeachment purposes, for example, if the questions are so vague as to give the witness wiggle room. Similarly, it is important that all the important questions are asked. The last thing a prosecutor wants to discover during a trial is that he or she failed to ask a necessary follow-up question, the adverse answer to which is revealed for the first time at trial.

Accordingly, prosecutors should prepare an outline of questions to ask a grand jury witness. Even experienced prosecutors are ill-advised to simply "wing it" with grand jury witnesses. A prosecutor should be prepared, however, to vary from the outline in response to the answers provided. In drafting outlines, prosecutors should at all times keep in mind elements of offense, and possible defenses, and the goal of calling the particular witness before the grand jury.

5. WHAT EVIDENCE TO PRESENT TO THE GRAND JURY

So, how much or little evidence must be presented to the grand jury? First, the government must present enough evidence to obtain an indictment. That means, the government must present at least enough evidence to show probable cause to believe that each element of the offense has been met. The government is not obligated to present more. So, the government does not have to present all the evidence it has to the grand jury. Nor is it barred, however, from using the power of the grand jury to obtain additional evidence, even if the evidence already presented to the grand jury is sufficient already to establish probable cause to believe the defendant committed the offense. *See United States v. Picketts*, 655 F.2d 837, 841 (7th Cir. 1981). Indeed, the grand jury has the obligation to thoroughly investigate the matters brought before it.

The government is under no duty to present exculpatory evidence to the grand jury. *See, e.g., United States v. Williams*, 504 U.S. 36 (1992); *United States v. Byron*, 994 F.2d 747, 748 (10th Cir. 1993); *United States v. Isgro*, 974 F.2d 1491, 1496 (9th Cir. 1992). Thus, although failure by a prosecutor to disclose exculpatory evidence will not result in dismissal of an indictment, it can result in ethical violations. *See ABA Standards for Criminal Justice* § 3–3.6(b) (3rd ed. 1993) ("No prosecutor shall knowingly fail to disclose to the grand jury evidence which tends to negate the guilt or mitigate the offense."). As previously mentioned, Department of Justice policy provides that if a prosecutor is personally aware of substantial evidence that directly negates the guilt of a subject of the investigation, the prosecutor must present or disclose that information to the grand jury before seeking an indictment. USAM 9–11.233. Regardless of the policy, such disclosures should be made for purely practical reasons. As stated above, a prosecutor should never be afraid of what comes out in the grand jury. It is far better to learn the information there, than later. Likewise, it is far better to see what a jury thinks of exculpatory evidence before the grand jury when the standard is probable cause, than find out later when the standard is beyond a reasonable doubt. In any event, the government will be required to disclose exculpatory evidence in discovery, so there is no legitimate reason not to disclose it during the grand jury proceedings.

CHAPTER 4

CRIMINAL CHARGES

■ ■ ■

To initiate a federal criminal case, the government may charge a defendant by filing a criminal complaint, a criminal information, or a grand jury indictment. The requirements for, and limitations of, each method for charging a defendant are significant. The decision to charge a defendant by means of a criminal complaint, instead of by means of a criminal information or grand jury indictment, is largely based on the particular circumstances of an investigation, the urgency surrounding the need to file charges, and the status of the target defendant. Below we will discuss each of the charging methods and discuss when and why each is appropriate in certain circumstances.

A. CRIMINAL COMPLAINT

The requirements for filing a criminal complaint are contained in Rule 3 of the Federal Rules of Criminal Procedure, and they are simple. A criminal complaint "is a written statement of the essential facts constituting the offense charged." Fed. R. Crim. P. 3. The government must submit a sworn affidavit in support of a criminal complaint. An agent signs the affidavit, swearing that the information contained in the affidavit is true and correct to the best of the agent's knowledge and belief. The affidavit submitted to the judicial officer must demonstrate probable cause to believe the defendant has committed criminal offense. If the judge agrees that probable cause exists to believe the defendant has committed a criminal offense, then the judge will issue a warrant for the defendant's arrest, unless the prosecutor asks for another means, such as a summons, to require the defendant to appear in court to answer to the charges. Fed. R. Crim. P. 4.

The government almost always utilizes criminal complaints as a temporary charging document. Criminal complaints are issued in situations where there is an immediate need to charge a person with a crime because the person poses a danger to the community or constitutes a flight risk. It follows, then, that criminal complaints are most often used in reactive cases. As will be explained in more detail below, a defendant cannot be brought to trial on a federal felony offense unless a grand jury has indicted him. Accordingly, a criminal complaint is a valid charging document for only 30 days, by which time the government must obtain a grand jury indictment or the charge is dismissed. If the underlying crime is a misdemeanor, then the government can replace the criminal complaint with a "criminal information."

B. CRIMINAL INFORMATION

A criminal information is another form of charging document. The United States may charge a defendant with a misdemeanor offense by criminal information without leave of the court and without any presentation of evidence to or review by a grand jury. Fed. R. Crim. P. 7(a). A misdemeanor crime is an offense punishable by one year or less in prison. Federal prosecutors are not barred from using the grand jury to investigate a misdemeanor offense, however, even if an indictment is never presented to the grand jury for deliberation.

The United States may file a criminal information against a defendant to charge a felony offense, but may try, or accept a guilty plea from, a criminal defendant only if the defendant waives his right to have the felony charge considered and returned by a grand jury in the form of an indictment. Fed. R. Crim. P. 7(a). *See also Duke v. United States*, 301 U.S. 492, 494–95 (1937). To constitute a valid waiver of indictment, the court must advise the defendant of the nature of the charge and his rights, and must waive his right to be indicted in open court. Fed. R. Crim. P. 7(b). Generally, defendants waive their right to require the government to submit a case to the grand jury only when they have already worked out a plea agreement with the United States, a part of which calls for them to waive presentation of the case to the grand jury.

Unlike indictments which must be returned by a grand jury, a federal prosecutor may issue a criminal information on his or her own authority. In form, a criminal information generally appears the same as an indictment, only the caption says "Information" and it is signed only by the prosecutor. The form of an indictment is addressed below.

C. INDICTMENTS

Rules 6 and 7 of the Federal Rules of Criminal Procedure set forth the requirements for a federal indictment. We have already discussed the grand jury process which, if probable cause is found to exist, results in the return of a "true bill," or in other words, a valid indictment charging the defendant with a criminal offense. When a true bill is returned, the government attorney and the grand jury present the indictment to a judicial officer, who after ensuring that the indictment and the grand jury voting ballot are complete and valid on their face, will order the indictment filed with the district court. Upon request of the United States, an indictment may be sealed until the defendants are arrested. Likewise, at the request of the United States, the judicial officer issues an arrest warrant, summons or notice requiring the defendant to appear in court for his arraignment. Fed. R. Crim. P. 9.

Under the Fifth Amendment to the United States Constitution, a person cannot be tried on a felony offense by the federal government unless a grand jury returns a "true bill" on an indictment charging that person with an offense. An indictment is simply a formal written document charging the defendant with committing an offense.

The Sixth Amendment to the United States Constitution provides that: "In all criminal prosecutions, the accused shall enjoy the right . . . to be informed of the nature and cause of the accusation. . . ." This mandate is reflected in the requirements set forth in the Federal Rules of Criminal Procedure. At a minimum, all charging documents must provide a "plain, concise, and definite written statement of the essential facts constituting the offense charged." Fed. R. Crim. P. Rule 7(c)(1). An indictment must contain sufficient detail (who, what, where, when, etc.) such that a defendant can understand the nature of the charges, can adequately prepare a defense to the charges, and can determine whether he is being charged in violation of the double jeopardy clause with a crime for which he has already been tried. *Russell v. United States*, 369 U.S. 749, 763–72 (1962). There are, however, no requirements of formal language as long as the essential information is contained in the charging document. The sufficiency of an indictment is judged on the face of the indictment and the charging document as a whole. *United States v. Critzer*, 951 F.2d 306 (11th Cir. 1992).

1. ESSENTIAL ELEMENTS

An indictment must charge every essential element of the offense, including the state of mind (scienter or mens rea) element. *Hamling v. United States*, 418 U.S. 87 (1974). Indictments which track the language of the statute are, therefore, usually legally sufficient. *Russell v. United States*, 369 U.S. 749 (1962). Some statutes, however, do not explicitly set forth every element of an offense; thus, it might not always work simply to track the statutory language. *Hamling v. United States*, 418 U.S. 87 (1974). So, for example, Title 18, United States Code, Section 1503, makes it a federal offense to obstruct a federal judicial proceeding. The statute itself says nothing about whether a defendant has to know that a judicial proceeding is pending, but the courts have found that to be an essential element of the offense, which must be alleged in the indictment and proved to a jury beyond a reasonable doubt. Accordingly, prosecutors should research relevant cases and model jury instructions to ensure that they are aware of and plead all of the essential elements of an offense.

In *Apprendi v. New Jersey*, 530 U.S. 466 (2000), the Supreme Court added a twist to this requirement of charging every essential element of an offense. In *Apprendi*, the Supreme Court held that the government must also specifically charge in the indictment any fact (except for the fact of a prior conviction), the existence of which if found could increase the statutory maximum sentence to be imposed. In addition, the government must prove that fact beyond a reasonable doubt and it must be so found by a jury. This development arose because some federal criminal statutes provide for increased penalties if certain facts are present, such as certain drug quantities, or in the case of *Apprendi*, the death of a car-jacking victim. Thus, after *Apprendi*, prosecutors must be intimately familiar with the statute and must specifically allege in the indictment any fact which could increase the statutory maximum facing a defendant.

Apprendi creates a "twist" on the requirement that indictments must allege every essential element of an offense because facts which only increase the maximum possible sentence are not "elements" of the offense, yet still must be alleged in the indictment. They are not elements in the sense that failure to prove the fact does not result in acquittal— rather, it simply results in less possible punishment. For example, in order to send a drug trafficker to jail for up to forty years (as opposed to up to twenty years), the government must allege in the indictment and prove to a jury beyond a reasonable doubt that the offense involved a certain quantity of drugs (say, more than 50 grams of methamphetamine). If the government proves all of the elements of the offense, but fails to prove the drug quantity, the defendant is not acquitted of the offense. He is convicted, but may only be sent to jail for up to twenty years, as opposed to up to forty years.

2.   DETAILS AND EVIDENCE

Depending on the nature of the case and the charges being brought, an indictment can consist of only a few lines, or may be scores of pages in length. In simple cases, an indictment need only contain the essentials. There is no requirement that the indictment describe the government's evidence, contain evidentiary detail, or identify all the facts supporting the allegations. *Wong Tai v. United States*, 273 U.S. 77 (1927). On the other hand, there is nothing prohibiting the inclusion of detail and evidence in an indictment. Thus, in complex cases, it may be appropriate to set forth in the indictment the entire scheme in some detail, including instances of particular acts essential to the scheme and the roles of various individuals in the criminal conduct. Called "speaking indictments" or "talking indictments," these detailed indictments can sometimes negate the need for a "bill of particulars" which a defendant may seek if the indictment contains insufficient detail for the defendant to mount a meaningful defense. *See United States v. Cole*, 707 F. Supp. 949, 1001 (N.D. Ill. 1989). A prosecutor should be careful in drafting a detailed indictment, however, as it may lock the government into a specific theory or claim. While this can sometimes be resolved by seeking a superseding indictment, timing may be such that this is not a viable option.

3. CONJUNCTIVE LANGUAGE

The government may charge a defendant using conjunctive language ("and") when a statute may be violated in more than one way. *Turner v. United States*, 396 U.S. 398 (1970). Yet, although a statute may be violated in more than one way, the government need only prove at trial that the defendant violated the statute in one of the listed ways. *Id.* So, for example, the government may charge that a defendant conspired to distribute marijuana *and* cocaine, in violation of Title 21, United States Code, Section 846. Yet, at trial, it is sufficient if the jury finds that the defendant conspired to distribute one drug, but not the other, as conspiring to distribute either is still a violation of the conspiracy statute. *Turner v. United States*, 396 U.S. 398 (1970). If there is more than one alternative, however, a jury should be instructed to unanimously agree as to how the defendant violated the statute. In short, the government charges in the conjunctive, but proves in the disjunctive.

4. ALLEGING THE DATE OF OFFENSE

The government does not need to allege the precise date of the offense in an indictment. Rather, it is sufficient for the government to allege an approximate date that the offense took place. *See, e.g., United States v. Severe*, 29 F.3d 444 (8th Cir. 1994); *United States v. Hernandez*, 962 F.2d 1152 (5th Cir. 1992). Accordingly, indictments will often use language like the crime occurred "on or about" a certain date, or "between about" certain dates. Too much ambiguity in the date of the alleged offense, however, can violate a defendant's due process rights if it prevents him from being able to determine if the instant prosecution is a violation of the Double Jeopardy Clause or prevents him from being able to mount a meaningful defense. Thus, the date of the offense must be reasonably close to the approximate date alleged in the indictment. *United States v. Summers*, 137 F.3d 597 (8th Cir. 1998).

5. MULTIPLE DEFENDANTS

Rule 8(b) of the Federal Rules of Criminal Procedure provides:

Two or more defendants may be charged in the same indictment or information if they are alleged to have participated in the same act or transaction or in the same series of acts or transactions constituting an offense or offenses. Such defendants may be charged in one or more counts together or separately and all of the defendants need not be charged in each count.

Fed. R. Crim. P. 8(b). Defendants joined in the same indictment need not be charged in each count together. *United States v. Madena*, 152 F.3d 831, 847 (8th Cir. 1998). Thus, the government may charge multiple defendants in a single indictment when the defendants have participated in the "same act or transaction" or when the defendants have participated in the "same series of acts or transactions." Fed. R. Crim. P. 8(b). In other words, under this rule the defendants must have acted together in some manner in order to be charged together in the same indictment. One defendant may be charged in all six counts of an indictment, for example, while another defendant may be charged in only one or two of the counts in the indictment.

A conspiracy charge is an obvious way of charging multiple parties in the same indictment by alleging that they acted together to commit a crime. *United States v. Vasquez-Velasco*, 15 F.3d 838 (9th Cir. 1994). Indeed, members of the same conspiracy generally should be charged together in the same indictment and tried together when possible. *United States v. Mathison*, 157 F.3d 541, 546 (8th Cir. 1998) (noting that courts have repeatedly held that defendants charged in a conspiracy should be tried together). This is the case even when one member of the conspiracy may have occupied a very minor role, while another member of the conspiracy occupied a leadership role.

On the other hand, it is not appropriate to charge multiple defendants in the same indictment if there is no real connection between them and their criminal conduct. Thus, it is not appropriate to charge multiple defendants in the same indictment simply because they committed the same offenses at approximately the same time, unless there is some further connection between them. *United States v. Vasquez-Velasco*, 15 F.3d 833 (9th Cir. 1994). In looking to determine whether joinder of defendants in the same indictment is proper, a court will look to the face of the indictment itself. In most cases, it is not appropriate for the court to look at the facts underlying the indictment to determine if joinder was proper. *Costello v. United States*, 350 U.S. 359 (1956).

6. MULTIPLE CHARGES

Similar to the joinder of multiple parties in a single indictment, the government can charge more than one offense in a single indictment. This is permitted when the offenses are: 1) of the same or similar character; 2) based upon the same act or transaction; or 3) are in some way connected together or part of a common scheme or plan. Fed. R. Crim. P. 8(a). The court, in determining if multiple charges are properly charged in the same indictment, will look at whether the crimes involved the same method of committing the offense (modus operandi) and whether they were committed reasonably close in time. *United States v. Edgar*, 82 F.3d 499 (1st Cir. 1996). There must be some logical connection between the offenses, just as there has to be some logical connection between defendants to charge them in the same indictment.

7. CONSPIRACY INDICTMENTS

There are some rules specific to the drafting of conspiracy indictments. A conspiracy is simply an agreement between two or more people to commit a crime. A conspiracy may have multiple objectives; in other words, two or more people could reach an agreement to commit multiple crimes. *Braverman v. United States*, 317 U.S. 49 (1942). On the other hand, the same two people may reach separate agreements to commit separate crimes. *United States v. Kotteakos*, 328 U.S. 750 (1946). To illustrate, imagine that two people, John Doe and Jane Doe, reached an agreement to distribute methamphetamine and cocaine. This would properly be charged as a single conspiracy with multiple objectives. On the other hand, imagine that John Doe and Jane Doe reached an agreement to rob a bank. Then, three months after robbing the bank, they reached an agreement to sell stolen vehicles through John's car dealership. This would best be indicted as two separate conspiracies.

Imagine, now, that John and Jane Doe agreed to rob a bank, and that three months later, John Doe and Steve Smith decide to rob a different bank. The first bank robbery could be charged as a conspiracy in one count, but the later bank robbery would not be deemed part of that conspiracy with Jane Doe. The second bank robbery could be charged in a separate indictment alleging a different conspiracy between John Doe and Steve Smith.

Common sense guide these determinations. If the parties and time frame of the criminal activity are the same or similar, and there is a common goal, it is more likely that there is one conspiracy with multiple objectives. *United States v. McCarthy*, 97 F.3d 1562 (8th Cir. 1996). On the other hand, if there are different people involved in committing the separate crimes, and/or the time periods do not overlap, and/or there are multiple goals, it is more likely that there are multiple conspiracies. *United States v. Barlin*, 686 F.2d 748 (5th Cir. 1991).

In any event, a prosecutor should take care to ensure that the evidence supports the duration, scope and nature of the conspiracy alleged in the indictment. An indictment should not allege that a conspiracy lasted for five years, for example, if the evidence only supports a conclusion that it lasted only two years.

Prosecutors should also be aware that it is inappropriate to name or identify by other means unindicted co-conspirators in an indictment.

United States v. Chadwick, 556 F.2d 450 (9th Cir. 1977); *United States v. Trujillo*, 714 F.2d 102 (11th Cir. 1983). Rather, such individuals should be referred to as "unindicted coconspirators" or as "other persons known and unknown to the grand jury" or by some other type of reference. On the other hand, there is nothing improper with identifying unindicted coconspirators in discovery or at trial. *United States v. Smith*, 776 F.2d 1104 (3rd Cir. 1985).

The United States is not obligated to name or indict all coconspirators in an indictment. *United States v. Delavanant*, 440 F.2d 1264 (3rd Cir. 1971). Indeed, the government may allege that a named defendant conspired with others, known and unknown to the grand jury, without ever identifying in the indictment the identity of any other coconspirator. *United States v. Howard*, 966 F.2d 1362 (10th Cir. 1992).

CHAPTER 5

PROCEDURE, DISCOVERY, AND PRETRIAL MOTIONS

■ ■ ■

This chapter is designed to provide an overview of the events which normally occur in federal criminal cases between the time the government charges the defendant in a felony case and trial. This pretrial period encompasses the defendant's arraignment on the charges, bond or detention hearings, discovery between the parties, and motions practice. Each of these topics is discussed below.

A. INITIAL HEARINGS

1. INITIAL APPEARANCE

Rule 5 of the Federal Rules of Criminal Procedure requires that, upon arrest, the government must bring the defendant before a judicial officer without unnecessary delay. What constitutes "unnecessary delay" depends on the circumstances, but generally more than 24 hours will require a justification. For example, it is permissible for a defendant arrested on a Friday night not to be presented for initial appearance until the following Monday because federal courts are not open on weekends. If the government is found to have violated the requirement of bringing a defendant before a judge in a timely manner under Rule 5, it may result in the suppression of any statements or evidence obtained during the period deemed to be unreasonable.

When the defendant appears before the judge for the first time, it is called, appropriately enough, the "initial appearance." Typically, this hearing occurs before a federal magistrate judge. An attorney is appointed to represent the defendant at the hearing, if the defendant does not already have one. During the brief hearing, the judge will apprize the defendant of the nature of the charges against him and explain to the defendant his rights under the Constitution. The judge will also determine if the government is seeking detention of the defendant pending trial.

In order to detain a defendant pending trial, the government must make a motion to detain the defendant at the initial hearing. 18 U.S.C. § 3142(f). If the government fails to move for detention at the time of the initial appearance, it is waived. The requirements for a detention hearing are discussed below.

2.   PRELIMINARY HEARING

When a defendant has been charged by a criminal complaint, and the matter has not yet been submitted to the grand jury, the defendant is entitled to a preliminary hearing. Fed. R. Crim. P. 5.1. A defendant may waive a preliminary hearing. *Id.* Otherwise, the court must hold a "preliminary hearing" or "probable cause hearing" within fourteen days of arraignment, if the defendant is in custody, or within twenty days of arraignment if the defendant has been released pending trial. Fed. R. Crim. P. 5.1(c). A court may, upon request of either party, extend these time limits, but absent such a request, the preliminary hearing must be held within the time frame established by the rule absent a showing of extraordinary circumstances. Fed. R. Crim. P. 5.1(d).

During a preliminary hearing, the government must present evidence to establish probable cause to believe the defendant committed the crime in question. Fed. R. Crim. P. 5.1(e). The government may satisfy the requirement for showing probable cause through hearsay evidence. *Id.* Furthermore, in determining whether probable cause exists, the court may rely upon evidence seized in violation of the defendant's constitutional rights. *Id.* The defendant has the right, at the preliminary hearing, to cross examine government witnesses, and also has the right to call his or her own witnesses. *Id.* If, as a result of the preliminary hearing, the court determines the government failed to establish probable cause the crime occurred, or that the defendant committed the offense, the court must dismiss the criminal complaint and discharge the defendant from custody. Fed. R. Crim. P. 5.1(b).

Dismissal of the complaint does not, however, prevent the government from instituting a subsequent prosecution of the defendant for the same offense. *Id.* In other words, even if the judge dismisses the criminal complaint, the government may still seek an indictment against the defendant. Like initial appearances, preliminary hearings are almost uniformly conducted by federal magistrate judges. Either party may appeal any decision of a federal magistrate judge to the district court judge, including decisions on preliminary or detention hearings.

3.   DETENTION HEARINGS

One of the decisions the government must make when arresting a defendant is whether to seek detention of the defendant in jail pending the trial in the matter. In the Bail Reform Act of 1984 Congress created a presumption that defendants will be released on bond pending trial in most cases. Whether a defendant is eligible for release pending trial is governed by Title 18, United States Code, Sections 3142 and 3144. Fed. R. Crim. P. 46(a). The district court has the power to impose on a defendant almost any condition of release necessary to ensure that the defendant will not pose a danger to the community and will appear, as required, at any subsequent court proceedings. 18 U.S.C. § 3142(b) & (c).

The government must move for detention at the defendant's initial appearance; if it fails to make such a motion, the government has waived the ability to seek detention. If the government does move for detention, however, the court must conduct a detention hearing to determine whether detention is appropriate. The detention hearing must be held at the time of the defendant's initial appearance, unless either party seeks an extension of time. 18 U.S.C. § 3142(f). The law provides, though, that "except for good cause," such an extension cannot exceed five days (if the defendant sought the extension) or three days (if the government sought the extension), not counting weekends and holidays. *Id.* During any such continuance, the defendant must be detained. *Id.*

At the detention hearing, the rules of evidence do not apply. *Id.* The burden is on the government to prove by a preponderance of the evidence that the defendant poses a flight risk, or by clear and convincing evidence that the defendant poses a danger to the community. *Id.* The defendant may, of course, cross examine the government's witnesses and may present his or her own evidence. *Id.*

As stated above, in most cases the law presumes that the defendant should be released pending trial. However, in certain cases, the contrary is true. If the defendant has been charged with: (1) a crime of violence; (2) any offense for which the maximum term of imprisonment is life imprisonment or death; (3) a drug trafficking offense punishable by a maximum term of ten years or more; or (4) any felony of the defendant has previously been convicted of two or more of the offenses described in (1) through (3) above, then there is a rebuttable presumption that the defendant is both a flight risk and poses a danger to the community, requiring his or her detention pending trial. 18 U.S.C. § 3142(f).

In deciding whether to detain a defendant, the court is required to consider: (1) the nature and circumstances of the offense, including whether the crime involves drugs or violence; (2) the weight of the evidence against the defendant; (3) the history and characteristics of the person, including such things as ties to the community, employment and financial resources, among other things; and (4) the nature and extent of the danger the defendant would pose to any individual or the community if released pending trial. 18 U.S.C. § 3142(f). Again, if the hearing is conducted by a magistrate judge, either side may seek de novo review by a district court judge. Further, either party may seek to have the issue of detention reconsidered at a later time should matters arise suggesting a change in circumstances.

4. ARRAIGNMENT

Once a grand jury has indicted a defendant and he has been arrested, the defendant must be arraigned before a federal judicial officer, which again often takes place before a federal magistrate judge. Fed. R. Crim. P.10. During the arraignment, the judge advises the defendant of charges pending against him. Unless waived, the judge must read verbatim the indictment pending against the defendant. At the time of arraignment, the defendant enters a plea. Fed. R. Crim. P. 10(a)(3). As a practical matter, the plea is always "not guilty," not only because a defendant is seldom prepared to plead guilty immediately after being charged with a crime, but also because, as mentioned above, arraignments are often conducted by federal magistrate judges who do not have the constitutional authority to accept guilty pleas (absent consent of the parties). At the arraignment, or shortly thereafter, the court will set a trial date and deadlines for other matters, such as the filing of dispositive and pretrial motions.

5. GUILTY PLEAS

It is a rare case where a defendant will enter a guilty plea without proceeding through discovery and pretrial motions, which are explained below in more detail. Thus, guilty pleas almost always follow chronologically after the discovery and pretrial motions stages of federal criminal practice have occurred. For the sake of organization in this book, however, description of the proceeding used for a defendant to change his plea from "not guilty" to "guilty" is most efficiently dealt with at this time.

Rule 11 of the Federal Rules of Criminal Procedure sets forth certain requirements, most premised upon constitutional guarantees, which a judge must follow when a defendant pleads guilty. The judge must make sure the guilty plea is knowingly made by the defendant, is voluntary, and is supported by a factual basis. Furthermore, the judge must make certain that the defendant is capable of understanding, and does, in fact, understand, the proceedings. A defendant must understand the constitutional and trial rights he will be giving up by pleading guilty instead of proceeding to trial.

Further, the judge must inform the defendant of the statutory maximum and minimum sentences that could be imposed as punishment for the crime. Finally, the judge must make sure that the defendant has not been unduly pressured to plead guilty, either by threats or promises.

Because a guilty plea involves a dispositive decision in the case, only an Article III judge, typically a United States District Court Judge, may accept a guilty plea. In many districts, however, federal magistrate judges preside over change of plea hearings and then issue a Report and Recommendation ("R&R"). The R&R summarizes the result of the hearing and recommends the district court judge enter an order accepting the guilty plea. The parties have ten days to object to the findings of the R&R. After that time, the district court judge can then rule on the R&R and formally accept the defendant's guilty plea.

B. DISCOVERY IN FEDERAL CRIMINAL CASES

To begin with, it should be understood that there is no general constitutional right to discovery. *Weatherford v. Bursey*, 429 U.S. 545, 559 (1977); *Wardius v. Oregon*, 412 U.S. 470, 474 (1973). Rather, discovery, the process by which one party learns about the evidence possessed by the other party, has developed over time as a matter of practice and practicality. The scope and nature of discovery permitted the parties in federal criminal cases are governed by statute, the Federal Rules of Criminal Procedure, and case law: 18 U.S.C. § 3500; 18 U.S.C. § 3505(b); Fed. R. Crim. P. §§ 12(I), 12.1, 12.2, 12.3, 16, 26.2 and 46(j); Fed. R. Evid. 404(b), 803(24), and 804(b)(5); *Brady v. Maryland*, 373 U.S. 83 (1963); and *Giglio v. United States*, 405 U.S. 150 (1972). These statutes, rules and cases are discussed in more detail below.

Although in practice most discovery in federal criminal cases is a one-way street with information flowing from the government to the defendant, the rules contemplate a degree of reciprocity. In theory, discovery "must be a two-way street." *Wardius*, 470 U.S. at 475.When the government provides discovery to a defendant, it triggers a requirement for the defendant to provide discovery to the government.

1. RULE 16, FEDERAL RULES OF CRIMINAL PROCEDURE

Fairness dictates that defendants are entitled to some basic information necessary for them to defend themselves against pending criminal charges. Rule 16 of the Federal Rules of Criminal Procedure requires the government to provide defendants with some of this basic information. There are some limitations, however, to discovery under Rule 16. First, a defendant is entitled to discovery under Rule 16 only after indictment. Further, Rule 16 obligations are triggered only by a proper request from the defendant.

Rule 16 of the Federal Rules of Criminal Procedure requires the government to provide a defendant with several categories of evidence, including a copy of any statements made by the defendant, his criminal record, documents and tangible objects, reports of examinations or tests, and expert information.

a. Defendant's Statements

Pursuant to Rule 16, a defendant is entitled to copies of any written or recorded statements the government alleges that he made. This entitlement, however, is limited to relevant *written* or *recorded* statements of defendant which are: (1) in possession or control of the government, including agencies; (2) regardless of whether the government intends to use those statements at trial; (3) to whomever those statements were made. In other words, the statements are not limited simply to those allegedly made in response to interrogation, but rather, encompass any statements made by a defendant to whomever.

The term "recorded" does *not* include statements "recorded" in reports or in grand jury testimony of third parties. It means actual recorded statements on audio or videotape, or recorded by a stenographer in the course of the defendant presenting testimony. Again, to be subject to Rule 16 discovery, the statement must be relevant.

In addition to recorded statements by the defendant, Rule 16 also requires disclosure of the portion of any written record containing the substance of any *oral* statements by the defendant if they are: (1) relevant; (2) made in response to interrogation; and (3) made to a person then known to the defendant to be a government agent. Even if not reduced to a written report, a defendant is entitled to the substance of any other relevant oral statement made by the defendant in response to interrogation by any person then known to him to be a government agent, if government intends to use that evidence at trial.

b. Defendant's Prior Criminal Record

Rule 16 requires the government to provide a defendant with a copy of his criminal history. This includes what is known, or could be known with due diligence, about the defendant's past criminal record. Except as required by the notice provisions of Federal Rule of Evidence 404(b), discussed below, the government is not required to indicate any intended use of this information.

c. Documents and Tangible Objects

Rule 16 requires advance disclosure to the defendant of any "books, papers, documents, photographs, tangible objects, buildings or places" that are: (1) in the government's possession and material to the defense; *or* (2) intended by the government for use as evidence in chief at trial, *or* (3) obtained from or belonging to the defendant. Disclosure of these items can be conditioned on safeguards necessary to protect the integrity of the government's evidence.

d.   Reports of Examinations and Tests

Rule 16 provides that the government must provide the defendant with reports of any examinations or tests. Examples might be ballistics tests, urinalysis tests or similar scientific analysis of evidence or data. To be discoverable, the result of examination must be either material to the preparation of the defense or intended for use by the government in its case.

e.   Expert Information

Rule 16(a)(1)(E) requires that, upon request by the defendant, the government must disclose to the defendant a written summary of expert testimony, describing the witness's opinions, "the bases and the reasons therefore," and his qualifications. The obligation to disclose under this rule is triggered by a request from the defendant. If no such request is made, the rule imposes no disclosure obligation on the government.

2.   JENCKS ACT (18 U.S.C. § 3500)

The Jencks Act provides that the government *must* produce to the defense copies of any prior statements made by government witness if: (1) the statements are in the possession of the government, which means in the possession of either the prosecutor or the investigative agency; (2) which relate to the subject matter on which the witness has testified; and (3) if the defense has moved for their production. The Jencks Act provides that the court may order the government to produce such statements only *after* a witness has testified on direct examination.

Rule 26.2 of the Federal Rules of Criminal Procedure substantially tracks Section 3500, but also applies it to all suppression hearings, sentencing hearings, probation revocation hearings, and, unless the Court orders otherwise, to preliminary and detention hearings. *See also* Rules 5.1, 12 (h), 32(e), 32.1(c), and 46(j). Rule 26.2 is reciprocal, meaning that a defendant has the same obligation to produce statements of his witnesses to the government.

What is a statement? The statutory definition in 18 U.S.C. § 3500(e) defines a statement as: (1) a written statement made by the witness and signed or otherwise adopted or approved by him; (2) a stenographic, mechanical, electrical, or other recording, or a transcription thereof, which is a substantially verbatim recital of an oral statement made by the witness and recorded contemporaneously with the making of such oral statement; or (3) a statement, however taken or recorded, or a transcription thereof, if any, made by the witness to a grand jury.

The key to the analysis is "whether the statement can fairly be deemed to reflect fully and without distortion the witness's own words."

Palermo v. United States, 360 U.S. 343, 352–3 (1959); *United States v. Morris*, 957 F.2d 1391, 1401 (7th Cir. 1992).

The most common issues in determining whether something is a "statement," pursuant to Section 3500, concern whether it is communicative, whether it is reasonably complete, whether it has been "adopted" by the witness, whether it is "substantially verbatim," and for what purpose it has been created. Portions of the statement that do not relate to the "subject matter of the testimony of the witness" can be excised on motion of the United States. 18 U.S.C. § 3500(c).

3.   WITNESS LISTS AND EXHIBIT LISTS

A defendant charged with treason or a capital offense is entitled to a list of the government's witnesses "at least three entire days" before trial. 18 U.S.C. § 3432. In noncapital cases, the defense is not statutorily entitled to an advance list of the government's witnesses or exhibits. As a practical matter, however, most federal district courts have adopted local rules requiring both the government and the defense to produce exhibit and witness lists at a reasonable time in advance of trial.

4.   BAD ACTS OF DEFENDANT

Federal Rule of Evidence 404(b) requires the prosecution to provide reasonable notice of "the general nature" of any uncharged crime, wrong or bad act in advance of trial or during trial, upon request of the accused. The degree of detail required under this notice requirement is not defined by statute. Likewise, there is no strict time frame provided for how far in advance of trial such notice is required. What constitutes reasonable and timely notice depends largely on the nature of the case and the nature of the other bad acts.

Rule 404(b) is not limited to use by the government. *See, e.g., United States v. McClure*, 546 F2d 670 (5th Cir. 1990) (acts of informant offered in entrapment defense). Nevertheless, the rule is silent as to a defendant's obligation to give similar notice to the government.

5.   *BRADY/GIGLIO* INFORMATION

Information tending to exculpate the defendant or mitigate his punishment, or tending to impeach government witnesses must be disclosed to the defendant. *See Brady v. Maryland*, 373 U.S. 83 (1963) (evidence that may tend to exculpate a defendant must be produced to the defendant); *Giglio v. United States*, 405 U.S. 150 (1992) (evidence which tends to impeach government witnesses must be produced to the defense). *Brady* and *Giglio* did not create new rules of discovery, but rather, require disclosure as a matter of due process that may void a conviction where the government does not disclose material evidence favorable to an accused.

As a practical matter, it may be difficult for the government to know whether it is in possession of information that could be exculpatory. If the government possesses a confession from another person that he or she committed a crime, that is clearly exculpatory. In practice, the distinction is more subtle and whether a piece of information or evidence is exculpatory may turn on the nature of the defense, which is generally unknown to the government until trial.

6.   ITEMS PROTECTED FROM DISCLOSURE

"Reports, memoranda, or other internal government documents made by the attorney for the government or other government agents in connection with the investigation or prosecution of the case" are not discoverable under Rule 16(a). Further, in contrast to the practice in some state courts, interrogatories and depositions are not permitted in federal criminal discovery. Although Rule 15 of the Federal Rules of Criminal Procedure provides a mechanism for preserving testimony of a party's own witnesses by evidence depositions under "exceptional circumstances," Rule 15 does not authorize discovery depositions. These depositions are permitted only when, for example, the witness lives overseas and is therefore not subject to the court's subpoena power, or where the witness is dying and a deposition is necessary to preserve the witness's testimony.

7.   ALTERNATIVES TO DISCOVERY

Although Rule 16 provides the basic discovery tools available by law, there are at least two other sources for discovery. Rule 17(c) permits the Court to order issuance of subpoenas for "books, papers, documents or objects" to be produced in court before the trial. This so-called "subpoena duces tecum" is available to both a defendant and the government to obtain documents from third parties that are relevant and necessary for either side to investigate the case or to prepare for trial.

In addition, counsel for the government and defense can reach agreements to provide discovery to each other beyond that required by the Federal Rules of Criminal Procedure. Many United States Attorneys' Offices have reached general agreements with the defense bar to allow for expanded discovery in exchange for broader reciprocal discovery. This is advantageous for both sides. It is helpful to the government, in these circumstances, because it prevents errors in nondisclosure which can be found to violate a criminal defendant's rights. It is advantageous to a defendant, of course, because it gives access to more information.

8. DEFENDANT'S DISCLOSURE OF EVIDENCE TO PROSECUTION

Rule 16 of the Federal Rules of Criminal Procedure provides an obligation on a defendant, albeit limited, especially in comparison to the government's obligation, to provide reciprocal discovery to the government. Rule 16(b)(1)(A) requires criminal defendants to provide reciprocal discovery of documents and tangible objects if the defendant has requested these from government. Likewise, the defendant is required to provide reports of examinations and tests, which are in the control of the defendant, which he intends to use at trial "as evidence in chief" or prepared by witness he intends to call at trial. Fed. R. Crim. P. 16(b)(1)(B).

In addition, Rule 16(b)(1)(C) mandates that defendants provide the government with a summary of expert testimony. Although generally speaking, mutual exchange of expert summaries is in the control of the defendant, who must make the first request, there is an exception. If the defendant files a notice of insanity or mental defect under Rule 12.2, the government can request discovery of expert information.

Under the probably unnecessary amendments to Rule 16(a)(1)(E), such a request by the government creates a reciprocal right in the defendant.

A defendant must also provide the government with statements of witnesses called by defendant, but only *after* the witness has testified. Fed. R. Crim. P. 26.2. This rule essentially requires the defendant provide the equivalent of the information the government must provide the defendant under the Jencks Act. For this reason, this is sometimes referred to as "reverse Jencks" information.

Should a defendant seek to present an alibi defense, he may need to provide notice to the government. Under Rule 12.1 the government may serve on the defendant a written demand stating the time, date, and place at which the offense was committed. This requires the defendant to serve on the government a written notice of alibi, stating the place the defendant claims to have been at the time and the names and addresses of supporting witnesses. If the defendant complies and provides the required information, this in turn creates a reciprocal duty for the government to respond at least ten days prior to trial with a written notice of the witnesses on whom the government intends to rely to prove the defendant's presence at the scene, or to rebut the alibi witnesses.

On the other hand, Rule 12.2. requires the defendant, *without request from the government*, to file within the time provided for the filing of pre-trial motions, written notice of his intent to rely on a defense of insanity, or a mental disease or defect. If the defense intends to introduce expert testimony concerning his mental condition, including conditions short of insanity, he must give notice to the prosecution of that intention within the time provided for filing pre-trial motions "or at such later time as the court may direct." Fed. R. Crim. P. 12.2(b). The filing of such a notice entitles the prosecution to request disclosure of the expert testimony. Fed. R. Crim. P. 16(b)(1)(C).

Similarly, Rule 12.3. requires the defendant, without a request, to give notice that he is relying upon a claim that he was acting on behalf of a law enforcement or intelligence agency. This so-called "Notice of Defense base on Public Authority" requires the government to file, within the time limits set out by the rule, a written response admitting or denying the defendant's claim. At that time, the government may, but need not, demand the names and addresses of the defense witnesses who will support the claim. After the defendant responds, the government must reply in kind, listing the names and addresses of its contrary witnesses.

Finally, a defendant may be obligated, upon demand by the government, to provide handwriting exemplars, fingerprints, and voice exemplars. Courts have uniformly held that a defendant's Fifth Amendment right against self-incrimination is not jeopardized by production of these things because it is not the equivalent of speech. *See, e.g., Gilbert v. California*, 388 U.S. 263, 266–67 (1967) (compelling defendant to provide handwriting exemplars was not a violation of the Fifth Amendment because it was not testimonial); *Kyger v. Carlton*, 146 F.3d 374, 381 n.2 (6th Cir. 1998) (taking fingerprints not a Fifth Amendment violation because it is not testimonial); *United States v. Dionisio*, 410 U.S. 1, 7 (1973) (compelling voice exemplars not a violation of Fifth Amendment because not testimonial).

C. PRETRIAL MOTIONS

The litigation of pretrial motions is a part of almost every federal criminal case. The number and complexity of the pretrial motions are directly proportionate to the seriousness and complexity of the indictment at issue. In some routine cases, defense counsel may not file any pretrial motions for the very simple reason that there is nothing of merit to litigate pretrial. On the other end of the spectrum, some complex cases can consume months or even years of pretrial litigation, sometimes resulting in interlocutory appeals and multiple subsequent delays in the trial date.

There are several categories of pretrial motions encountered in federal criminal cases. Generally they consist of motions to dismiss the indictment, motions to change the indictment, motions to change the trial, motions to suppress evidence, discovery motions and motions in limine. We will briefly discuss each in turn.

1. MOTIONS TO DISMISS THE INDICTMENT

Indictments may be attacked for a number of reasons. An indictment may be challenged for being insufficient as a matter of law. Fed. R. Crim. Pro. 12. In other words, the allegation is made that the indictment fails to allege a federal offense. In addition, a court may dismiss an indictment because it is barred by the statute of limitations. On occasion, challenges are brought to an indictment alleging that the government has abused the grand jury in some manner. On even more rare occasions, defendants assert that the court should dismiss an indictment because of outrageous government conduct.

One important point to remember in federal criminal practice is that a defendant cannot challenge an indictment based on an assertion that it is not supported by the facts, or on the ground that the undisputed facts mandate judgment in favor of the defendant. In civil practice, litigants can bring such motions, called motions for summary judgment, in which the court is called upon to render judgment in one party's favor based upon a finding of certain facts. In federal criminal practice, trial is the only time that the judgment is rendered based upon the facts of the case.

2. MOTIONS TO CHANGE THE INDICTMENT

In some instances, defendants do not dispute that the indictment is sufficient as a matter of law, but may allege that the indictment should be changed for some reason. One of the more common pretrial motions of this nature is a motion alleging improper joinder. Rule 8(a) of the Federal Rules of Criminal Procedure provides:

> **Joinder of Offenses.** Two or more offense may be charged in the same indictment or information in a separate count for each offense if the offenses charged, whether felonies or misdemeanors or both, are of the same or similar character or are based on the same act or transaction or on two or more acts or transactions connected together or constituting parts of a common scheme or plan.

Rule 8(b) of the Federal Rules of Criminal Procedure provides:

> **Joinder of Defendants.** Two or more defendants may be charged in the same indictment or information if they are alleged to have participated in the same act or transaction or in the same series of acts or transactions constituting an offense or offenses. Such defendants may be charged in one or more counts together or separately and all of the defendants need not be charged in each count.

Motions alleging improper joinder, either of offenses or defendants, therefore assert that the indictment failed to comply with these rules of Federal Criminal Procedure because it failed to meet the requirements set forth in the rules.

Another, albeit less common, pretrial motion to change an indictment is a motion to strike language in the indictment. Rule 7(d) of the Federal Rules of Criminal Procedure provides that "[t]he court on motion of the defendant may strike surplusage from the indictment or information." Defendants may file motions to strike when they believe that the indictment contains allegations, whether true or untrue, which the defendants claim are unnecessary to the pleading and which is somehow prejudicial or damaging to the defendants.

3. MOTIONS TO CHANGE THE TRIAL

Rule 14 of the Federal Rules of Criminal Procedure provides for the severance of offenses or defendants, even if properly joined in the first place under Rule 8. Rule 14 provides:

> If it appears that a defendant or the government is prejudiced by a joinder of offenses or of defendants in an indictment or information or by such joinder for trial together, the court may order an election or separate trials of counts, grant a severance of defendants or provide whatever other relief justice requires. In ruling on a motion by a defendant for severance the court may order the attorney for the government to deliver to the court for inspection *in camera* any statements or confessions made by the defendants which the government intends to introduce in evidence at trial.

To be clear, a defendant filing a motion under Rule 8 is alleging that the offenses or defendants were wrongfully joined in that the indictment fails to meet the requirements of Rule 8. A motion under Rule 14 asserts that, even though the joinder of offenses or defendants complied with Rule 8, the offenses or defendants should nevertheless be severed to ensure a fair trial.

One reason either a defendant or the government may move to sever defendants, pursuant to Rule 14, is because one defendant made a confession in which he incriminated a co-defendant. That confession would be admissible against the confessor as an admission of a party opponent. Fed. R. Evid. 801(d)(2). The Sixth Amendment, however, mandates that a defendant be able to cross examine an accuser. Yet, the confessor (in this case, the codefendant) has a right under the Fifth Amendment to remain silent and cannot be compelled to take the stand to be questioned about his confession. This *Bruton* problem, so named after the case of *Bruton v. United States*, 391 U.S. 123 (1968), is one reason why properly joined defendants may be prejudiced by a joint trial.

Another pretrial motion aimed at the manner in which the trial is to occur, versus an attack on the indictment itself, is a motion for change of venue. Rule 18 of the Federal Rules of Criminal Procedure provides, in pertinent part, that "[e]xcept as otherwise permitted by statute or by these rules, the prosecution shall be had in a district in which the offense was committed." Thus, a defendant may file a motion to move the trial to another district on the ground that the offense occurred in another district. Even when the venue is properly in the district, pursuant to Rule 18, a defendant may nevertheless seek to change venue for other reasons.

Rule 21(a) of the Federal Rules of Criminal Procedure provide that a court "must transfer the proceeding against the defendant to another district if the court is satisfied that so great a prejudice against the defendant exists in the transferring district that the defendant cannot obtain a fair and impartial trial there." Pretrial publicity or notoriety of the offense, such as in the Timothy McVey trial, may be a ground for seeking a change of venue under this rule. Only the defendant may file a motion under this Rule. In addition, Rule 21(b) allows the court to transfer a criminal case to another district "[f]or the convenience of parties, any victim, and witnesses, and in the interest of justice." Again, only a defendant may move for a change of venue under this rule.

4. MOTIONS TO SUPPRESS EVIDENCE

The most common motion filed in federal criminal cases is a motion to suppress evidence. Although the Constitution does not explicitly provide for the suppression of evidence obtained in violation of a defendant's Constitutional rights, the courts have fashioned this remedy, sometimes referred to as the exclusionary rule. *See Arizona v. Evans*, 514 U.S. 1 (1995) (exclusionary rule is a judicially created remedy). The purpose of the exclusionary rule is to punish law enforcement officers for violating a defendant's constitutional rights and to deter wrongful government conduct in the future by suppressing or excluding evidence obtained in violation of the Constitution. *Evans*, 514 U.S. at 14–15.

Motions may be filed to suppress statements obtained from a defendant in violation of the Fifth Amendment right to remain silent, or the Fifth or Sixth Amendment rights to counsel. Likewise, a defendant may move to suppress evidence obtained in violation of the Fourth Amendment prohibition against unreasonable searches and seizures. Under the Supreme Court's decision in *Wong Sun v. United States*, 371 U.S. 471, 484 (1963), a defendant may seek to suppress not only the specific evidence obtained directly as a result of a violation of his constitutional rights, but also any other evidence derived from that violation—the so-called "fruit of the poisonous tree."

5.　DISCOVERY-RELATED MOTIONS

Defendants sometimes file pretrial motions in an effort to obtain greater discovery from the government. For example, Rule 7(f) provides that "[t]he court may direct the filing of a bill of particulars." A motion for a bill of particulars may be made before arraignment or within fourteen days after arraignment or at such later time as a court may permit. *Id*. A court may permit the government to amend a bill of particulars at any time before the verdict is returned. *Id*. A motion for a bill of particulars is simply a request that the government explain its indictment in more detail. Although mere notice pleading is required under the Federal Rules of Criminal Procedure, a defendant may be entitled to a bill of particulars if the indictment nevertheless lacks sufficient detail for the defendant to know what crime he has been accused of committing, or if necessary for him to mount a meaningful defense or determine if he is being subjected to double jeopardy.

Defendants may also seek to find out the identity of confidential informants. As a general matter, the courts are reluctant to require the government to reveal the identity of confidential informants who are not going to be witnesses at trial, but will compel disclosure if justice requires. A defendant must make a showing in these cases for why the identity of the informant is necessary.

6.　MOTIONS IN LIMINE

Before a trial commences, the government or a defendant may file Rule 104 motions or motions in limine. Rule 104 of the Federal Rules of Evidence allows trial courts to make pretrial rulings on the admissibility of evidence. So, a Rule 104 motion requests the trial court rule in advance of trial that certain evidence is admissible pursuant to the Federal Rules of Evidence. A motion in limine, on the other hand, seeks a court order finding that certain evidence is inadmissible pursuant to the Federal Rules of Evidence. Each motion is an attempt to anticipate an evidentiary problem that may arise at trial and have the court rule on the admissibility of the evidence before the trial begins. These motions, generically referred to as motions in limine, have the advantage of permitting the parties to carefully craft their arguments in favor of, or against, admission, rather than simply making arguments off the cuff during the middle of trial. Further, it prevents surprises from occurring at trial, allows the court time to make clearly analyzed evidentiary rulings, and avoids the possibility of error.

Although the term "limine" is derived from the term "limit," suggesting that the goal is to limit the evidence admitted at trial, in practice the term "motion in limine" is not so limited. Rather, the term is used rather imprecisely to refer to a motionfiled in advance of trial requesting an order to find that certain evidence is admissible or that certain evidence is inadmissible.

To be clear, although both a motion to suppress and a motion in limine may have the same result, that is, keeping evidence out of the trial, they are different. Motions to suppress are based on allegations that the evidence was obtained in violation of the Constitution or some other law. Motions in limine do not allege that the evidence was obtained improperly. Rather, motions in limine are based on assertions the evidence should not be admitted under pursuant to the Federal Rules of Evidence.

CHAPTER 6

JURY SELECTION

■ ■ ■

Jury selection in federal court may be less important than it is in state court for the simple reason that most federal courts strictly limit the length, scope and nature of voir dire by attorneys. Lawyers practicing in state courts often use voir dire to try their cases, not so much questioning prospective jurors as engaging in long explanations of their cases and theories, punctuated by occasional questions of no real importance asked solely to maintain the facade of conducting jury selection. Using this method, jury selection sometimes takes days, at the end of which the presentation of the evidence may be anticlimactic and largely academic.

Federal judges seldom permit such antics in their court rooms. It is completely within the court's discretion to control the scope and nature of voir dire, and a trial judge can limit questions by counsel to those "it deems proper." *United States v. Rosales-Lopez*, 451 U.S. 182, 189 (1981). Indeed, Rule 24(a) of the Federal Rules of Criminal Procedure leaves it totally within the judge's discretion whether to permit the parties to conduct voir dire at all. The rule does not even require the judge to conduct voir dire. *See* Fed. R. Crim. P. 24(a) (the court "*may* examine prospective jurors or may permit the attorneys for the parties to do so.") (emphasis added). Thus, in practice, the degree to which federal judges restrict jury selection varies by judge and by district to a greater degree than probably any other aspect of a federal criminal trial. Although some judges permit wide latitude in conducting voir dire, other judges permit none at all. Despite, or perhaps because of, these limitations, when a lawyer has an opportunity to engage in jury selection, it is important to make the most of it.

After all, the jurors are the most important people in the court room during jury trials. They are the decision-makers. And jury selection is important not only because lawyers want to select the best possible jury, but also because this is the first time the jury will see the lawyer in action. First impressions are lasting ones. Therefore, jury selection is, perhaps, one of the most important parts of a jury trial in federal court because it is through this process that the parties choose their judges (of the facts) and jurors formulate their initial impression of the lawyer and his or her client.

There are important Constitutional, statutory and case laws that control jury selection in federal criminal cases, which will be reviewed here. We will also discuss voir dire as an advocacy skill, one which is all too seldom taught.

A. A BRIEF HISTORY OF JURY SELECTION

The Western jury system dates back to ancient Greece—indeed, a Greek jury (called a dicastery) convicted Socrates of atheism in 399 B.C. The nature, content and purpose of Western juries, however, have changed dramatically over time. For a period, juries were chosen from among witnesses who already knew the facts underlying the dispute, as opposed to our current system of seeking out those who are totally ignorant of the underlying facts. The process of conducting voir dire for the purpose of examining prospective jurors is believed to date back to medieval times. The nature of the questioning obviously changed with the nature of the juries.

Although England has largely abandoned the lawyer-led jury selection process, it has remained a mainstay of the American judicial system, at least in state courts. Jury selection, however, has developed haphazardly. There are very few laws, rules or regulations governing the jury selection process. As a consequence, jury selection in state court differs significantly from jury selection in federal court, while still further differences exist between courts within the same system.

As a general matter, however, the American jury trial involves a process through which the court and the parties attempt to empanel a group of people from the surrounding community who can fairly and impartially evaluate the evidence presented and render a just verdict. To choose from among a group of citizens a certain number of impartial jurors, we have adopted a system of examining or questioning prospective jurors in order to make that decision. That questioning process is commonly referred to as "voir dire."

"Voir dire," pronounced "vwar dear," derives from the French verbs "voir" and "dire," and means, literally "to see, to tell." In Old French, "voir dire" meant "to speak the truth." *See* David Mellinkoff, THE LANGUAGE OF THE LAW, 101–02, 106 (1963). Voir dire generally refers to the process of conducting a preliminary examination of a person to determine competency, interest, bias or some other factor that would disqualify the person from appearing in court as a juror or witness. BLACK'S LAW DICTIONARY (7th ed. 1999). Thus, incidentally, the process of voir dire is used not only to examine potential jurors, but is also used to examine witnesses if one party believes that there exists some fundamental flaw that should prevent them from giving testimony.

B. THE RIGHT TO A JURY AND THE PURPOSE OF JURY SELECTION

The Constitution commands juries in criminal cases. U.S. Const. Art. III, § 2, ¶ 3 ("The trial of all Crimes, except in Cases of Impeachment," shall be by Jury. . . ."). The Supreme Court has concluded that this right to trial by jury does not extend, however, to petty offenses, that is to crimes punishable by less than six months in prison.

The Constitution is silent, however, as to the size or composition of a criminal jury. At common law, juries typically consisted of twelve people. That common law practice has been codified in federal practice in Rule 23 of the Federal Rules of Criminal Procedure. There are provisions in the rule for a jury of less than twelve to decide a case either by stipulation of the parties or if a juror is excused for good cause after trial begins. The rule also provides that a defendant can waive trial by jury, but only with consent of the government. The government does not have to explain or justify its decision if it declines to agree to a bench trial.

The Constitution is also silent as to voir dire. As mentioned above, the purpose of jury selection in the United States courts is to arrive at an impartial jury. This purpose is reflected in and now founded upon the Sixth Amendment to the United States Constitution, which provides:

> In all criminal proceedings, the accused shall enjoy the right to a speedy and public trial, by an impartial jury of the State and district wherein the crime shall have been committed.

U.S. Const. amend. VI. Voir dire is deemed critical to achieve the goal of an impartial jury. *See Rosales-Lopez v. United States*, 451 U.S. 182, 188 (1981) ("Voir dire plays a critical function in assuring the criminal defendant that his Sixth Amendment right to an impartial jury will be honored. Without an adequate voir dire the trial judge's responsibility to remove prospective jurors who will not be able impartially to follow the court's instructions and evaluate the evidence cannot be fulfilled."). Nevertheless, as mentioned above, Rule 24 of the Federal Rules of Criminal Procedure does not require either the judge or the parties to engage in voir dire. As a practical matter, judges will invariably engage in some voir dire, however limited it may be.

The Sixth Amendment does not define what makes a juror "impartial." True impartiality is an idealistic, unmeasurable, and largely unattainable goal. Humans, by nature, bring to jury service certain inherent, inherited, and learned biases, prejudices, and points of view such that the concept of having a truly "impartial" juror is not dissimilar to the Declaration of Independence's concept of "the pursuit of happiness." Nevertheless, an impartial juror is generally one who can assure the court and the parties that he or she can set aside any inherent biases or prejudices and decide the case based on the facts presented in evidence as applied to the law given by the court.

In practice, jury selection is not selection at all. It is an effort to de-select certain prospective jurors who appear to carry the strongest and most disagreeable beliefs or values. The reason for this is because the parties do not have the privilege of striking prospective jurors ad infinitum. Rather, each side is provided only a limited number of strikes, to be discussed in more detail later. Therefore, at best a party has only a limited ability to eliminate the most partial prospective jurors, rather than select the most impartial ones. The purpose of jury de-selection, then, is to arrive at a group that is as fair as possible, or at least a group not partial toward the other party. If all goes well during jury selection, parties are able to remove the worst prospective jurors and end up with the most impartial jurors possible, given the panel.

C. THE MECHANICS OF JURY SELECTION

To understand jury selection, it is important first to become familiar with the mechanics of the jury selection process. Unfortunately, these mechanics often differ in some degree from district to district, and from judge to judge. There are some basics, however, that are at least similar from courtroom to courtroom which we will discuss below.

1. THE JURY POOL AND VENIRE

To begin with, prospective jurors are selected at random from the district. *See Duren v. Missouri*, 439 U.S. 357. 363–64 (1979) (holding that a defendant has right to trial by a jury selected from a fair cross-section of the community). If there are multiple divisions within a district, prospective jurors are generally selected from the division where the trial will be held, although prospective jurors can be pulled from anywhere within the district. Most courts submit basic jury questionnaires to prospective jurors before they ever set foot in the courtroom. These questionnaires typically solicit information on certain basic topics and recurring issues, such as the prospective juror's occupation, education level, involvement in prior jury selection, and the like. You should determine if your district issues jury questionnaires. If they are used, become familiar with them for they can often provide some key information.

Typically, once the clerk of court has identified a pool of prospective jurors, the clerk will draw from that pool a smaller group to appear at a given trial. This smaller group, called a venire, constitutes the body of citizens from which the trial jury will ultimately be chosen. The size of the venire depends on the number of trials set on a given day, the length of the trial, or the complexity of the case. Before jury selection begins, the potential jurors are administered an oath which requires them to answer truthfully all questions posed to them regarding their qualifications to serve as jurors.

2.   COURT VOIR DIRE

In federal court the trial judge will conduct the initial questioning of prospective jurors. Typically the court provides a brief description of the case, then questions the panel as a whole. These questions usually cover topics which relate to obvious biases or prejudices. The court's sole interest is in weeding out prospective jurors who cannot be impartial. Some judges will ask follow-up questions, while other judges will simply elicit answers which suggest that a prospective juror may be biased, depending on the attorneys to ask the necessary follow-up questions. So, in courts where judges permit the lawyers to directly question the prospective jurors, lawyers need to be prepared to ask follow-up questions, if necessary, either to determine if a prospective juror is prejudiced or to rehabilitate a prospective juror who may at first appear prejudiced or biased, but who turns out not to be biased upon further examination.

One of the judge's primary obligations during jury selection is dealing with prospective jurors who claim they are unable to serve as a juror because of some other commitment, such as work or family obligations. Most judges handle these issues with tact and in a manner designed to discourage prospective jurors who simply want to shirk their civic duties. Quite often, however, you will have prospective jurors left on the panel who clearly do not want to serve as jurors and have been frustrated in their attempts to fabricate reasons for being excused. Parties may want to use their peremptory strikes to eliminate such prospective jurors, as they likely will not do justice to the case, to the United States or to the defendant.

3.   QUESTIONS BY PARTIES

After the court conducts its voir dire, many federal judges will permit the government to conduct voir dire, though it is not required by Rule 24. The latest survey of federal judges suggests that a majority of federal judges permit some voir dire by the attorneys. *See* John Shapard & Molly Johnson, *Federal Judicial Center Memorandum to Advisory Committee on Civil Rules* (Oct. 4, 1999). Again, it is fully within the trial court's discretion to permit or deny direct participation by the parties in voir dire as there is no Constitutional requirement that it even occur. *Mu'Min v. Virginia*, 500 U.S. 415, 430 (1991) (district courts have broad discretion in deciding whether to allow specific questions by attorneys during voir dire).

The Federal Rules of Criminal Procedure provide no time limits on voir dire by the parties. A trial judge's discretion in controlling jury selection extends to the time permitted attorneys to conduct voir dire, if they're allowed to do it at all. Therefore, judges will often give a time limitation to counsel. These are often reflected in local rules or in court scheduling orders.

Once the attorney has completed questioning, he or she is generally required to pass "for cause" or move to remove prospective jurors "for cause." A "for cause" challenge is one where the prospective juror should be removed because he or she cannot be fair and impartial. Some courts require the lawyers to exercise these for cause challenges in front of the prospective jurors. Understandably, this could rankle the prospective jurors, especially the prospective jurors whom the lawyer claims cannot be impartial. Preferably, challenges to remove a prospective juror for cause are conducted at a side-bar and outside the presence of the jury. If a lawyer loses a for-cause motion, the lawyer will probably want to use a peremptory strike to remove the prospective juror, or risk having a very unfriendly juror on your panel.

If the government was permitted to conduct voir dire, then of course defense attorneys will be permitted to question prospective jurors. When there are multiple defendants the courts will usually permit counsel for each defendant to conduct separate voir dire. When complete, each defense attorney is required to "pass for cause" before sitting down.

4. CHALLENGES AND STRIKES

There are two methods of removing prospective jurors from a venire. The first method we have already discussed, known as "for cause" challenges. These are instances where a person's prejudice or bias is so clearly obvious that the prospective juror simply cannot be impartial. *See Wainwright v. Witt*, 469 U.S. 412, 424 (1985) (standard for determining whether a venire member may be removed for cause depends on whether the "juror's views would prevent or substantially impair the performance of his duties as a juror in accordance with his instructions and his oath") (internal quotations omitted). Either party can challenge a juror "for cause," but it remains in the court's discretion whether to grant the motion. *See United States v. Parmley*, 108 F.3d 922 (8th Cir. 1997) (striking for cause is a matter committed to the discretion of the district court). There are no limits on the number of for-cause challenges.

The other method of removing a prospective juror is by use of peremptory strikes. Each side is provided the opportunity to strike a number of prospective jurors for any constitutionally permissible reason. In other words, either side may strike a number of potential jurors for any reason whatsoever, so long as the reason is not based on the race, national origin, or gender of the prospective juror. This prohibition against prejudicial application of peremptory strikes applies to both parties in a criminal case. *United States v. Martinez-Salazar*, 528 U.S. 304, 315 (2000) ("Under the Equal Protection Clause, a defendant may not exercise a peremptory challenge to remove a potential juror solely on the basis of the juror's gender, ethnic origin, or race.").

In contrast to "for cause" challenges, the number of peremptory strikes allowed for each side is limited. The exercise of peremptory strikes is not a constitutional right, but a "means to the constitutional end of an impartial jury and a fair trial." *Georgia v. McCollum*, 505 U.S. 42, 58 (1992). The number of peremptory strikes provided to parties in a federal criminal case is government by Federal Rule of Criminal Procedure 24(b), and depends on the number of defendants, nature of the case and other factors. Generally, in a federal felony trial, the government is given six peremptory strikes and the defendant is granted ten. The manner or method used by the court in how the parties exercise the strikes is not prescribed in the Rule, however, and is again left to the trial court's discretion.

Remember that the voir dire process is more accurately described as juror de-selection. Peremptory strikes provide lawyers with the opportunity to eliminate prospective jurors they believe are biased against their case or, for whatever reason, may not be the best juror for their side. The reality is that lawyers are stuck with the panel pulled by the court and have only a limited ability to remove certain prospective jurors. Thus, the appropriate perspective is not determining which prospective jurors a lawyer wants on the jury, but rather, which prospective jurors the lawyer would least like on the jury.

Given that perspective, lawyers should exercise peremptory strikes with careful thought. Obviously, a lawyer would want to strike those prospective jurors who are clearly biased against his or her party. More often than not, however, there will still be a large number of prospective jurors who are not clearly against the lawyer's party, but appear as if they would be better for the other side. The best strategy is to strike those who are leaders and are unfavorable to your side. If a lawyer runs out of peremptory strikes, it's preferable to have left on the jury those who are followers; although they may be unfavorable to the lawyer's client, they are less likely to influence the outcome of the case.

Out of the venire (which can be 30, 50, or more people) the questioning is usually, but not always, directed to a smaller group drawn from the venire. It is at this point that the mechanics of the jury selection process often differ the most from one court to the next. Some courts will choose 12 potential jurors, seat them in the box, and all questioning is directed at those initial 12 until and unless one or more of them are removed for cause, at which point other members of the venire replace those stricken. When all "for cause" challenges have been exercised, the parties may exercise peremptory strikes, or may not, as they choose. If they exercise peremptory strikes, the stricken jurors are replaced again from the venire, and the peremptory striking process continues until the appropriate number of prospective jurors is left.

In other courts, 26 or so prospective jurors are placed in the well of the courtroom and questions are directed at them. Again, if some are stricken for cause, they are replaced by other members of the venire. When all "for cause" challenges have been exercised, the court then directs the parties that they must exercise a given number of peremptory strikes, regardless of whether they wish to strike any juror.

There are a number of other variations on this theme that are utilized in the federal court system. The key is that lawyers should learn and become familiar with the method used in their jurisdiction.

5. THE IMPROPER EXERCISE OF PEREMPTORY STRIKES

During the process of exercising peremptory strikes, lawyers for both the government and the defendant must ensure that their exercise of peremptory strikes is not motivated by an improper or unconstitutional reason. In exercising peremptory strikes, attorneys often rely in part on stereotypes, assuming that certain types of people from particular areas or with similar socioeconomic backgrounds or professions, for example, share certain belief systems favorable or unfavorable to one side or the other. For example, prosecutors may believe wealthy, well educated, or politically conservative people are more likely to be favorable to the government in a criminal case. In contrast, defense attorneys may believe that actors, writers, and artists are better for criminal defendants. Studies have shown, however, that attorneys often draw inaccurate conclusions about prospective jurors relying on such stereotypes.[1]

As inaccurate as reliance on stereotypes may be, attorneys may nevertheless still exercise their peremptory strikes relying on them so long as the stereotype is not based on a constitutionally protected area. An attorney may choose to strike a juror for any legitimate reason—even something so vague as not feeling that the attorney was "connecting with" the juror. However, an attorney cannot strike a juror because of the juror's race, sex, or national origin. *See Batson v. Kentucky*, 476 U.S. 79 (1986) (government's use of peremptory challenges to remove African-Americans from jury panel unconstitutional). This prohibition is based on

---

[1] Caroline C. Otis, et al., *Hypothesis Testing in Attorney-Conducted Voir Dire*, 38 LAW & HUM. BEHAV. 392, 401–02 (2013) (summarizing the conclusion from one such study, showing it was consistent with past studies finding that attorney generalizations about prospective jurors are often mistaken).

a defendant's right under the Equal Protection Clause and juror's rights in the judicial system. Thus, a white defendant can object to the government using peremptory strikes to remove minorities from the jury (*Powers v. Ohio*, 499 U.S. 400 (1991)), an African-American defendant can challenge the government's use of peremptory strikes to remove white prospective jurors (*Roman v. Abrahms*, 822 F.2d 214, 227–28 (2d Cir. 1987)), and the government can object to a defendant's similarly improper use of peremptory strikes (*Georgia v. McCollum*, 505 U.S. 42 (1991)). Just as race is irrelevant to whether a person can serve as an impartial juror, to too other characteristics, such as gender, are irrelevant. Thus, it is improper to use a peremptory strike to remove a juror simply because of the juror's gender. *See J.E.B. v. Alabama ex rel TB*, 511 U.S. 127 (1994). The Supreme Court has not expanded scope of this prohibition beyond race, gender and national origin. So, for example, there is no prohibition for a lawyer to use a peremptory strike to remove a potential juror based on sexual orientation or religious beliefs.

If one side believes that the other exercised a peremptory strike for an unconstitutional reason, that is one side believes the opposing counsel based the peremptory strike on the prospective juror's gender, ethnicity, or nationality, then the party may make a so-called *Batson* challenge, which requires the trial court to hold a *Batson* hearing. This three-part procedure, borrowed from a similar process used in employment discrimination cases, begins with the objecting party making an initial prima facie showing that the peremptory strike was unconstitutionally motivated. If the moving party is able to make such a showing, the burden shifts to the party who exercised the peremptory strike to articulate a neutral explanation for the challenges. The standard here is not high. "Although the prosecutor must present a comprehensible reason, '[t]he second step of this process does not demand an explanation that is persuasive, or even plausible'; so long as the reason is not inherently discriminatory, it suffices." *Rice v. Collins*, 546 U.S. 333, 338 (2006) (quoting *Purkett v. Elem*, 514 U.S. 765, 767–68 (1995)).

If the non-moving party articulates a non-discriminatory reason, the court must then decide whether it was the real and legitimate reason, or rather, was merely a pretext for striking the prospective juror for an unconstitutional reason. "This final step involves evaluating the 'persuasiveness of the justification' proffered by the prosecutor, but 'the ultimate burden of persuasion regarding [the alleged discriminatory] motivation rests with, and never shifts from, the opponent of the strike.'" *Rice*, 546 U.S. at 338 (quoting *Purkett*, 514 U.S. at 768). If the trial court finds the peremptory strike was motivated by a constitutionally improper reason, the court may remedy the improper use of peremptory challenges by discharging the entire venire and selecting a new panel, or by disallowing the improper challenge and seating the struck juror. If the

Batson objection is incorrectly dismissed but found on appeal, the remedy is a new trial.

D. GOALS OF JURY SELECTION

In order to conduct effective voir dire and to intelligently exercise peremptory strikes, it is important first to understand the goals of jury selection. These include eliminating biased prospective jurors, learning about the prospective jurors, educating prospective jurors about the case and the law, and preparing the prospective jurors for the evidence. We discuss each of these goals below.

1. ELIMINATE BIASED PROSPECTIVE JURORS

The removal of biased prospective jurors is the most obvious purpose for conducting jury selection. The goal is to populate the jury with individuals who know nothing about the case or the parties and come to the case with no preconceived biases for or against either party. Thus, the court and the lawyers will ask questions of the prospective jurors to discover whether someone is biased so that they can seek to remove the prospective juror for cause or, failing that, so that they can exercise a peremptory strike to eliminate that prospective juror.

In order to question prospective jurors to uncover biases, however, you must first identify potential biases or prejudices. There are, of course, the obvious biases and the ones that the trial judge is most concerned about uncovering—those of a Constitutional nature, such as prejudices against people because of the race, religion, national origin, sex or other protected status. Obviously, we cannot have a fair judicial system if we permit people to sit in judgment of others when they are basing their decisions not on the facts of the case, but on the color of the lawyer's, agent's, or defendant's skin.

There are other biases and prejudices, however, that are not so obvious, but to an advocate almost as important. There are, for example, potential party-specific biases. For example, a venire member may simply hate all defense attorneys, regardless of their race, national origin, etc. Or a prospective juror may detest the United States government because of a prior dispute with the IRS or for some other reason unrelated to the case. Your questions during voir dire, therefore, must be tailored to root out these potential party biases.

Further, there may be case-specific biases you need be concerned about. For example, if the case involves the prosecution of a medical doctor, the lawyers should ask questions during voir dire to determine if there are prospective jurors who view doctors as second in stature only to God, or whether any believe that doctors are greedy incompetent hacks. Lawyers should structure questions to uncover prejudices among prospective jurors that, because of the unique facts or issues in the particular case at trial, may make prospective jurors inappropriate for that case, even though they may be perfectly suited to sit as an impartial juror in some other type of case.

The questions lawyers will ask to uncover such bias or prejudices will depend largely on the facts of the case. For example, if the government is prosecuting a defendant for being a felon in possession of a firearm, the lawyers will obviously want to determine the prospective jurors' attitudes about weapons and possession of weapons. There is an art, however, to asking questions in such a way that it uncovers the bias without necessarily alerting the prospective juror of the purpose of the question. Imagine in a firearms case that you have a venire member who believes so strongly that the Second Amendment gives everyone the right to bear arms that he would never vote to convict regardless of whether the government proves its case. Asking that prospective juror, point blank, whether he holds such beliefs is unlikely to generate a frank response, either because the prospective juror wants to be able to exercise the power to prevent such a conviction or out of fear of being attacked for holding such beliefs. Accordingly, a prosecutor may approach the issue more gingerly by asking about prospective jurors' understanding of the Second Amendment and, if anyone believes strongly that it guarantees everyone the right to bear arms, whether prospective jurors can imagine circumstances where it might be wise to adopt exceptions to that general principle.

Sometimes it is impossible to determine whether prospective jurors are biased, or to get them to admit publicly that they hold unpopular beliefs. For example, if you ask a group of people whether they would hold it against a defendant for not testifying truthfully, most will tell you, if they are being honest, that they would, despite the Constitutional right to remain silent. Of course, it would be nice during jury selection to ask that question and have prospective jurors admit such views. That seldom happens. When it does, and the lawyer is convinced that the prospective juror will maintain that belief despite instructions from the court that jurors cannot to consider the defendant's silence in any way, then the lawyer can challenge that prospective juror for cause. More often, however, prospective jurors will not admit that they have that belief because they recognize that it is generally improper, however logical it might seem. Therefore, the only thing a lawyer can do is attempt to instill in the jury panel the importance of following the instructions. This can be done in a mild way, such that the prospective jurors will feel a sense of obligation and pride by following the rules. Rather than berate the prospective jurors that they must follow the rules, therefore, the better practice is to talk about why those rules are important, and then ask if the prospective jurors all understand and agree that the rule is important and should be followed.

2.   LEARN ABOUT THE PROSPECTIVE JURORS

Another goal of voir dire, and one less understood and exercised by attorneys, is learning about the jury panel. Lawyers can learn about the prospective jurors, and the resulting jury, through written questionnaires and through the voir dire process.

As mentioned previously, many courts require prospective jurors to fill out written questionnaires before they appear in court. Copies of the completed questionnaires are usually provided to the attorneys several days before trial. These questionnaires typically provide only basic information, such as the juror's age, residence, job, prior jury service and the like. In complicated or controversial cases, attorneys may want to petition the court to submit special questionnaires to prospective jurors oriented toward the specific issues that are anticipated at trial.

The other way of learning about prospective jurors, of course, is to question the individual prospective jurors during the voir dire process. Some attorneys find that there are certain questions that tell them a significant amount about a person's personality. For example, some attorneys ask each prospective juror to name their favorite television show or magazine, believing that the answer to such questions reveal something about the prospective juror's personality. The difficulty with this approach is that this type of stereotyping may be inaccurate. Another approach is to engage each juror in some questioning with the nature of the question sometimes being less important than your judgment of the manner in which the juror answers the question. In other words, it's important to hear each juror speak about something, anything, so you can judge how he or she behaves, the tone of voice, and confidence level displayed when speaking in a courtroom. Whatever method is used, the goal is to learn about the prospective jurors' background (education, jobs, etc.) as well as their personalities (leader, follower, easily intimidated or confused, etc.).

As a general rule, one of the most important things lawyers want to learn about the prospective jurors is their leadership quality. The reason has to do with group dynamics. Keeping in mind, again, that lawyers are not able to pick the jury they want, but rather, have a limited opportunity to deselect bad prospective jurors, then it is critically important to take off the bad leaders first. People who are generally followers are more apt to follow any leader. A leader who is prejudiced against the government or a defendant for some reason may turn the entire jury against that party, taking the followers along with him or her. Therefore, all things being equal, lawyers want to uncover among the prospective jurors those who appear to be bad for their case, and those who are more likely to be leaders, so that they can use their limited peremptory strikes against the bad leaders.

Lawyers also want to learn as much as possible about the prospective jurors to determine the intellectual capacity and general attitude of the potential jury. The reason for this is that you may need to alter presentation of your evidence based on nature of jury. For example, if the trial involves very complex securities fraud charges and the jury is generally not college educated, the parties may need to spend much more time educating the jury during the trial than would be necessary if the jury was generally college educated. Remember always that the jury is the audience and the judge. It is important to tailor the case to the audience and not just assume all juries are alike.

3. EDUCATE THE JURY

Voir dire presents an opportunity to educate a jury about certain issues or concepts that may arise in a criminal case. During jury questioning, lawyers may want to ask the prospective jurors about their understanding of certain legal concepts that we, as lawyers, take for granted but which may be foreign to the average juror. The purpose of this questioning is to teach the prospective jurors certain concepts then quiz them to make sure that they understand and accept the concept.

In federal criminal cases there are certain legal concepts that arise on a regular basis. For example, the legal concept of possession is often at issue. Lawyers may want to advise the prospective jurors during voir dire that the law recognizes several forms of "possession," including sole and joint possession, as well as actual and constructive possession. Then the lawyer may want to ask the prospective jurors if they understand and accept the concept that the law makes no distinction between the various forms of possession, such that a person can be held responsible for possession whether it was sole or joint, actual or constructive. Some courts permit discussion of legal issues, such as "possession," while others will not. If there are key legal concepts upon which the case will turn, such as possession, then the lawyers need to address this during voir dire if permitted. If a lawyer is not aware of whether the judge will permit questioning prospective jurors on their understanding of and willingness to accept key legal concepts, then the lawyer should file a motion with the court before the trial to seek permission to ask such questions. If the court bars such questions, then the lawyer should ask the court to cover the topic during the court's voir dire.

In some cases lawyers may want to expand this education function to the subject matter of the case. This need arises quite often in complex white collar cases. For example, if the case involves the prosecution of a doctor or a business person, the lawyers may want to explain certain medical terms or business relationships to make sure that, when the case is presented, the jury has the mental capacity to follow along with the evidence.

Lawyers should also view voir dire as an opportunity to de-program the jury. People have been conditioned now by decades of television crime shows. They expect to see certain things in the court room because it's what they see on T.V. Lawyers may consider taking the opportunity during voir dire to find out how addicted the panel is to the television crime shows, and to find out whether they are able and willing to make a distinction between Hollywood and reality. This is particularly important in criminal cases lacking in scientific evidence. According to television crime shows, fingerprints are always recoverable from any surface, regardless of how long they have been present, and are always identifiable, and always match up to some suspect. Reality is far from this fiction. If the government is prosecuting a case where fingerprints were not recovered, or were smudged, or partial, or did not result in a match, for example, the prosecutor may want to strongly consider discussing this topic with the prospective jurors and educate them about the differences between television and reality.

4.   PREPARE THE JURY

A final goal of jury selection is to prepare the jury for the case. This means that the lawyer can use the jury selection process to front certain issues to not only test the jury's comprehension and acceptance, but to acclimate the jury to what the case will involve. For example, if the case involves explicit crime scene photographs, the prosecutor will want to advise the prospective jurors that they will see such pictures and determine if they can handle viewing such photographs and still be fair jurors. In addition, though, presenting that issue to the jury during voir dire prepares them for what they will see during the trial. It helps them begin to accept mentally the issue they will later encounter. This process can be used for any aspect of your case which may be controversial (such as the use of cooperators), or disturbing (crime scene photographs), or conceptually or intellectually difficult to understand (money laundering or complex accounting procedures).

E.   PREPARING FOR JURY SELECTION

As we discussed above, jury selection is a very important part of every trial. Yet, our experience has been that attorneys rarely spend much time preparing for jury selection. Lawyers should prepare for jury selection to the same extent as they would for direct examination or cross examination, or any other part of the trial.

This means that, to begin with, lawyers should research prospective jurors to extent possible. Attorneys should take full advantage of jury questionnaires submitted by the court and, in appropriate cases, prepare special questionnaires to be presented to the prospective jurors. Lawyers should learn about the areas from which the prospective jurors are drawn. For example, some towns are very blue color, while others are more professional; some communities have a reputation for being liberal while others for being conservative. None of this information is alone determinative, and involves some assumptions based on stereotypes, but is nevertheless important information for lawyers consider in order to ask appropriate questions and make intelligent decisions in exercising their limited peremptory strikes.

There are a large number of professional jury consultants who market themselves as experts in the area of evaluating and selecting juries. They can provide a wealth of information to a lawyer. Indeed, in important cases, jury consulting firms will have several consultants sitting in the courtroom watching each prospective juror, making notes, evaluating answers, interpreting body language, and providing advice to the lawyers. Jury consultants can provide a variety of services, including polling of the potential community from which the jury will be drawn, demographic studies, statistical juror profiling, and many other activities designed to provide you with the greatest amount of information available to utilize in conducting voir dire.

As with every resource, there are real and potential drawbacks to jury consultants. Their services do not come cheap and the cost can be justified only in the most important cases. In addition, there is a danger of over-reliance on the advice of jury consultants at the expense of the lawyer's own experience and judgment. Finally, complications may arise, depending upon the type or work performed, regarding obligations to divulge the results of the analysis to the opposing party, thereby potentially impairing if not eliminating any tactical advantage that may have been gained by retaining the services of a jury consultant.

Lawyers should also think about their case in light of what it means for jury selection. That means they should think about whether there are certain aspects to the case that some prospective jurors may dislike or about which they may possess a predisposed bias, whether there are key legal concepts at issue, and whether there are complex areas about the case that are going to require the lawyers to educate the jury. Lawyers should then formulate questions to deal with those issues, to identify the leaders who are bad for their side, to uncover biases, educate, and prepare the jury. In doing this, lawyers should write out an outline of topics to be covered during voir dire. Just as in conducting any examination, however, it is generally best not to write down full questions because lawyers will then find themselves reading the question to the prospective jurors in a monotone voice, effectively putting them to sleep before the lawyer even begin the trial.

F. THE SKILLS OF CONDUCTING EFFECTIVE JURY SELECTION

Jury selection should be viewed as a trial skill to the same degree as any other aspect of trial. It is a form of advocacy that requires critical thinking, effective methods, and a persuasive style, just like opening statement, direct or cross examination, or closing argument. Jury selection is, after all, the first time the jurors will hear the lawyers speak and jurors will form instant and lasting impressions based on the lawyers' performances during voir dire.

1. THE STYLE OF QUESTIONING PROSPECTIVE JURORS

Conducting questioning during jury selection is unlike almost any other form of questioning conducted during trial practice. It is not direct examination. It is not cross examination. It is, in many ways, a combination of the two, with aspects of opening statement thrown in.

To begin with, the most disconcerting thing about questioning the jury is the utter lack of response. The silence, in response to many questions, is deafening. Prospective jurors typically will not respond audibly to a lawyer's questions unless the lawyer is questioning an individual prospective juror. Instead, at most, a lawyer may get prospective jurors to raise their hands in response to a question posed to the panel as a whole. Thus, in practice, voir dire can take on the appearance of talking at the prospective jurors, as opposed to questioning them.

Further, jury questioning is not like direct examination because the lawyer seldom knows what the prospective jurors are going to say in response. The lawyer has not prepared them like the lawyer would prepare witnesses. A lawyer typically knows very little about prospective jurors and can only guess how they may respond to any given question. Likewise, questioning prospective jurors is not the same as cross examining them. A lawyer does not ever want to adopt the tone of conducting cross examination of prospective jurors. They are the potential judges of the case. A party cannot afford to antagonize them. Yet, because the parties know so little about what they may say in response to any question, and some probing may be necessary to uncover sincere beliefs and views, jury selection is somewhat similar to cross examination in those respects.

If questioning prospective jurors is similar to any other aspect of criminal trial work, it may be closest to questioning civilian witnesses before a grand jury. In a grand jury when you are questioning a civilian third-party witness (for example a bank employee in a case where you suspect that another employee has conducted bank fraud), a prosecutor may often ask open-ended questions in an effort to explore and search out answers, while at other times the prosecutor may engage in low-key leading questions to test the employee's recollection or potential for bias. Yet, even grand jury examination is still different from voir dire because grand jury witnesses will never be the ones judging the facts of the government's case and returning a verdict.

Knowing that the people the lawyer is questioning in voir dire will ultimately decide the fate of the case, lawyers must always conduct themselves in a professional, polite, manner. This means that lawyers must carefully consider the people they are questioning and what they are going through. It is important for the lawyer to keep in mind that court rooms are intimidating to most people. Speaking in public is also very stressful for most people. Add to that the prospect of being questioned by a lawyer, whom many people find intimidating, and you will begin to see the difficulty of the task ahead of a lawyer in conducting jury voir dire. In order to conduct an effective voir dire it is important to connect as much as possible with the prospective jurors so as to generate the most honest and open responses. The more intimidating the lawyer or the lawyer's questioning appears, the more distant the lawyer will be from the goals of effective voir dire. Use of a friendly tone of voice, simple language, a respectful distance from the jury, and eye contact, all make the process easier for the prospective jurors.

Lawyers should not ask "Does anyone have a problem with" questions. For example, lawyers should not ask "Do any of the jurors have a problem with the government using cooperators?" The form of the question is judgmental and suggests that there may be a problem with the government's use of cooperators, or if someone doesn't like cooperators, that they have a "problem." Instead, lawyers should find a way of asking the question without using the word "problem." For example, a lawyer could ask whether the prospective jurors recognize that the government sometimes uses cooperators as witnesses and whether the prospective jurors would listen fairly to testimony from cooperators, and judge that testimony like they would testimony from other witnesses. A prosecutor could then simply ask: "What do you think about the government's use of a cooperator?"

It is important for lawyers to listen to answers and ask appropriate follow-up questions. All too often lawyers conduct voir dire like they do direct or cross examination—they ask questions and do not listen to the answers, but rather, go to the next item on their list. It is especially important during jury selection to pay close attention to what prospective jurors say, how they say it, and to ask appropriate follow up questions.

There are volumes of books, articles and studies regarding body language and the nonverbal messages conveyed through body language. This chapter is not the place, and we are not the authorities, to discuss body language. Lawyers should, however, be aware of the subject matter and the potential it provides for evaluating prospective jurors. Law enforcement agents often receive training in this area as part of their education on conducting interrogations, so prosecutors may want to use the skills of the case agent, who will be sitting at counsel table with the prosecutor, to help "read" these non-verbal cues from the prospective jurors.

Finally, be brief. Prospective jurors dislike waiting, dislike being questioned, and dislike anything they perceive to be grandstanding by lawyers. Lawyers should conduct the most concise, succinct voir dire possible while still achieving the goals, and then sit down.

Conducting jury selection is simply a unique part of trial, and a separate trial skill lawyers must work hone, develop and master to be an effective advocate.

2. METHODS OF QUESTIONING PROSPECTIVE JURORS

So, how does a lawyer go about questioning prospective jurors to achieve the goals of jury selection we have discussed? A lawyer could just ask questions of the panel as a whole. Alternatively, a lawyer could ask questions of each prospective juror, going down the rows, one prospective juror at a time. Or, a lawyer could just ask questions of particular prospective jurors in whom the lawyer has a specific interest. Of course, lawyers could, and often do, use a combination of one or more of these techniques.

As a general matter, it is often preferable to initially direct questions to the panel as a whole. Keep in mind that most prospective jurors are intimidated by the setting. By asking questions to the group to begin with, it allows them to become more comfortable with the lawyer before the lawyer takes them on individually. Further, it makes sense to ask questions to the group as a whole at the beginning to cover some of the issues that are applicable to the entire panel. For example, if the lawyer is going to discuss a legal concept with the prospective jurors, it would be important to make sure that the entire panel understands and accepts the concept, not just an individual prospective juror.

It is probably best to ask questions of individual prospective jurors which are intended to uncover potential bias in the middle of the voir dire questions. The reason to conduct these questions in the middle of the voir dire examination is the same reason to bury negative topics with trial witnesses in the middle of their direct examinations—the primacy and recency effect of memory. The prospective jurors are most likely to remember the first part and the last part of the voir dire, and forget the questions asked in the middle.

One technique to keep in mind is how to insulate the rest of the prospective jurors from the effects of one or two prospective jurors who show an animosity toward the lawyer's party. Say, for example, a prospective juror claims he can be fair and impartial, but hates the government because he was audited by the IRS five years ago. The prosecutor may want to ask questions of this prospective juror in a manner intended to guilt the rest of the prospective jurors, if not this particular prospective juror, into making sure they will not let that incident enter into their judgment. The prosecutor can do this by asking questions that emphasize why that prospective juror's view is not relevant to this case. For example, the prosecutor may ask: "You understand, sir, that this case does not involve the IRS?" "Would you agree with me that it would be unfair to let your bad experience with a completely different part of the government cloud your fair judgment of the facts of this unrelated matter?" Lawyers should be sure not to pass judgment on, or condemn or argue with, prospective jurors about their view points. Every person is entitled to his or her own views and beliefs. Lawyers should be thankful when prospective jurors divulge their views instead of hiding them. So, lawyers should not suggest that a prospective juror is "wrong" or mistaken. Rather, lawyers should acknowledge and respect the prospective juror's view and distinguish the instant case from the basis for prospective juror's bias or prejudice.

It is often best for a lawyer to end voir dire with questions tending to emphasize the key points or legal issues in the case. Prosecutors should not end by asking the prospective jurors if they will hold the government to the burden of proving the case beyond a reasonable doubt. Rather, prosecutors should end voir dire with questions focused on the key element in dispute, such as a question describing all the different ways a person can be in "possession" of an illegal item. In contrast, a defense attorney may very well want to end voir dire focused on the government's burden of proof. Finally, lawyers should end voir dire by telling the prospective jurors that the lawyer does not have any more questions, thanking them for their time and attention, and (if you can) announce to the court that the lawyer does not wish to challenge any prospective jurors for cause.

G. IMPROPER JURY SELECTION

As mentioned previously, there are certain things that are improper and unethical during voir dire. In federal criminal cases, where a person's liberty is at stake, it is especially important that prosecutors conduct proper jury selection. There are several matters to keep in mind.

Neither party, nor their agents (including law enforcement agents as well as paralegal assistants or other support staff), or witnesses should have any contact with prospective jurors. The concern here is not only those thankfully rare cases of actual jury tampering, but also the appearance of impropriety. Even if the DEA agent is only passing the time of day with a prospective juror, a defendant or another prospective juror who happens to witness the exchange may believe that something inappropriate has occurred.

During voir dire itself the government must remember a defendant's constitutional rights and ensure that in asking questions of prospective jurors, those rights are never jeopardized. In other words, it is improper for a prosecutor ever to suggest during voir dire that the defendant is obligated to present any evidence in his own defense, or that the jury should take into consideration in any way the defendant's exercise of his right to remain silent. For instance, even referencing an anticipated opening statement by the defense or an anticipated affirmative defense can be error because a criminal defendant has no obligation to speak even in an opening statement or to present any defense, even if in pretrial discussions it is apparent that one is likely. It is also improper for the government to suggest in voir dire that the jury's ultimate decision will be between guilt and innocence; the verdict is for "guilty" or "not guilty"—a jury is not called upon to determine whether a defendant is innocent. Further, the government must be particularly careful never to make reference to matters not in evidence or to seek during voir dire to prejudice the jury by appealing to their emotions.

Furthermore, it is improper to suggest that jury has right, or should exercise the power, to ignore law and facts to render what a party believes to be the "right" or "fair" decision. This includes pandering to the jury's sense of "duty" to the country or community.

Finally, attorneys should not use voir dire to ingratiate themselves to the prospective jurors. Some lawyers try to do this by telling about themselves during voir dire, referencing their prior military experience or humble upbringing, or in some other manner attempt to enhance their appearance in front of the prospective jurors. Voir dire is for the purpose of questioning the prospective jurors to help inform the exercise of for-cause challenges and peremptory strikes, not as part of a popularity contest. Lawyers who seek to ingratiate themselves to the jury are, in a way, seeking to have the jury base its verdict on how well they like one lawyers over the other instead of whether the evidence shows the defendant to be guilty or not guilty.

H. CONCLUSION

This chapter has attempted to familiarize the reader with the primary issues involved in jury selection in federal criminal cases, and to provide some advice regarding style and techniques to use in jury selection. There are many excellent resources available to learn far more about jury selection than was provided here. Lawyers who are serious about trying federal criminal jury trials should avail themselves of these resources and treat jury selection as an important and integral part of federal criminal practice.

CHAPTER 7

TRIAL PREPARATION

■ ■ ■

Preparation for trial, in the larger sense, should begin during the investigation and continue up until the last day of trial. In other words, an attorney should be thinking of the trial with regard to everything that is done during an investigation. During the criminal investigation, a federal prosecutor should think not just about what evidence is necessary to make a case, but what evidence will make the case persuasive. Prosecutors should be actively involved in the investigation, therefore, and not simply accept the evidence uncovered by the agents. Rather, prosecutors should help determine how to conduct the investigation to uncover the type of evidence that will be necessary to prove all of the elements of the crime but also will persuasively show the defendant's guilt. A prosecutor must likewise think about how he or she will lay a foundation for the evidence uncovered through an investigation. Defense attorneys must similarly think into the future about possible defenses at trial and seek out evidence that will be sufficient and persuasive for the defense.

Thus, although attorneys must prepare for trial from the start of the investigation through the end of trial, this chapter addresses a narrower concept of trial preparation—that is, how an attorney prepares for trial once the evidence has been accumulated and trial is around the corner. There are a great number of tasks that must be performed to get ready for trial, such as preparing jury instructions, motions in limine, opening statements and closing arguments. The actual presentation of the case to the jury, however, can generally be broken down into the two main categories of evidence: witnesses and evidence. Preparation for questioning witnesses also consists of two tasks: preparing an outline of questions and meeting with the witness to review the questions and otherwise prepare the witness for trial. This chapter will only deal with preparing for the presentation of the case through witnesses and evidence, as other chapters address the other matters.

A. WITNESS LIST

In preparing for trial, an attorney should begin by drafting a list of the witnesses he or she plans on calling to the stand. In many cases, prosecutors will be formulating the witness list during the investigation, even if it is not reduced to writing. When it is clear, however, that the case will proceed to trial, lawyers need to draft an actual witness list. In practice, this is a task for the prosecutor and only sometimes a task that falls on defense attorneys. The reality is that in most federal criminal cases the government calls witnesses and the defense does not. In white collar cases, it is more likely the defense will present witnesses. This is a product, of course, of the burden of proof. Absent some type of affirmative defense, the government has the sole burden of proof, and therefore the sole burden to present witnesses and evidence. Moreover, it is often the case that criminal defendants simply do not have witnesses they can call to prove their innocence. So, in the typical criminal case, the government calls witnesses, the defense attorney cross examines them, and the defense calls no witnesses.

Whether prosecutor or defense attorney is drafting it, a witness list should include the witnesses in the order that the attorney anticipates that they will be called at trial. That order, of course, should be logical and organized in the manner best designed to tell the story and persuade the jury. It is best to start and finish with strong witnesses, and place weak witnesses in the middle, under the theory that the jury will remember best that which they first hear and last hear. Indeed, not only should the entire witness list be organized in this manner, but if the evidence will take more than one day to present, an effort should be made to have strong witnesses at the beginning and the end of each day of trial. Each day of trial, in that sense, should be treated like a mini trial.

In drafting a witness list, an attorney must be careful to remember to include each witness necessary to lay foundations for the evidence and to authenticate the evidence. When possible, a party should ordinarily seek stipulations from the opposing party for foundation and authenticity to avoid calling witnesses solely for that purpose. For example, if a prosecutor has bank records that need to get into evidence, the prosecutor should normally try to get a stipulation that the bank records are what they claim to be to avoid the necessity of calling a document custodian at trial for the sole purpose of identifying the records. Sometimes, however, a prosecutor may want to call such a witness when it may be more persuasive, such as when the prosecutor wants to emphasize that the bank record is authentic if for some reason the authenticity of the document is in question.

In determining the order of witnesses, the government should also consider the placement of corroborating witnesses. For example, if the government is using a cooperator, it is often best to present a witness or two before and after the cooperator who will corroborate some aspect of what the cooperator will say. This can have the effect of bolstering the credibility of the cooperator by showing that the cooperator's testimony does not stand alone.

In drafting a witness list—in determining who to actually call at trial—lawyers should not fall into the trap of calling everyone with knowledge of the case. In many federal criminal investigations there are scores of witnesses who know something about the case. For example, when agents execute search warrants there are often a half-dozen or more agents participating in the search. Likewise, in controlled buys of narcotics, there may be a dozen agents conducting surveillance of the transaction. It is not necessary, and is actually counter-productive, to call every one of these agents unless absolutely necessary to lay the foundation for a piece of evidence. Agents will often try to conduct the investigation with this in mind. For example, during the execution of a search warrant agents will often not move an item of evidence from where it was found, leaving the item for a single agent to collect so that a single agent can lay the foundation for all the evidence collected during a search. So, in determining who to call, lawyers should use judgment. Just because a witness exists does not mean the witness is necessary or persuasive.

On the other hand, the government in particular should be cautious not to call too few witnesses. There is the saying sometimes used during an argument, "don't make a federal case out it," implying that a federal case is something particularly significant. There is a sense that a federal case is an important, significant case. Therefore, when the government presents a federal criminal case, it should have the appearance of an important, significant case. In some federal criminal cases, such as a single controlled-buy drug case, or the seizure of a firearm from a felon, it may be possible for the government to present its entire case with only two or three witnesses, particularly if the defense stipulates to certain elements of the offense or to the foundation for or admission of certain evidence. Although there is a temptation to make the case and quick and easy as possible, prosecutors should also keep in mind the appearance that may create in the jury's mind. Therefore, prosecutors should call as few witnesses as necessary, but enough witnesses to fully present the evidence in a persuasive manner.

Finally, lawyers should be prepared to adjust the witness list, even in the middle of trial. As a lawyer talks with the witnesses in preparing for trial, it may become apparent that more or fewer witnesses are needed, or that the order of witnesses needs to be adjusted so as to make the best presentation. Further, as the case is actually presented at trial, lawyers may determine that witnesses can be eliminated as unnecessary or that they should be shifted to make a more persuasive case. It is difficult to add witnesses during the trial, particularly for the government, because local rules and practice typically require a list of witnesses be provided to the opposing party in advance of trial. In some cases, however, witnesses can be added if there is good cause or the opposing party acquiesces in the addition. The bottom line is that lawyers should be constantly reconsidering their list of witnesses and the order in which they are calling the witnesses, and not feel wedded to the initial list drafted well before trial.

B. EXHIBIT LIST

Once a lawyer has identified all of the witnesses and figured out the order in which the lawyer intends to call them, the next step is to develop an exhibit list. Of course, throughout the investigation and preparation for trial, the lawyer should be thinking about what exhibits will constitute the evidence in the case should it go to trial. Once trial is at hand, however, the lawyer needs to review all of the potential evidence to determine which pieces of evidence are actually needed or desirable to introduce at trial. There is no substitute for an attorney to personally inspect every piece of evidence in a case. During this review of the evidence an attorney must think not only of evidence that is necessary and persuasive for the case-in-chief, but also evidence which may be needed during the other side's case or as rebuttal evidence.

As with identifying witnesses, lawyers also need to use judgment and discretion in determining what evidence to present as exhibits at trial. Marking too much evidence as exhibits can be counter-productive. Simply because you have documents or items in the file does not mean that you have to make them trial exhibits. If the jury is presented with an avalanche of exhibits, it will be difficult for them to discern the important evidence from the less important evidence, and may cause confusion. For example, in a complex white collar case, it is incumbent upon the lawyers to sort through the volumes of bank records and mark just the checks or deposits or other transactional documents that are (1) essential to prove the elements of the offense and (2) tell the story persuasively. On the other hand, marking too few exhibits can create the appearance of a weak case. For example, in a simple drug interdiction case where a state trooper interdicted a car carrying methamphetamine, there may not be a lot of evidence from the investigation. Indeed, perhaps the only evidence from the stop itself may be the controlled substances. This is where the prosecutor needs to think creatively about how to tell the story using exhibits. In other words, the prosecutor should think about what he or she would say in closing argument to persuade the jury that the defendant who was driving the car from Texas to Minnesota knew that the car contained methamphetamine, and then work backwards to determine what exhibits might help tell that story. A prosecutor will probably want to use photographs from the scene, for example, and if none were taken, have them taken after the fact. Perhaps the prosecutor would also mark a map of the defendant's route as an exhibit. A search of the car and defendant's pocket litter may reveal receipts or other items that would show the route and hours of driving, or other indicators that the trip was made in a hurry. It is important, again, for a prosecutor in particular not to simply accept what the agent identifies as exhibits and feel bound to use only those items.

Drafting the actual exhibit list for use in the case may seem an easy and obvious task, but in complex cases or cases involving a lot of evidence, there is a skill to the task. An exhibit list, and hence the exhibits, can be organized in many different ways. One way is by starting with what you believe will be the first piece of evidence you will introduce at trial and ending with your last piece of evidence. However, this is not always the best way. If there are parts or stages to the case, say for example multiple searches or multiple controlled buys, you should consider marking your exhibits in groups. For example, the prosecutor could mark all the evidence from the first search as exhibits 1 through 50, and the evidence from the second search as exhibits 51 through 100. Thus, by adopting this pattern the attorney will know from the exhibit number assigned to an exhibit the source of that piece of evidence. A lawyer need not use all of the exhibit numbers in the range, so if the first search warrant generated only 37 pieces of evidence, for example, the prosecutor would simply not use exhibit numbers 38–50. This same method can be used with other logical categories, be it searches, transactions, victims, charges, or some other type of event. Avoid using both numbers and letters. For example, you may want to mark five photographs of a crime scene as Exhibits 12A, 12B, etc., but if you have more than twenty-six such photographs, using that system becomes confusing. It would be far better to simply mark each exhibit by a different number or mark a group of photographs as a single exhibit number, but then mark each page by a page number. So, reference in trial would then be made during trial to Exhibit 12, page 3, for example.

In addition to identifying and reviewing each document or tangible object that you intend to use as an exhibit at trial, lawyers also need to prepare any demonstrative exhibits they intend to use at trial. Demonstrative exhibits can be anything that will help the jury understand the evidence. The most common demonstrative exhibits are things like maps, floor plans, or charts, but a lawyer may also want to use objects as demonstrative exhibits. For example, in a methamphetamine clandestine laboratory prosecution, a prosecutor may want to mark lithium batteries of the type used by the defendant in the manufacturing process as demonstrative exhibits. The actual batteries would not exist, in this example, because they would have been destroyed during the manufacturing process. Lawyers should take full advantage of, and be creative with, the use of demonstrative exhibits. People, including jurors, often learn better if they get information both visually and orally. Therefore, a lawyers should try to create a demonstrative exhibit for any important part of the case that can visually depicted in some way by a chart, summary, diagram, or object.

To be clear, the difference between an exhibit, that is a piece of evidence from the case, and a demonstrative exhibit, is that an exhibit will go back to the jury room during deliberations while a demonstrative exhibit will not. A demonstrative exhibit is not actual evidence from the case which has been authenticated and for which a foundation has been laid. Rather, it is a visual aid and, as such, typically cannot be relied upon by the jury to establish an element of the offense. An exhibit may be accepted by the court as an exhibit, or a demonstrative exhibit, based upon the type of foundation was laid for it. For example, if a witness testifies that a floor plan of a house where a crime occurred fairly and accurately reflects the crime scene, then a foundation has been laid such that the court should admit the floor plan as an exhibit. If, however, the prosecutor simply creates a floor plan of the crime scene based on descriptions of the witnesses, the court may permit the prosecutor to use the floor plan as a demonstrative exhibit, but not permit it to go back to the jury as an actual exhibit.

C. MATCHING WITNESS LIST TO EXHIBIT LIST

Once a lawyer has developed both a witness list and exhibit list, the next task is to match them. In other words, a lawyer should chart out exactly which witness is necessary to introduce which piece of evidence. Further, the lawyer should also determine not just who must testify with respect to a given exhibit, but rather, who the lawyer wants to testify regarding a given exhibit. For example, in a drug case a prosecutor will need to have the agent who found the drugs during a search testify about the drugs in order to lay the foundation, but may want to also have a chemist or an experienced narcotics agent testify about the exhibit as well.

During the exercise of matching the witness and exhibit lists, holes and weaknesses sometimes appear. For example, it may occur to the prosecutor during this exercise that another witness is needed to lay the foundation for an exhibit. Conversely, the prosecutor may realize that there are no obvious exhibits to introduce during the testimony of a key witness. The prosecutor may, therefore, want to create a demonstrative exhibit for this witness to enhance the persuasiveness of that witness's testimony. Finally, it may also become apparent when matching up witnesses with exhibits that a single witness is responsible for laying the foundation for a large number of exhibits. A lawyer may want to consider how this will work and appear at trial, and consider whether to add a witness to share responsibility for laying the foundation for the exhibits. For example, as mentioned above, law enforcement agencies intentionally try to conduct searches so that a single agent can lay the foundation for all exhibits seized during a search. But, if there were scores of exhibits seized, it may be more persuasive and less tedious to split it up by room in the house, for example, and have several agents describe what was found in the rooms and lay the foundation for the exhibits found in the various rooms.

D. DRAFTING AN OUTLINE OF QUESTIONS

After the lawyer conducts the exercise of matching witnesses to exhibits, the lawyer should turn to drafting outlines of questions for each witness. This should be an outline, not a list of questions typed out in full. Lawyers should refrain from writing out every question because it creates a temptation to read the questions at trial. This often makes the questions sound rehearsed and monotone, and it also tends to makes the lawyer inflexible and unable to adapt the questions to testimony. Rather, the outline of questions should be a series of bullet points of subjects the lawyer wants to cover during the questioning. The exception to this practice of preparing bullet points, versus full questions, is when it comes to asking questions in key areas, like laying the foundation for an exhibit. There are basic questions to ask to lay the foundation for different types of exhibits, and it can be important to cover each part of the foundation requirement to lay a proper foundation. To make sure it is done correctly, it is often helpful to write these questions out in full in the witness outline.

In the draft of questions for a witness, the lawyer should also note which exhibits will be used with the witness. In the outline, it is helpful to make notes regarding specific rules of evidence which provide the basis for introducing certain exhibits the lawyer thinks may be challenged at trial, so that the notes are handy when needed. The lawyer should also carefully review the questions from the opposing party's view and identify questions that could draw an objection. The lawyer should then determine if the questions can be re-worded in such a way to avoid the possibility of drawing an objection. If not, the lawyers should make a note in the outline identifying the rule of evidence upon which the lawyer is relying for admissibility of the evidence. For example, the lawyer may have a question that calls for hearsay, but the answer falls within a recognized exception to the hearsay rules. The lawyer should note that evidentiary exception in the margin of the witness's outline.

It is important that lawyers revise the witness outline as necessary to adjust to information learned during trial preparation and not get wedded to the initial draft. It is helpful to have draft outlines of questions before sitting down with the witnesses and preparing them for trial. It would be uncommon to go through a witness preparation session, however, and not see a need to adjust and change the outline in response to what the witness tells the attorney during the witness preparation session. Likewise, as the trial commences the testimony will likely come out slightly different than what the lawyer anticipated. So, it is important for lawyers to change the outline of questions for witnesses to adjust for the testimony as it actually comes out in the courtroom. Finally, lawyers should always treat the outline as just that—an outline. Lawyers should adjust questioning of the witness to respond to what the witness says and not blindly follow a script.

E. PREPARING THE WITNESSES

The final step in trial preparation is to prepare the witnesses. There are several parts to witness preparation. First, the lawyer needs to explain the process and logistics of testifying in federal court. Second, the lawyer needs to describe direct and cross examination and provide some advice to the witness on how to think about questions. Third, the lawyer will want to walk through the questions the lawyer intends to ask the witness, and the questions the lawyer anticipates the opposing counsel will ask the witness. We will discuss each aspect of witness preparation below. It is important, however, to start and end each witness preparation session with an admonition to the witness that the single most important rule for the witness to follow is to tell the truth. This is especially important for the government to emphasize, both because it is manifestly the obligation of the Department of Justice to make sure that the truth comes out and justice prevails in every case, but also because some government witnesses, like cooperators, have a motivation to exaggerate or lie and it is incumbent upon the prosecutors to do everything they can to counter this motivation. It is also important for prosecutors never to meet with a witness without a law enforcement agent present so that a witness cannot make a false allegation that the prosecutor pressured or threatened or promised something to the witness during the preparation session.

1. PROCESS AND LOGISTICS

The first part of the witness preparation session should be devoted to describing the trial process to the witness. Trial lawyers take knowledge of the process for granted and often assume everyone knows how a courtroom works. The truth is that most witnesses have never been in a courtroom before and have no idea how the process works, what the courtroom looks like, or who the people are in the courtroom. Most witnesses will be very intimidated and often scared of testifying in a federal courtroom. If the lawyer explains the process to the witness, it can decrease the witness's anxiety.

A good trial lawyer will approach each witness preparation session as if the witness is completely ignorant of the entire process and explain it to the witness in simple terms. The lawyer should start with what date and time the witness should arrive at the courthouse, where the witness should go to in the courthouse to meet with the lawyer or staff before the witness testifies, how the witness will proceed from that location (like a waiting room) to the courtroom. The lawyer should even explain to the witness how the witness should enter the courtroom, where the witness should walk in order to get to the witness box, how the witness will be sworn in as a witness, and where the witness will sit.

It is very helpful in this stage of the preparation session to have a diagram of the courtroom to show the witness. The lawyer can use the diagram to point out who else will be in the courtroom, where the judge sits, where the jury sits, and identify and explain the role of other people in the courtroom (such as the court reporter, the judge's law clerk, court security officers, and Deputy United States Marshals). For the prosecutor, it is very important not to tell the witness during the preparation session where the defendant will be sitting in the courtroom. That is because many witnesses will be asked during their testimony to identify the defendant in the courtroom. If the prosecutor tells the witness in advance where the defendant will be sitting, the prosecutor is essentially feeding answers to the witness and coaching the witness's testimony.

The lawyer should describe the order of questioning, that is, for example, explaining that the prosecutor will go first and ask questions followed by the defense attorney asking questions, with the possibility of follow up questions by both sides. It is helpful to label these for the witness as direct examination and cross examination, etc. Witness have often heard these terms, and may hear them from the judge or lawyers during trial, so explaining the terms will help acclimate the witness to the courtroom lingo. The lawyer will ultimately want to explain how the testimony will end, that the witness will be excused, and how to exit the courtroom. The lawyers should ask if the witness has any questions after explaining the process.

2.   DIRECT AND CROSS EXAMINATION EXPLANATION

Having covered the process and logistics of testifying, the lawyer should spend some time describing what direct and cross examination will sound like, and provide some advice to the witness on how to handle certain questions. It is important, especially for the government, to emphasize that the lawyer will never be telling the witness what to say. Rather, the lawyer will only be providing advice for how to think about certain questions to aid the witness in telling the truth. It is best to reiterate that the only job the witness has is to tell the truth.

Lawyers should again try to place themselves in the shoes of someone completely unfamiliar with a trial when trying to explain direct and cross examination to a witness. A lawyer should imagine how one would explain the manner of questioning to a child or a foreigner. So, for example, a lawyer will want to explain the difference between a leading and non-leading question, and explain during direct examination that the lawyer will only be asking non-leading questions, while on cross examination the lawyer will often, if not always, use leading questions. The lawyer will want to emphasize the need for the witness to listen carefully to questions and answer just the question asked of the witness, and to ask for clarification or rephrasing by the lawyer if the witness does not understand the question. The lawyer should explain what the witness should do if they cannot recall an answer and explain the process of refreshing recollection. The lawyer should explain what an objection is, what is will sound like at trial, what the judge will do in handling objections, and the role of the witness to stop talking and wait for the judge to rule when an objection is made. The lawyer will also want to explain how exhibits will be handled in the courtroom and what the witness can expect if presented with an exhibit. In most federal courtrooms the technology allows most exhibits to be presented electronically, so this process should be explained to the witness.

It is very important for lawyers to prepare witnesses for cross examination. This is the most intimidating part of a trial for a witness. Lawyers know what cross examination sounds like, and what techniques are used in cross examination, so the lawyer should explain all this to the witness. This means describing what impeachment by a prior inconsistent statement sounds like. The lawyer should explain how a lawyer may try to impeach the witness with bias, prior criminal record, or lack of memory. A lawyer can provide advice to witness on handling these types of questions. That advice is often that the witness should readily admit the facts and not be defensive or argumentative with the lawyer. Again, however, it is important to emphasize to the witness that they should always tell the truth and if they do that, cross examination cannot hurt them.

This is the time during the preparation session to make sure the witness divulges to the lawyer any information that could be used to impeach the witness. A prosecutor may, for example, explain to the witness that the defendant will be whispering in his lawyer's ear every bad thing the defendant knows about the witness and the lawyer will use it in cross examination if permitted by the Federal Rules of Evidence. If the prosecutor knows about those bad things, like drug use or prior bad acts or lies, then the prosecutor may be able to prevent the defense from bringing them out if they would violate the Federal Rules of Evidence, or if that is not possible, the prosecutor can bring it out during direct examination to soften the blow and to show that the government and witness are not trying to hide anything from the jury.

3.   REVIEW OF TESTIMONY

The final stage of witness preparation is to run through the questions the lawyer intends to ask the witness and the questions the lawyer anticipates the opposing attorney will ask on cross examination.

Regarding direct examination, the lawyer should go through the outline of questions that the lawyer should have prepared in advance of the witness preparation session. The lawyer should take notes or interlineate changes on the question outline as necessary in response to the witness's responses. For example, the lawyer may want to word a question slightly differently, or with different terminology, if it would make the question more understandable to the witness. During the run through of questions, the lawyer should show the witness any exhibits the lawyer would anticipate using with the witness during trial. This is the opportunity to make sure that the witness is familiar with the exhibit, and can lay the foundation for admission of the exhibit. It is also an opportunity to make sure the lawyer fully understands everything important about the exhibit there is to know. For example, if the exhibit is a photograph of a crime scene, the lawyer may have chosen the photograph because it shows the murder weapon on the floor. The lawyer should ask the witness during the preparation session, however, if there is anything else in the photograph that is of evidentiary value. Perhaps, for example, the lawyer did not realize that the blood spatter pattern on the wall depicted in the picture explains how the victim was attacked. Finally, the lawyer should use the witness preparation session to make sure there are not additional items of evidence that should be marked, or demonstrative exhibits that should be created, for trial. Lawyers should constantly be re-evaluating their choice of exhibits and witnesses. So, for example, in preparing a crime scene investigator the prosecutor should show the witness all of the photographs of the crime scene the lawyer has chosen as exhibits, but also show the witness all of the crime scene photos and make sure that there are no other photos that the witness believes would be helpful during the witness's testimony. Likewise, it may become apparent during the trial preparation session with the witness that a demonstrative diagram, chart, or object would be helpful in presenting the witness's testimony. This will require changes in the exhibits and exhibit list, of course, but lawyers must recognize that trial preparation is an evolving process.

Finally, the lawyer should explain the cross examination the lawyer anticipates will be used by the opposing counsel. This is difficult for lawyers to do. It requires the lawyer to step out of their own role and imagine the case from the view of the opposing attorney. The lawyer needs to look at the weaknesses in the lawyer's case, and in this particular witness's testimony. If done well, this often exposes problems that require the direct examination to be changed to address the issues uncovered.

CHAPTER 8

DEFENSES IN FEDERAL CRIMINAL CASES

■ ■ ■

Defendants have a variety of defenses available in federal criminal cases. Many of these defenses are essentially the same as those available to a defendant facing charges brought by a state or county. Some federal statutes, however, contain somewhat unique defenses within the statutory language, or court have read defenses into the statutory language. Moreover, under the Federal Rules of Criminal Procedure and Federal Rules of Evidence there are nuances to presenting some defenses in federal criminal cases. Both prosecutors and defense attorneys should be aware of these peculiarities with regard to the presentation of defenses in federal criminal cases. Thus, in this section we will discuss defenses to criminal charges generally, and in the process explore how federal criminal law may affect the preservation and presentation of some traditional defenses.

Generally speaking, there are two parts to every crime: an act (*actus reas*) and mental state (*mens rea*). Defenses to criminal charges can thus be divided into two corresponding categories: those attacking the alleged act, and those attacking the alleged mental state of the defendant. In federal criminal practice, there is a third category—statutory defenses sometimes found in specific federal statutes which may go to either the act or the criminal intent. We will discuss below various defenses under each of these categories. Keep in mind that we are not here attempting to set forth every possible defense, but rather, the more common defenses and those which are addressed in the Federal Rules of Criminal Procedure or the Federal Rules of Evidence.

A. DEFENSES BASED ON THE ACT

1. "I DIDN'T DO IT" DEFENSE

The most obvious and simple of all defenses is, of course, the one where the defendant simply claims that he did not commit the alleged criminal act. This is sometimes referred to by practitioners humorously as the "SODDI" defense: Some Other Dude Did It. Here the defendant is not specifically denying that, if the government proves he committed the act, that he somehow lacked the mental state to be found guilty of the crime. Rather, the defendant is simply denying performing the act that constituted the crime. A simple example would be a defendant who claims that he did not commit the bank robbery. During trial his defense attorney will strive to persuade the jury that he did not commit the act, but normally will not address whether, if found to have robbed the bank, he had the requisite mental intent to do so. Often this type of defense consists mostly, or solely, upon attacking the adequacy of the government's case during cross examination, as opposed to the defense putting on any evidence.

It may become important, when considering this classic defense, to keep in mind Rule 404(b) of the Federal Rules of Evidence. As we discussed earlier, Rule 404(b) permits the introduction of evidence of other acts committed by the defendant if introduced for some purpose other than propensity. Sometimes the government offers Rule 404(b) evidence in response to the "I didn't do it" defense for the purpose of showing some type of pattern. In other words, the government may introduce evidence that the defendant previously robbed a bank to show a modus operandi (if the nature of the bank robbery was distinctively similar). Rule 404(b) would also allow the government to introduce evidence of another bank robbery to prove defendant had the intent to rob this bank, knowledge of how to rob a bank, or the absence of mistake in robbing the bank. On the other hand, a defendant may conditionally concede that he had the necessary mental state (i.e., he had the intent) if the government proves that he committed the act, in which case evidence of the other robbery may not be admissible pursuant to Rule 404(b). The point here is only to point out that Rule 404(b) evidence can have a significant impact on what type of defense can or should be presented.

2. "I COULDN'T HAVE DONE IT BECAUSE I WASN'T THERE"—ALIBI DEFENSE

An alibi defense is a type of "I didn't do it" defense. Here the defendant is affirmatively claiming that he has evidence to prove that he was somewhere other than the scene of the crime when the crime was committed. A judge may instruct a jury as to this defense only if there is a factual basis for the instruction and it was necessary for the defendant to be present to be found guilty of the offense. *See United States v. Webster*, 769 F.2d 487, 490 (8th Cir. 1985). In other words, if the indictment alleges that the defendant robbed a bank on a particular date, and the defendant has presented some factual basis to support a claim that he was somewhere else at the time of the bank robbery, then a court may instruct a jury that it can consider this defense. On the other hand, if the indictment charges that the defendant aided and abetted the bank robbery by providing a gun to a cohort, who actually entered the bank to rob it, it is no defense to the charge to establish that the defendant was not present at the bank. *See United States v. Anderson*, 654 F.2d 1264, 1270–71 (8th Cir. 1981).

An alibi defense is governed by Rule 12.1 of the Federal Rules of Criminal Procedure. Under this Rule, if the government requests notice, a defendant must provide evidence in support of the alleged alibi defense. In other words, the defendant must provide the basic facts of the alibi defense to the government, such as stating where the defendant claims he was at the time of the offense and the name and contact information for witnesses he claims will establish the alibi. Failure to provide such evidence can result in the court prohibiting a defendant from presenting the evidence at trial. Fed. R. Crim. P. 12.1(d). On the other hand, if the government fails to request to be notified of an alibi defense, the defendant has no obligation to provide alibi notice. If the defendant asserts an alibi defense and provides the requisite information, it triggers a reciprocal obligation by the government to provide the defendant with similar rebuttal information, such as the name and contact information of witnesses the government believes would rebut the defendant's alibi defense.

3. "I DIDN'T DO EVERY PART OF IT"— THE TECHNICAL DEFENSE

The typical "I didn't do it" defense is based upon a claim, either through an attack on the government's case or through affirmative evidence, that the defendant had nothing to do with the criminal act. In some cases, however, a defendant may mount a more limited "I didn't do it" defense by focusing upon a single element of the government's case. For example, as we have explained previously, the federal government generally has limited jurisdiction in criminal cases requiring proof of some federal interest in the crime. In most cases this requires a showing of interstate commerce or travel, and in other cases involves a showing that the crime involved federal property or taxes. A defendant accused of some type of mail fraud may not deny committing the fraudulent acts alleged in the indictment, but rather, may attack the jurisdictional element by claiming that there was, for example, no mailing involved.

This type of technical defense may be applied to any essential element of a crime. Because many federal crimes are complex, particularly in the white collar area, this can sometimes raise the possibility of such a technical defense. Thus, both prosecutors and defense attorneys should very carefully review the evidence with each essential element in mind so as to determine whether there is evidence, beyond a reasonable doubt, as to each essential element.

B. DEFENSES BASED ON THE MENTAL STATE

1. "I DID IT, BUT I DIDN'T MEAN TO DO IT"

Since each crime contains some element going to a defendant's mental state, a defendant may defend against the charge by claiming that he or she lacked the necessary mental state to be guilty of the crime. The necessary mental state will differ depending on the crime, but the government must always prove some mental state. For example, a defendant may defend against a charge that he was a felon in possession of a firearm by claiming that he did not know he was in possession of the weapon. Here he is not denying the act, possession, but rather, is denying the mental state—knowing that he had possession. This can be an effective defense because, of course, it is always difficult to prove what is in someone's mind. Indeed, defense theories often rely on attacking the mental state element or elements of criminal charges because there is seldom direct evidence of the defendant's state of mind. Rather, the government often must rely on circumstantial evidence to establish the defendant's mental state. This, then, is a logical area for a defense attorney to focus a defense in a case where the government can otherwise establish beyond a reasonable doubt the defendant committed the act.

2. "I DID IT, BUT I WAS TRICKED INTO DOING IT"—ENTRAPMENT

When a defendant presents an entrapment defense, he is not denying that he committed the act; rather, he is claiming that he did not have the intent to commit the crime and only did so when he was wrongfully induced or persuaded to commit the crime by the government. The "government" can include people working on behalf of the government, such as cooperators. An entrapment defense has two prongs: first, a jury must conclude that the defendant was induced or persuaded to commit the crime; second, the jury must find that the defendant did not have a prior intent or predisposition to commit the crime absent the inducement. *United States v. Pfeffer*, 901 F.2d 654, 656 (8th Cir. 1990). If evidence is lacking as to either prong, then there was no entrapment. *See United States v. LaChapelle*, 969 F.2d 632 (8th Cir. 1992).

For the court to instruct the jury on entrapment, the defendant must present a prima facie case of entrapment. *United States v. Felix*, 867 F.2d 1068, 1074 (8th Cir. 1989). If he does that, the burden then shifts to the government to prove beyond a reasonable doubt that the defendant was not entrapped. Entrapment defenses arise most often in investigations using undercover operations, and most often when the government uses a cooperator. In conducting such operations, therefore, the government must anticipate this defense and take steps to prevent entrapment. This is why, for example, that a cooperator is searched before being sent in to make a controlled buy of drugs from a target; it eliminates the possibility the cooperator will provide the target with drugs under some pretense and then point the finger at the target.

3. "I DID IT, BUT THEY SAID I COULD"— CLAIM OF LEGAL AUTHORITY

Under this defense, although the defendant admits committing the act, the defendant claims he did not intend to commit a crime because he was acting under a claim of legal authority. This is also sometimes called "entrapment by estoppel." An example of this defense might be a claim by a drug dealer that he believed he was working for the DEA at the time of the offense. He may claim that the reason he was selling drugs is because he was helping the DEA gather evidence on drug dealers. This legal authority defense also arises sometimes in complex regulatory offenses where the defendant corporation, for example, claims that conflicting government laws or statements by regulators or inspectors led it to believe that its conduct was lawful. Under this defense, a defendant must establish a factual basis for claiming that he was misled by the government into believing he had the legal authority to commit the crime. Otherwise, the court will not instruct the jury as to the defense. *United States v. Austin*, 915 F.2d 363 (8th Cir. 1990). Further, Rule 12.3 of the Federal Rules of Criminal Procedure requires a defendant to give the government notice of this defense. This notification is similar to the one for an alibi defense, in the sense that the defendant must provide the identity and contact information for the government official he claims gave him authority to commit the act. It is different from the alibi defense notification provision, however, because the defendant must provide this notice to the government regardless of whether the government requests such notice, whereas a defendant needs to provide an alibi defense notice only if the government requests the information.

4. "I DID IT, BUT HE MADE ME DO IT"—COERCION

Another defense to the mental state defense is to claim that the defendant was coerced to commit the crime, or committed it under duress. Coercion may excuse the commission of a crime if the defendant had a well-grounded belief that death or serious bodily injury would result if he did not commit the crime. *United States v. Campbell*, 609 F.2d 922, 924 (8th Cir. 1980). The harm can be to the defendant, or to a third party. *See LaFave & Scott, Criminal Law*, 374–75, 385–88 (1972). The defendant has the initial burden again of introducing facts sufficient to establish a basis for presenting the defense to the jury. As always, however, the government must ultimately prove beyond a reasonable doubt that the defendant had the requisite intent, which in the case of this defense requires rebutting the coercion defense. *Id.* at 925. If the defendant had a reasonable opportunity to avoid the harm or could prevent the harm by committing a lawful act, then the defense is not available. *United States v. Uthe*, 686 F.2d 636, 637 (8th Cir. 1982).

5. "I DID IT TO PROTECT MYSELF OR ANOTHER"—SELF DEFENSE

Similar to coercion, this defense claims that the person was compelled to commit the crime because of a fear that force was necessary to protect himself or another. A claim of self-defense presumes that the victim was the source of the force which compelled the defendant to act, while a claim of coercion does not. Similarly, self-defense implies that the crime committed involved force. In other words, a person may feel coerced by a third party to embezzle funds from a bank, but that is not regarded as self-defense.

The difference between coercion and self-defense is also found in the nature of the outside pressure on the defendant. As stated above, a defense of coercion requires a showing that death or serious bodily injury will result if the defendant does not commit the crime. On the other hand, self-defense (or defense of another) is permissible only if the defendant uses force proportionate to the amount of force used by the victim. In other words, a defendant may claim self-defense for striking a person who is threatening to strike him—he need not show that he was fearing death or serious bodily injury. On the other hand, a defendant may not be justified in killing a person under a claim of self-defense if the person was only going to strike him, unless the defendant can demonstrate that he had a reasonable basis for believing that the strike would kill him or cause serious bodily injury. Although it is not necessary for a person to retreat in order to claim self-defense, a jury may consider the defendant's ability to retreat in determining whether reasonable force was used. *United States v. Goodface*, 835 F.2d 1233, 1235–36 (8th Cir. 1987). As a practical matter, outside of special federal jurisdiction (like federal park land, or Indian Reservations) the federal government seldom prosecutes these types of violent crimes, so these defenses are seldom encountered in federal criminal practice.

6. "I DID IT, BUT I WAS CRAZY"—INSANITY DEFENSE

If a defendant suffered from a severe mental disease or defect at the time he committed the offense, such that he could not appreciate the nature and quality or the wrongfulness of the act, then he lacked the necessary mental state to be held criminally liable for the act. Title 18, United States Code, Section 17. The burden of proof with regard to insanity is, significantly, placed upon the defendant. The defendant must prove insanity, under federal law, by clear and convincing evidence. Remember too that Rule 12.2 of the Federal Rules of Criminal Procedure, a defendant must provide advance notice to the government of his intent to rely on this defense, regardless of whether notice is requested by the government. Failure to provide such notice can result in the court barring the defendant from presenting the defense at trial. Rule 12.2(a), Federal Rules of Criminal Procedure.

Insanity defenses are relatively rare in federal criminal practice, and very seldom are they successful. When asserted, however, the insanity defense can make the case very complex. Experts will be necessary for both side. Both experts will need to examine the defendant and will rely heavily on collateral information about the defendant. A claim of insanity opens the defendant's entire life to examination in order to determine if the defendant has a mental disease or defect and what may or may not have caused a mental disease or defect. Moreover, an insanity defense ultimately takes over the focus of the case. Whether the defendant committed the crime is no longer at issue as much as how the defendant committed the crime and whether there are signs in the way the defendant committed the offense that sheds light on the defendant's sanity.

7. "I DID IT, BUT I WAS DRUNK"— INTOXICATION OR DRUG USE

Under some federal laws, a defendant may not be found guilty if, due to alcohol or drug intoxication at the time of the offense, he was unable to possess the requisite mental state. An intoxication defense is available only with regard to specific intent crimes, however, and only upon a factual showing to support the defense. *See United States v. Fay*, 668 F.2d 375, 377 (8th Cir. 1981). Generally, a specific intent crime is one where the defendant intends to not only commit the act but also intends the outcome or result of the crime. Which crimes are deemed specific intent crimes and which are general intent crimes are not always easy to determine from the plain reading of the statutes. For example, assault with a deadly weapon is a specific intent crime under Title 18, United States Code, Sections 1153 and 113(c), while assault on a federal officer, under Title 18 United States Code, Section 111, is a general intent crime. Thus, voluntary intoxication may be available as a defense to the first crime, but not the second. Lawyers will need to research the case law where a violent crime is charged to determine whether an intoxication defense is available. Generally, this defense is rarely used in federal criminal cases outside of murder and assault cases.

8. "I DID IT, BUT I THOUGHT I COULD"— GOOD FAITH DEFENSE

Under some federal statutes, a person cannot be found guilty if he had a good faith belief which negates the requisite criminal intent. A good faith defense arises most often in the context of crimes charging that the defendant acted with the intent to defraud. Good faith is, essentially, the antithesis to intent to defraud. *United States v. Scherer*, 653 F.2d 334, 338 (8th Cir. 1981). Therefore, a good faith belief by the defendant that the act was not going to deprive another of money or goods is a defense in any fraud case. For example, a defendant who is charged with mail fraud because he solicited money from the elderly claiming his meditation tape will prolong life by 30 years is not guilty of the fraud if the jury believes that the defendant in good faith believed that his meditation tape could prolong life by 30 years. This is so even if no reasonable person would believe it. On the other hand, a good faith belief that a law is wrong or unconstitutional is not a defense. In other words, a person who believes that the federal income tax is unconstitutional has no good faith defense.

Like most of affirmative defenses, a court need not instruct a jury on a good faith defense absent some evidentiary showing to support the defense. *Id.* at 337. Good faith defenses are tricky for both prosecution and defense. Jury instructions regarding good faith defenses must be specifically tailored to reflect the statute involved and the nature of the good faith basis claimed.

A variation on the good faith defense is an advice of counsel (or advice of an accountant or other professional) defense. Reliance on advice of counsel is not, by itself, a defense; rather, it is a factor that may be considered in determining whether someone acted in good faith. *United States v. Poludniak*, 657 F.2d 948, 958–59 (8th Cir. 1981). For a defendant to be entitled to an advice of counsel theory of defense, the defendant must demonstrate that he disclosed all relevant facts to his attorney prior to receiving the allegedly errant advice, the attorney provided advice to the defendant to act in in a particular manner, and the defendant followed the attorney's advice to the letter. *United States v. Hecht*, 705 F.2d 976 (8th Cir. 1983). Because of the complexity of federal law, this defense is not uncommon in federal white collar criminal cases.

C. STATUTORY DEFENSES

In some cases, Congress has provided defenses within the language of the statute itself. This statutory language is often reflective of a compromise or a recognition that there ought to be exceptions for criminal liability under certain circumstances. These statutory defenses arise most often in statutes which involved highly regulated areas. For example, under Title 21, United States Code, Section 841, it is a crime for anyone to distribute a controlled substance to another person. Under this Title, however, it is lawful for a medical doctor to distribute a controlled substance if it is done for a legitimate medical purpose and in the course of the defendant's medical practice. Thus, a doctor accused of illegally prescribing controlled substances to others may defeat the charge if she can prove that her prescriptions were for a legitimate medical purpose as part of her regular practice. Similarly, in most federal environmental criminal statutes, there are exceptions written into the statute for small business or businesses that generate a small amount of waste product. This is because Congress recognized the costs of complying with environmental laws can be very expensive and beyond the means of small business.

Thus, it is important when prosecuting or defending federal criminal cases to carefully read the pertinent statute and conduct some preliminary research to become aware of any statute-specific defenses established by Congress or recognized by the courts.

CHAPTER 9

OPENING STATEMENTS

■ ■ ■

Many books and commentators assert that the opening statement is the most important part of a trial. Of course, you are likely to find other authorities argue that jury selection, direct examination, cross examination and closing argument are each, in turn, the most important part of a trial. We hold that the opening statement is an important, critical stage of any trial, but have difficulty ranking it, or any other part of the trial for that matter, as the most important,

Common sense tells you that opening statements are important because of first impressions. Even though in some courts the jury may have already heard you speak during jury selection, the opening statement is still the first time in any case the jury will hear a lawyer speak about the merits of the case. Accordingly, what you say and how you say it is bound to have a lasting impression. You know through your personal experience that first impressions make a big difference in how you perceive others. Studies similarly show that most jurors vote consistently with their first impressions made after opening statements.[1]

Thus, it's important to lock the jury into a belief. People don't like to be wrong. Therefore, if the jury determines after opening statement that your side is correct, they will tend to interpret the evidence in a way to reinforce that belief.

A. PURPOSE OF OPENING STATEMENT

Opening statement is the opportunity for you to tell the facts of the case in a clear, coherent, narrative manner. This will be your *only* chance to do so in a clear, unobstructed manner. Opening statements allows you to put emphasis on the facts that you choose in the order of your choosing. During opening statements, a lawyer has the option of presenting bad facts to the jury first, before the other side reveals them in a manner suggesting that you are hiding the bad facts. An opening statement allows you to establish yourself and your case as worthy of belief. It's your

---

[1] *See, e.g.,* E. Allan Lind & Gina Y. Ke, *The Relative Importance of Opening and Closing Statements*, in THE PSYCHOLOGY OF EVIDENCE AND TRIAL PROCEDURE 229 (Saul M. Kassin & Lawrence S. Wrightsman eds., 1985); Thomas J. Pyszczynski, Jeff Greenberg, David Mack & Lawrence S. Wrightsman, *Opening Statements in a Jury Trial: The Effect of Promising More Than the Evidence Can Show*, 11 J. APPLIED SOC. PSYCHOL. 434 (1981).

opportunity to present yourself to a jury as honest, open, and confident in the jury and the quality of your case. If juries believe you, you will more easily have them believe your case.

B. PREPARING OPENING STATEMENT WITH THE JURY IN MIND

Jury pools run the entire range of sophistication and intelligence. All that is commonly required to serve as a juror is a driver's license or voter registration card. There is no test or evaluation to ensure a person has a specific level of education or even a basic level of common sense before they serve as a juror. Jurors generally do not have long attention spans. Moreover, most jurors are unfamiliar with the criminal justice system, except for what they see on television or in movies. Therefore, jurors may base their expectations of you and your case on a Hollywood version of court room drama. With their limited attention spans, and their television-based understanding of the justice system, jurors expect quick, stimulating performances by the attorneys. You must be aware of jurors' expectations, and in appropriate cases deal with it directly during your opening.

Yet, collectively, a jury as a decision-making body generally exercises sound, intelligent judgment. A jury usually (but not always) exercises common sense. Although jurors may start the trial with little knowledge, collectively they pick it up quickly. Accordingly, have faith in the jury system, because it works. Trust that if you do your job well, the jury will do its job well, also. Even though individually most jurors will be less educated and far less knowledgeable than you about the justice system, collectively they are sharp. *Never* be condescending to your jury.

C. THE STRUCTURE OF OPENING STATEMENTS

1. THE INTRODUCTION

In every opening statement there is some form of introduction. The common beginning phrase is something like: "May it please the court, ladies and gentlemen of the jury, . . ." Your introductory statement should be no longer. From that phrase forward, you must seize the moment. The first five minutes of your opening statement is the only time that you are guaranteed to have the entire jury's undivided attention. Determine the most important thing you want to tell the jury and get it out in the first five minutes of your opening.

Do not waste the beginning of your opening on a lengthy introduction or trivial preliminaries. Do not explain how a trial works, that your opening is "like a puzzle," or that what you say isn't evidence. Do not speak of generalities or lofty goals of the criminal justice system. Rather, get to the point. Describe the case or your client in a compelling nutshell. Establish the theme of your case, if you have one, in the first minute of the case. Then move on to tell the story of your case.

2.   THE STORY

Every case is a story about some alleged crime. Your goal in the opening statement is to tell the story to the jury in a way that is understandable, interesting, and persuasive. As in fiction, there are countless ways to tell a story. Authors decide how to structure or order their stories to grab and retain the reader's interest, and to shape their views of events and characters. Crafting an opening statement is similar. An attorney must learn to tell the story of the case in a compelling manner that immediately captures the jury's attention and retains it throughout the opening statement. Through the opening, an attorney can shape the way the jury perceives the facts and judges the witnesses.

Every case is different, so there is no absolutely "right way" to order an opening. Usually it makes the most sense to structure your opening in a chronological manner by walking the jury through the events of the crime from start to finish. You might give some consideration, however, to other orders if you think it is appropriate in a given case. For example, some events may be confusing or lose emphasis if placed in strictly chronological order. Perhaps the story is more persuasive if told from the point of view of the investigation, structuring the facts in the order they were discovered during the investigation and led inevitably to the conclusion that the defendant was guilty. Likewise, you may choose to reveal some fact at the end of your opening because it has the greatest impact, even if chronologically it fits in time earlier in the story. For example, in a case involving the interstate travel to engage in sexual relationship with a minor, you may want to tell the story of this case, then at the end of your opening reveal to the jury that you will also prove that the defendant was previously convicted for the same offense (of course, before you try something like this make sure that the evidence is admissible).

You should also give some thought about the point of view of the narration. The typical method of presenting an opening statement is in third-person, as if you are a narrator of the story. Example: "On April 13, 2001, officers arrived at the house and found blood on the steps." You should consider, though, whether the story can be better told from the view of one of the people involved in the story. Perhaps the story is more persuasive if told from the point of view of one of your witnesses. Example: "Officer John Malone walked slowly up to the house. As he cautiously approached, he saw blood on the steps." Again, think about the general fiction you read; novels are written in many different ways, all of which can contribute to a persuasive opening statement.

As you tell your story, you should introduce the characters (witnesses) who are essential to your story. Do it in a manner that is a natural part of the story, not as a list. For example, don't get caught in the habit of saying "you will also hear Mr. Smith testify, and he will tell you. . . . Then you will hear Mrs. Beasley testify, and she will say. . . ." Rather, make it fit into the story you are telling. For example: "As Officer Malone came in the front door of the house, he saw Barbara Smith, kneeling behind the sofa. Ms. Smith had just seen the defendant beat her mother and was hiding from the defendant, her ex-husband."

In every case there will be many unimportant people who had something to do with the events, just in like in many books there are unimportant background characters. In your opening you should introduce the jury to the main witnesses from whom they will be soon hearing. Be careful as you tell your story, however, not to overwhelm the jury with too many names. The jury need not know in the opening statement of every witness. Indeed, the jury will be overwhelmed with too many names and will lose focus on the most important facts you are trying to impart during opening statement. Likewise, except for the truly key witnesses, avoid using names altogether in opening statement. Rather, refer to secondary witnesses by their role or position. Example: "When the defendant entered the bank, the guard was just emerging from the Vice President's office." Even if you will be calling both the guard and the Vice President as witnesses at the trial, it is those witness's positions that are important to the story, not their names.

One of the goals of opening statement is to persuade the jury to believe your side of the case. For witnesses to be persuasive, it helps if the jurors can identify and empathize with the witness. This is hard to do if the jurors see witnesses as something less than human beings with real lives. Therefore, you may consider humanizing your key witnesses in the opening statement. Tell a little about important witnesses, so the jury can begin to connect with the witnesses even before they see them. Example: "Officer John Malone, a twelve-year veteran of the force, was tied after working the night shift when he walked slowly up to the house. . . ." Recall, however, that an opening statement reflects what you anticipate the evidence will show, so you will need to make sure you later elicit these facts from the witness when they testify.

Every part of your opening should have a purpose. But, not every part of your story is as important as every other part. Sometimes, small details are important. Stress those important parts. Ignore the trivial parts. Exercise judgment about the winning facts of your case.

You may also consider using foreshadowing in your opening statement. Foreshadowing is a technique used in fiction whereby the author provides some facts earlier in the narrative that suggest what facts will later be revealed. Foreshadowing is an effective way to engage readers because when the foreshadowed fact is later revealed, the reader feels a sense of triumph, having guessed at that fact because of the foreshadowing. The same technique can be used in an opening statement. Instead of providing the jury with the concluding fact, an engaging opening statement may provide the facts that lead to the conclusion, without stating it. Consider, for example, a bank robbery case in which the police recovered fingerprints belonging to the defendant on the demand note. An opening statement using foreshadowing may tell the jury about the use of a demand note, the fact it was left by the robber with the teller, that the teller carefully preserved it, that the FBI dusted it for prints, but stop short of saying in opening statement that officers found a latent print that came back as belonging to the defendant. Rather, the prosecutor may just want to look the defendant's way when indicating a latent print was found on the note. When later, during trial, the forensic expert testifies that the latent print belonged to the defendant, jurors may feel confirmed in the conclusion they think they reached on their own.

You may also want to consider leaving out some facts from your opening statement that are unnecessary, but nevertheless persuasive. You do not need to tell the jury about every fact you have in opening statement. If the opening statement leaves the jury leaning toward your side, and then they learn during the course of trial even more facts that they didn't know before that support your side, it can be very effective. In our bank robbery example, motive is not an element of the crime and therefore need not necessarily be discussed during opening statement. Although a prosecutor could reveal in opening statement that the defendant incurred a massive gambling debt and received an eviction notice days before the bank robbery, it may be more effective to reveal these facts during the course of the trial so as to save a surprise for the jury that will convince it even more that the defendant is guilty of the offense.

You should also strive to make the story compelling. Every story has some natural drama. Find that drama, the human interest angle, the most interesting or fascinating part of the case and emphasize it during the opening. Even with the most mundane of cases, you can use pacing, foreshadowing, and suspense to create a sense of tension and meaning.

3.   THE ELEMENTS OF THE OFFENSE

If necessary, briefly describe the elements of the offenses. In many federal criminal trials, the elements of the offense often are not complex and need not be covered in any detail during opening. For example, the elements of bank robbery involve the taking of money without permission from a bank insured by the FDIC. It is not difficult for a jury to understand why robbing a bank is bad and what it takes to be guilty of the crime. The federal jurisdiction element (insured by the FDIC) is not an important part of the story and would not need to be addressed in opening statement.

In other federal cases, however, the crime may be very complex and the elements of the offense not so clearly understood. In those cases you will need to explain to the jury what the government needs to show to prove the defendant committed a crime. When you do explain the elements during an opening statement, don't call them "elements" or "counts." Rather, refer to them as "things" or "facts" the government must prove. Don't try to turn jurors into lawyers. Juries need to know the law in opening only as it relates to the facts and what you are trying to prove. Just provide them a very quick, common-sense discussion of what constitutes the crime you are prosecuting. To the extent you discuss the things the government has to prove, limit this discussion to the elements that are really in dispute. If the case involves a mail fraud charge and the defendant is not really contesting that a mailing was involved, then there is no reason to spend any time in opening statement talking about a mailing.

4. ADDRESS POTENTIAL PROBLEMS

Every case has weaknesses, or it would not be going to trial. Before the end of the trial the jury will become fully aware of those weaknesses and problems. Accordingly, it is far better for you to acknowledge and front the difficulties in your own case during opening statement, before the other side does, and attempt to either minimize them, or sensitize the jury to the fact that the problems will make no difference in your case. If possible, turn negatives into positives.

Often your "problem" will be a problem witness. For the government, the witnesses in this category are often coconspirators or cooperators testifying on behalf of the government. Stress (without arguing) that these witnesses are probably no worse than the defendant:

> *John Smith was one of the people who bought drugs from the defendant over a long period of time. As you might imagine, people who deal in drugs are not always the finest citizens, and Mr. Smith is no exception. He has been convicted of drug crimes in the past, and he will admit them.*

Again, when possible, turn a negative into a positive:

> *During this trial, you will hear from witnesses in a position to know about the defendant's criminal acts, people who worked beside the defendant as he committed his crimes, and who took orders from the defendant to carry out the scheme.*

You must, however, resist the temptation to argue witness credibility during your opening. It is perfectly appropriate, however, to point to facts which make your witnesses look credible.

Other times, the government's difficulty is with the lack of direct evidence of a crime. Many cases are proven by circumstantial evidence. Prosecutors should not apologize for circumstantial cases. If possible, find a way to shift blame to the defendant:

> *There will be no witness who can conclusively identify the defendant as the person who robbed the bank. Because the defendant wore a ski mask, none of the bank tellers could identify him. The evidence will show, however, that the defendant had some of the stolen money in his apartment, that agents found a similar ski mask in his car, and that he was heard bragging to his friends about the robbery.*

Or again, turn a negative into a positive:

> *There will be no evidence that the defendant dealt directly with the undercover agents, or handled the cocaine that was seized in this case. Rather, the evidence will show that the defendant was the one who controlled other people, who directed the operation, who tried to insulate himself by having others do the dirty work, but who ultimately stood to profit from the sale of the cocaine.*

As we mentioned earlier, jurors come to trial with certain expectations borne of too many hours in front of the television. They will often expect you to provide them with evidence you don't have. In other cases, the expectations arise from the nature of the alleged crime. For example, if you charge a defendant with being a felon in possession of a firearm, the jury may naturally expect you to present evidence that he was seen with the gun in his hands, when your evidence may consist of proving constructive, joint possession as a result of the gun being found in the house he shared with his wife. Likewise, in a fraud or false statements case, the defendant may not have succeeded in his scheme, and therefore there was no loss to the victim or advantage to the defendant. In a drug case, there may be no drugs seized, or the conspiracy may have been ultimately unsuccessful. In such cases, you may want to touch on that fact, but don't make a big deal out of it. Oftentimes, there is good reason that you will not prove an expected fact.

Even if your case doesn't have a "problem," like a bad witness or a missing piece of evidence, you may have a case with boring parts to it. Again, it is sometimes appropriate in opening statement to acknowledge that there will be a boring part, but explain its necessity to the jury. This helps prepare the jury for the boring part, while also emphasizing its importance at the same time. For example, in a bank fraud case, you may want to forewarn the jurors they will be hearing from a forensic accountant who, though the testimony may be complex and lengthy, will explain the machinations the defendant engaged in to conceal the fraud from the bank by doctoring the corporate records.

Whatever your problem or difficulty, you should front it during your opening, but do not be defensive, and do not dwell on it. Raise it, deal with it, and move on to better parts of your story.

5. CONCLUSION

The last part of your opening is your closing—the end portion or conclusion to your opening statement. Your conclusion should concisely summarize the essential thrust of the evidence and your theory of the case. This is the time to remind the jury of your theme, if your case has one. Be cautious, however, not to make your "theme" seem trite by concocting clever phrases. Keep it simple and sincere.

One thing you should never forget is to tell the jury what you want from them. You need to tell them directly. For example:

> *It is based on this evidence that at the conclusion of the trial, I will stand before you and ask that you return a verdict of guilty on all charges.*

Or:

> *After all the evidence has been heard, it will be clear that the government has failed to meet its heavy burden, that the government has failed to prove beyond a reasonable doubt that [name] is guilty.*

While it may seem premature in the opening to be asking for the verdict, it is not. It is important for the jury to keep in mind throughout the trial what you want from them.

D. COMMON TECHNIQUES FOR OPENING STATEMENTS

Opening statements are, in some measure, a form of public performance. As with any public performance, there are issues of execution—such as where to stand, what language is best, what props to use—that need be addressed. In this section we will discuss the most common issues and relate our judgment on each.

1. SCRIPT, NOTES OR MEMORY?

Lawyers differ significantly on the degree to which they rely on notes during opening statements. Some write out their opening statements word for word and read it to the jury without deviation from the printed word. Others use notes of varying degree of detail as guides to their opening. Still others memorize the essence of what they want to say during opening and speak without a script or notes. Which method you adopt will depend on your own speaking style and may depend on your level of experience or the complexity of the case.

Regardless of which method you use, there are certain fundamental pointers that will make your opening more persuasive. First, you need to understand that eye contact with your jury is important. If you do not look the jurors in the eye, they will not be as likely to listen to you or trust you. Second, the first and last five minutes of your opening are your most important, due to the primacy/recency effect. Accordingly, even if you use notes for the remainder of your opening, you should try to memorize the first and last five minutes of the opening, and use an outline for the rest. Third, whether you use notes or memorize your opening, you should think carefully about how you state certain key issues or facts and practice them to ensure that they will come out as you intend them. A slip of tongue in a federal criminal case, especially by a prosecutor, may lead to a mistrial.

2. WHERE TO STAND, HOW TO MOVE

The rules differ widely in federal court rooms regarding the freedom of movement that the judges afford the attorneys. Some federal judges allow lawyers to move fairly freely about the court room, especially during opening statement or closing argument, while others will chain lawyers to the lectern. Most allow only limited movement around the area of the lectern. You should, of course, check out the rules in the court room where you will appear in advance of trial so that you acclimate yourself to the restrictions, if any.

Even in court rooms where the judges restrict lawyers to the lectern, you generally should be able to move the lectern from its usual place to a place in front of the jury. Stand behind the lectern to start, but don't hesitate to move from it to emphasize the important parts, if your judge permits. Even when you have complete freedom of movement in the court room, however, you do not want to stand too close to the jury. It makes jurors uncomfortable and may anger even the most reasonable judge.

If your trial judge permits free movement in the well of the courtroom during opening statements, use that freedom to effect. If a lawyer moves with purpose, and builds that movement into the telling of the story, it can aid in keeping the jury's attention and in their comprehension of the facts. On the other hand, if a lawyer moves without purpose—simply pacing back and forth in front of the jury box while droning on—it can distract the jury and detract from its comprehension.

Purposeful movement can be built into the story by using it as a way to mark the passage of time, to indicate a change in topic, or to re-enact some aspect of the events being related. For example, in Western cultures time is seen as linear, moving from left to right. If you have structured your opening statement in a way that you are relating the facts in chronological order, you can move your position in the courtroom to demonstrate the passage of time as you chronologically tell the story. So, you might deliver your opening remarks—your first five minutes where you summarize the case and state your theme—standing in a middle location before the jury box. Then, when you start to describe the events in chronological order, move to the right (as you are facing the jury box) and talk about the first events standing far right. As you move to each set of new events, you can slowly move to a position to the left, stop, talk about those events, and then move again to the left before talking about the next set of events. Remember to consider your movement from the point of view of the jury; as you move from right to left as you face the jury box, the jury will view you moving from its left to right, like a time line, during your delivery.

If your opening is not structured chronologically, you can still use movement in the courtroom to mark the change in topics during opening statement. For example, you may start with the basic facts of the bank robbery by moving to a location to the right of the jury as you face the jury box. Then, perhaps, when you change topics to discuss the forensic evidence from the bank or the evidence found at the defendant's house that link him to the robbery, you could move to a position in the center before the jury box. Then, when you finish by talking about the defendant's motive for robbing the bank, you could take a final position to the left as you face the jury box.

Finally, movement can be used to reflect actual events during the crime as you recount them during opening statement. Lawyers should be cautious in doing this—a courtroom is not a stage and lawyers are not actors—so movement in this respect should be representative, not a re-enactment. Consider, for example, a case where a bank robber pulled down a ski mask while entering the bank and then approached the teller while withdrawing a pistol from his pocket. During opening statement, the lawyer may reflect these movements, using the witness box as if it were the teller's counter, and generally make the movements the robber made while approaching the teller's counter. In an example like this, a lawyer should not act as if the jurors were behind the teller's station. As a general rule, lawyers should not explicitly or implicitly place the jurors in the role of any party, witness or victim. Lawyers should also use subdued, representational movements when attempting to represent actual movement during the crime, as opposed to dramatic movement. The goal is the help the jury visualize the events, not to re-enact them as if on a stage.

3. USE OF LANGUAGE

Language is the key to opening statements. It is largely through your words that you must persuade the jury. Accordingly, you should pay particular attention to the words you chose and the meaning they convey.

For example, the government generally will want to emphasize the defendant's status by referring to him as "the defendant" instead of by a respectful "Mr. Smith" or a familiar "Bob." Defense counsel, on the other hand, generally want to humanize criminal defendants and, therefore, should never refer to defendants as "the defendant," but rather by more human and familiar terms. Defense attorneys should refrain from referring to the defendant as "my client." The relationship the defendant bears to the lawyer is irrelevant, turns the focus on the lawyer, and dehumanizes the defendant.

You should also strive to use clear, understandable language. Don't talk like a lawyer or a cop. Non-lawyers are sensitive to the use of ten-dollar words when ten-cent words will do. Lay people do not take kindly to having lawyers flaunt their allegedly superior knowledge, education, and vocabulary, and will soon forget the message from dislike of the messenger. Similarly, cop-talk (e.g., "After the officer responded to the 10–29, he exited his government-issued patrol vehicle. . . .") lacks description, and therefore fails to persuade. Use simple language, while not talking down to the jury. You should also always explain unfamiliar words and names the first time you use them.

4. USE OF EXHIBITS OR DEMONSTRATIVE AIDS

Many studies of human retention report significantly higher levels of short and long term memory when the spoken word is combined with visual aids. Thus, demonstrative aids (such as charts, maps, diagrams and the like) are generally a good idea, especially in long, involved cases. Demonstrative aids are good for very technical factual issues, or to explain a very complicated factual scenario. When constructing demonstrative exhibits, the simpler, the better.

You may also use actual evidence from the trial during opening statements. You may want to hold up the gun used in the crime, or show a photograph of the bank robbery scene. Obviously, these pieces of key evidence can have significant impact. You should take care not to use too many demonstrative aids or actual exhibits during an opening statement as it may dilute the impact.

Whether you use a demonstrative exhibit or an actual exhibit during opening statement, you must always make sure the demonstrative aid or exhibit is admissible. Before using either in your opening, ensure that the other side and the court do not object. Only bad things can result from an opening that begins with the court reprimanding you for showing the jury a demonstrative or actual exhibit without prior approval. Furthermore, a mistrial could and likely would result if a lawyer used an exhibit during opening statement that was not then later admitted into evidence during the trial.

5. LEVEL OF DETAIL AND LENGTH OF OPENING

There are no clear guidelines regarding the degree of detail to include in an opening statement. The more detail, the harder it will be for a jury to follow, to retain your theme, and to stay awake. Also, the more detail, the greater the likelihood that your evidence will not meet the promises you make. On the other hand, vague, broad-brush openings without sufficient detail lack persuasive quality.

Keep in mind that you are giving a "snapshot" of the case, not a blow by blow description. Therefore, adjust the amount of detail you provide. Give more detail on the important parts, less or no detail on the unimportant ones. Dates and times are only important for their relation to other dates and times. "Two days after the fire" means much more to a jury hearing about a case than "Tuesday, August 22."

Juries have difficulty remembering a large number of names. During opening statement you will want and need to introduce the jury to the names of the key figures in the drama. Again, it is better to refer to less important witnesses by title or function (e.g., "the arson investigator" or "the medical examiner").

Finally, you should take only the amount of time necessary to provide the jury with a snapshot of the case, and no more. That amount will vary, of course, depending on the length and complexity of the trial. To avoid nasty surprises, however, be sure to ask the court how much time will be allowed for opening before you start. It is better to make your opening too short than too long. The authors of this text have tried cases that lasted months, yet kept opening statements to less than an hour. In the typical three or four day jury trial, an opening statement often can be delivered in fifteen minutes, or less.

E. DEFENSE OPENING STATEMENTS

Although many of the suggestions discussed above apply with equal force to a defense opening statement as they do to a government's opening statement, defense attorneys have unique considerations that prosecutors do not.

First, a defendant need not make an opening statement at all. Although it is hard to conceive of a case where waiving opening statement completely would be wise, perhaps in an appropriate case it could work.

Short of waiving opening statement completely, a defendant may reserve his or her opening statement and deliver it at the conclusion of the government's case in chief and before the defense case-in-chief. Some experienced defense attorneys will suggest that it is best to reserve opening statement in every case because the government's evidence may not come in as planned and the defense can therefore adjust its case (as summarized in the opening statement) to the evidence as presented. Other experienced defense attorneys will advise never to reserve an opening statement. They reason that the defense should never let the government get up and speak without responding to the government's assertions in some manner. They may also point out that in many federal criminal cases, defendants do not call any witnesses. A defense attorney can only present an opening statement to comment on what the attorney anticipates the evidence to be. If the defendant has reserved opening statement, the government has presented its case, and the defendant has no case to present, a reserved opening statement in that case is a waived opening statement. The middle ground is to reserve opening statements in those (probably rare) cases where the defendant will present witnesses on substantive matters that could be a surprise to the government. In these cases, if the defendant presents an opening statement at the beginning of the trial before the government's case-in-chief, it will alert the government to the defendant's defense and allow the government to change or add to the evidence it otherwise might present.

Defense attorneys also have a unique difficulty in dealing with the issue of whether their clients will testify. No matter how certain an attorney may be that the defendant will not testify, or will testify, it is risky business to promise either one to the jury during an opening statement. A defendant has the absolute right to testify or not to testify, and can change his or her mind several times during the course of the trial. Until the defense "rests," a defendant can testify. Accordingly, most experienced defense attorneys suggest leaving this issue alone during an opening statement. Some defense attorneys, however, recommend spending a lot of time during opening statement talking about a defendant's constitutional right not to testify, but only if the defense attorney is absolutely certain the defendant will testify. They reason that this shows how extraordinary it is for the defendant to waive his or her constitutional right and implies that this would be done only because the defendant knows he or she is innocent.

Often in federal criminal cases, defendants do not present any evidence at all. Particularly in those cases, but probably in all defense opening statements, defense attorneys are well advised to emphasize the government's burden of proof, and the presumption of innocence. Defense attorneys often spend a significant amount of the opening statement discussing these bedrock Constitutional principles, attempting to persuade the jury to internalize these concepts. In some cases, this may be all a defense attorney can do in opening statement.

Defense attorneys sometimes talk about the lack of the government's evidence, the strength of the defendant's evidence, or both, during opening statement. A defendant can always talk about government's omissions, mistakes, or lack of evidence—no criminal investigation is perfect and, therefore, there is always something a good defense attorney can dream up that the government "coulda, shoulda, woulda" done if it had been competent. In some cases the defense will actually have some evidence, and a defense attorney may want to discuss it during opening. Be aware that by telling the jury about a defense, the defendant creates expectations in the jury that a defendant will present evidence of innocence, a burden not imposed upon a defendant by the Constitution. Accordingly, a defense attorney must seriously weigh the consequences of suggesting to the jury that the defendant will mount his own defense, as opposed to attacking the government's evidence.

Finally, unlike in closing arguments where the government has a right of rebuttal, there is no rebuttal opening statement. Therefore, the defense counsel is the last to speak to the jury before the evidence begins, and the government cannot respond. Defense counsel can exploit this in some instances by posing hypothetical or rhetorical questions they want the jury to keep in mind as the evidence is presented. For example, a defense attorney may say something like: "As you listen to the government's case, ask yourself why the police never dusted for fingerprints at the crime scene." There may be a fact that easily explains this that the government could provide, but the government doesn't have the opportunity to do so now. So, the jury is left with the impression that there is something important or sinister in the failure to take prints that may linger even when the facts later come out that explain why this should not really be an issue.

F. THE "DON'TS" OF OPENING STATEMENTS

For every piece of advice regarding how to conduct an opening statement, there are an equal number of things we recommend you do not do when preparing for and presenting your opening statement. We will discuss a few of those below.

Although we suggest above that you write an outline of your opening statement, don't write your opening on the morning of trial. Last minute preparation is no preparation at all. Write it out in advance and practice it, either presenting it to others in your office or presenting it to your spouse or partner or, if necessary, to yourself in front of a mirror. Remember, the appearance you present during opening will likely create a lasting impression on the jury.

Don't argue during an opening statement. Why not? Argument in opening statements is objectionable, and a good attorney on the other side will object to your opening statement if, for no other reason, than to interrupt your flow. An objection to your opening statement, when sustained by the court, hurts you in the eyes of the jury at a time when you are trying to look credible. What constitutes an argumentative statement is not always clear. One test is to ask yourself: "Do I have a witness who will say this, or an exhibit that will show this?" If the answer is no, then it is likely a conclusion you are asking the jury to reach from evidence, and not a statement of fact that will be presented through testimony or exhibits. Thus, another test is to ask yourself: "Am I asking the jury to draw inferences from facts?" Generally, if you talk about witness credibility, you are arguing.

If, despite your best efforts, you slip into argument during your opening statement, you may have to deal with an objection by opposing counsel. One of the easiest ways to deal with such an objection is, after the objection is voiced, rephrase your point, beginning your statement with the phrase: "The evidence will show. . . ." This makes it clear that you do have evidence that will establish the point you are making.

Remember that sequencing of facts is not argument. In other words, if you place facts in proper order, they can lead to a conclusion, but yet not be argument. For example, lining up the facts in proper order— defendant lost his job, defendant bought a gun, defendant drove a red car, the bank was robbed by a man with a gun who jumped into a red car that fled the scene—can lead to the conclusion defendant robbed the bank without constituting argument.

Don't talk about evidence if you are not sure it will be admitted. To do so carries the potential for a mistrial—particularly if you represent the United States. At the very least, opposing counsel will try to discredit you and your case by pointing out later your failure to produce that which you promised during opening statement. Use motions in limine to determine what will come in, and what will stay out so that you know the answers before you present opening statement. If the judge refuses to rule pretrial, then err on the side of caution. They key is not to overstate your case, or over promise. Opening statements are promises—promises of what you will prove to the jury through the evidence. Be sure to keep your promises, and note carefully the promises the other side makes, but fails to keep. Your credibility, and the credibility of your party, are at issue

Don't make other objectionable statements during opening. One of the most common errors is to express your personal opinions during opening statement. Your personal opinion does not belong anywhere in the trial. Furthermore, the government must be extremely cautious not to comment on the defendant's silence. This extends to speculation as to whether a defendant will testify or present evidence. Suggesting, during your opening, that the defendant has an obligation to present any evidence at all constitutes a comment on the defendant's right to remain silent and can be reversible error if the defendant does not, in the end, testify or present evidence. Indeed, prosecutors should not assume the defense counsel will even make an opening statement, let alone say anything during the government's opening statement about what the prosecutor predicts defense counsel may say during the defendant's opening statement. A defendant has a constitutional right to say nothing at all, which means the defense attorney need not even deliver an opening statement.

Attorneys representing the United States must also refrain from invoking larger societal goals during opening statement. The government must stick to the facts of the case. Do not ask the jury to "send a message" or "clean up the streets." Do not suggest that a guilty verdict in this case will benefit society or advance the war on drugs or the like. Why congress made certain conduct a crime is not a fact of the case. For example, it is improper for the government to explain why sawed-off shotguns are particularly dangerous or how criminals use them because they are easily concealed. Try the case on the facts of the case and leave policy making to Congress.

G. CONCLUSION

Opening statements can be an enjoyable challenge—a first opportunity to persuade others through the use of words. It is an art form, however, that can only be mastered, if ever, after years of practice. At the end of this section we have reproduced a couple opening statements by experienced, skillful attorneys who demonstrate the power an effective opening statement can have.

EXCERPT FROM GOVERNMENT'S OPENING STATEMENT, *UNITED STATES V. TIMOTHY MCVEIGH*

May it please the Court . . .

THE COURT: Counsel.

MR. HARTZLER: Ladies and gentlemen of the jury, April 19th, 1995, was a beautiful day in Oklahoma City—at least it started out as a beautiful day. The sun was shining. Flowers were blooming. It was springtime in Oklahoma City. Sometime after six o'clock that morning, Tevin Garrett's mother woke him up to get him ready for the day. He was only 16 months old. He was a toddler; and as some of you know that have experience with toddlers, he had a keen eye for mischief. He would often pull on the cord of her curling iron in the morning, pull it off the counter top until it fell down, often till it fell down on him.

That morning, she picked him up and wrestled with him on her bed before she got him dressed. She remembers this morning because that was the last morning of his life.

That morning, Mrs. Garrett got Tevin and her daughter ready for school and they left the house at about 7:15 to go downtown to Oklahoma City. She had to be at work at eight o'clock. Tevin's sister went to kindergarten, and they dropped the little girl off at kindergarten first; and Helena Garrett and Tevin proceeded to downtown Oklahoma City.

Usually she parked a little bit distant from her building; but this day, she was running a little bit late, so she decided that she would park in the Murrah Federal Building. She did not work in the Murrah Building. She wasn't even a federal employee. She worked across the street in the General Records Building.

She pulled into the lot, the parking lot of the federal building, in order to make it into work on time; and she went upstairs to the second floor with Tevin, because Tevin attended the day-care center on the second floor of the federal building. When she went in, she saw that Chase and Colton Smith were already there, two year old and three year old. Dominique London was there already. He was just shy of his third birthday. So was Zack Chavez. He had already turned three.

When she turned to leave to go to her work, Tevin, as so often, often happens with small children, cried and clung to her; and then, as you see with children so frequently, they try to help each other. Little—one of the little Coverdale boys—there were two of them, Elijah and Aaron. The youngest one was two and a half. Elijah came up to Tevin and patted him on the back and comforted him as his mother left.

As Helena Garrett left the Murrah Federal Building to go to work across the street, she could look back up at the building; and there was a wall of plate glass windows on the second floor. You can look through those windows and see into the day-care center; and the children would run up to those windows and press their hands and faces to those windows to say goodbye to their parents. And standing on the sidewalk, it was almost as though you can reach up and touch the children there on the second floor. But none of the parents of any of the children that I just mentioned ever touched those children again while they were still alive.

At nine o'clock that morning, two things happened almost simultaneously. In the Water Resources Building—that's another building to the west of the Murrah Building across the street—an ordinary legal proceeding began in one of the hearing rooms; and at the same time, in front of the Murrah Building, a large Ryder truck pulled up into a vacant parking space in front of the building and parked right beneath those plate glass windows from the day-care center.

What these two separate but almost simultaneous events have in common is that they—they both involved grievances of some sort. The legal proceeding had to do with water rights. It wasn't a legal proceeding as we are having here, because there was no court reporter. It was a tape-recorded proceeding, and you will hear the tape recording of that proceeding. It was an ordinary, everyday-across-America, typical legal proceeding in which one party has a grievance and brings it into court or into a hearing to resolve it, to resolve it not by violence and terror but to resolve it in the same way we are resolving matters here, by constitutional due process.

And across the street, the Ryder truck was there also to resolve a grievance; but the truck wasn't there to resolve the grievance by means of due process or by any other democratic means. The truck was there to impose the will of Timothy McVeigh on the rest of America and to do so by premeditated violence and terror, by murdering innocent men, women and children, in hopes of seeing blood flow in the streets of America.

At 9:02 that morning, two minutes after the water rights proceeding began, a catastrophic explosion ripped the air in downtown Oklahoma City. It instantaneously demolished the entire front of the Murrah Building, brought down tons and tons of concrete and metal, dismembered people inside, and it destroyed, forever, scores and scores and scores of lives, lives of innocent Americans: clerks, secretaries, law enforcement officers, credit union employees, citizens applying for Social Security, and little kids.

All the children I mentioned earlier, all of them died, and more; dozens and dozens of other men, women, children, cousins, loved ones, grandparents, grandchildren, ordinary Americans going about their business. And the only reason they died, the only reason that they are no longer with us, no longer with their loved ones, is that they were in a building owned by a government that Timothy McVeigh so hated that with premeditated intent and a well-designed plan that he had developed over months and months before the bombing, he chose to take their innocent lives to serve his twisted purpose.

In plain, simple language, it was an act of terror, violence, intend—intended to serve selfish political purpose.

The man who committed this act is sitting in this courtroom behind me, and he's the one that committed those murders.

EXCERPT FROM PLAINTIFF'S OPENING STATEMENT, *RONALD GOLDMAN V. O.J. SIMPSON*

MR. PETROCELLI: Thank you, Your Honor.

On a June evening, the 12th of June, 1994, Nicole Brown Simpson just finished putting her ten-year-old daughter, Sydney, and her six-year-old son, Justin, down to bed.

She filled her bathtub with water. She lit some candles, began to get ready to take a bath and relax for the evening.

The phone rang. It was 9:40 p.m. Nicole answered. And it was her mother, saying that she had left her glasses at the restaurant nearby in Brentwood, where the family had all celebrated Sydney's dance recital over dinner, just an hour before.

Nicole's mother asked if Nicole could please pick up her glasses from the restaurant the next day. Nicole said, of course, good-bye, and hung up.

Nicole then called the restaurant and asked to speak to a friendly young waiter there. Nicole asked this young waiter if he would be kind enough to drop her mother's glasses off.

The young man obliged and said he would drop the glasses off shortly after work, on his way to meet his friend in Marina Del Rey. The young man's name was Ron Goldman. He was 25 years old.

With the glasses in hand, Ron walked out of the restaurant, walked the few minutes to his apartment nearby, to change. He left the restaurant at 9:50 p.m.

After Ron changed, he got into his girlfriend's car parked in his garage, and drove the short distance to Nicole Brown Simpson's home at 875 South Bundy Drive in Brentwood.

Ron parked the car on the side street, walked to the front of Nicole's condominium, and turned up the walkway to the front gate. Just past the front gate were steps leading to Nicole's condominium.

Ronald Goldman never made it past those steps. It was at that front gate that Ron spent the last few savage minutes of his life. It was there that his brutalized body was found next to Nicole Brown Simpson's slain body, with her mother's glasses lying next to him on the ground in an envelope.

Ron Goldman's young life ended because he agreed to do a friend a favor, only to come upon her rageful killer and his.

He might have run from danger, but he did not. Ron Goldman died, ladies and gentlemen, with his eyes open. And in the last furious moment of his life, Ron saw through those open eyes the person who killed his friend Nicole. And for that reason, he too had to die.

And the last person Ron Goldman saw through his open eyes was the man who took his young life away: The man who now sits in this courtroom, the defendant, Orenthal James Simpson.

Ladies and gentlemen, we will prove to you that Ronald Lyle Goldman and Nicole Brown Simpson died at the hands of the defendant, Orenthal Simpson.

Let me again introduce myself and my colleagues to you.

My name is Daniel Petrocelli. With me are Edward Medvene, Peter Gelblum, Yvette Molinaro, Thomas Lambert. We all represent the Estate of Ronald Goldman and Ronald's father, Fred, in this, his last fight for justice for his son.

Mr. Brewer represents Ronald's mother, Sharon Rufo, and Mr. Kelly represents the Estate of Nicole Brown Simpson. And they will each talk to you after me.

In this trial, we will present to you an extraordinary amount of evidence undeniably pointing to O.J. Simpson as the person who killed Ronald Goldman and Nicole Brown Simpson on the evening of June 12.

This evidence includes:

Mr. Simpson's blood leaving the scene of the murder at Nicole's condominium;

His blood dripping to the ground from the fingers of his left hand;

Mr. Simpson's blood on the glove he wore when he killed Ron and Nicole;

Mr. Simpson's blood in his car that he used to drive from Bundy to his home at Rockingham, five minutes away;

Mr. Simpson's blood on the driveway of his home;

Mr. Simpson's blood inside his home;

Ron's blood in Mr. Simpson's car;

Nicole's blood in Mr. Simpson's car;

Ron's blood on Mr. Simpson's glove;

Nicole's blood on Mr. Simpson's glove;

Nicole's blood on the socks in Mr. Simpson's bedroom;

Mr. Simpson's own blood on his socks;

Mr. Simpson's size 12 shoe prints in the blood of Nicole, leaving the scene of the murder, exiting towards the back of the condominium;

Hair matching Mr. Simpson's hair in the knit cap he left behind at the scene of the murders;

Hair matching Mr. Simpson's hair on Ronald Goldman's shirt;

Strands of Nicole's hair and Ron's hair on the glove Mr. Simpson dropped on the side of his house, trying to get onto his property so no one would see him;

Carpet fibers, rare carpet fibers from Mr. Simpson's Bronco found in the knit cap that he left at the scene of the murders;

Matching blue-black cotton fibers found on Ronald Goldman's shirt;

The glove at Rockingham and Mr. Simpson's socks in the bedroom, tying all three together.

Cuts and bruises to Mr. Simpson's left hand during his brief but violent attacks on Ron and Nicole;

Cuts to this day that Mr. Simpson cannot and will not explain.

We will prove to you that Mr. Simpson has no alibi during the time when the murders were committed.

He cannot identify a single person who can account for his whereabouts during the time of the murders. Not one person will take this stand and testify that he or she was with Mr. Simpson or spoke to Mr. Simpson during the time of these murders.

We will prove how Ron and Nicole were killed quickly and savagely. They were defenseless against a man so large, powerful, strong, armed with a six-inch knife, and in a total state of rage.

Nicole had no chance to fight, and died within moments of the gaping cut to her throat.

Ron tried to fight, but trapped in a small, caged area, he was cut down swiftly.

We will prove to you that Mr. Simpson committed the murders and sped back home, just in time to drive to the airport and catch a plane that he desperately needed to catch to have any hope of an alibi. In his extreme panic and hurry, Mr. Simpson left behind a trail of incriminating evidence, starting right at the murder scene and leading right into his bedroom.

We will prove to you that Mr. Simpson was embroiled in a deeply emotional conflict with Nicole Brown Simpson after she had just ended any last attempt at reconciliation between the two.

We will describe to you the rejection and pain this caused Mr. Simpson in detail, the build-up of tension, emotion, and anger between Mr. Simpson and Nicole in the last weeks and days leading up to her murder.

We will prove that Mr. Simpson killed Ronald Goldman because he would have been a witness to the rageful attack and murder of Nicole, a witness who would have testified in this trial, a young man who simply, and frankly, happened to be at the wrong place at the wrong time.

We will prove to you how Mr. Simpson's own words and actions following the murders revealed then, and still reveal today, his guilt for these deaths.

You will hear Mr. Simpson on tape, just hours after the murder, unable to explain his actions the night before, during the time of the murders.

You will hear him make very incriminating statements, statements that he will now try to contradict or vary.

We will tell you about Mr. Simpson's flight from the police when they came to arrest him and his apparent thoughts of taking his life, thoughts that are consistent, ladies and gentlemen, only with a person who had killed, and that are totally inconsistent with a man whose children had just lost their mother at the hands of a stranger.

MR. BAKER: Your Honor, I'm going to object. This is argument, not opening statement.

THE COURT: Overruled.

MR. PETROCELLI: Thank you.

You will hear how this man came back to Los Angeles on the day after the murders and huddled with lawyers, rather than huddle with his children.

MR. BAKER: I object, Your Honor. That's argument.

THE COURT: Sustained.

MR. PETROCELLI: We will reveal to you lies and deceptions in the sworn testimony of Mr. Simpson when questioned under oath for the first time.

MR. BAKER: I'll object again, Your Honor. That's argument.

MR. PETROCELLI: Your Honor, this is what we will introduce.

THE COURT: Overruled.

MR. PETROCELLI: We will reveal to you lies and deceptions in the sworn testimony of Mr. Simpson when questioned under oath for the first time about his involvement in these murders.

We will prove to you that when asked all the important questions about his involvement in these murders, O.J. Simpson could not, would not, and did not tell the truth.

MR. BAKER: Your Honor, I'll object again. This is argument.

THE COURT: Overruled.

MR. PETROCELLI: And finally, ladies and gentlemen, we will show that when faced with the truth of his blood, his hair, his clothing, his gloves, his shoes, his Bronco, his rage, his motive, his words, and his actions, you will see how Mr. Simpson in this trial will resort to theories of police conspiracies, frame-ups, cover-ups and incompetence, to try to explain away all of the incriminating evidence.

And we will show you that there is not one ounce of evidence, not one ounce of proof, and not one ounce of truth to any of these things.

We will demonstrate to you that far from these theories born out of desperation, there is only one.

MR. BAKER: I object. Again, this is simply argument theory. "Born out of desperation" is argument.

THE COURT: Sustained.

MR. PETROCELLI: We will prove to you, ladies and gentlemen, that there is only one real and true and honest answer why all the evidence in this case points to O.J. Simpson. And that is because he is the person who killed Ronald Goldman and Nicole Brown Simpson.

Now, let me review this evidence with you in detail.

CHAPTER 10

DIRECT EXAMINATIONS

■ ■ ■

Direct examination of witnesses is the core of a litigator's case. Through direct examination of witnesses, the party presents the evidence upon which the party rests its case, and upon which the jury must decide the merits of the dispute. Attorneys sometimes see direct examination, however, as something one has to get through after opening statement and before the fun of presenting a closing argument. In reality, without direct examination, there is no case.

Skillfully presented, a party's case-in-chief can be as persuasive as the most compelling closing argument. The direct examination of each witness should be structured in light of how that witness will contribute to the case-in-chief in connection with each of the other witnesses. Further, the direct examination of each witness should be structured as a self-contained presentation so that, standing alone, it is as compelling and persuasive and logical as possible.

In this chapter we will discuss how to conduct a direct examination of a witness is a manner that best advocates for your party.

A. THE PURPOSE OF DIRECT EXAMINATION

The purpose of direct examination is to argue your case to the jury through your witnesses and exhibits. Direct examination is not to be used simply to store up snippets of evidence for your closing argument where you will tie it all together in an amazing and clever fashion. Jurors will be making up their minds as you present your evidence. Therefore, it benefits your case if the jurors know how the evidence supports your theory of the case as they hear the testimony or see the evidence. You can effectively argue your case by making the testimony clear and memorable, credible, and, hopefully, invulnerable to cross-examination.

The role of the attorney in direct examination is to facilitate the witness's ability to tell his or her part of the story in a compelling and logical manner. Each witness has a story to tell, and that story is important to understanding the entire case or else you would not be calling that witness. An attorney needs to understand where each witness's story fits into the larger picture, and then develop that story with the larger picture in mind. In other words, be careful not to be diverted into details or side issues which, although perhaps interesting in relation to a particular witness's story, are unimportant to the case as a whole and which may distract from the larger case.

For example, in a bank robbery case the teller may have a fascinating background as an immigrant who worked his way through college washing dishes in a dormitory kitchen. Although that may make the witness interesting, those details do nothing to advance the case as a whole. In contrast, had the teller worked his way through college as a campus security guard, during which time he received training on observation and retention of details, then that background could enhance the overall case by demonstrating why the teller's identification of the defendant has greater reliability.

Finally, the overall purpose of direct examination is to prove your case. For that reason, it is important to view direct examination of all of your witnesses as a whole, and individually, to ensure that you will introduce evidence sufficient to meet your burden of proof. For the government, that means it must make sure through direct examination that it presents sufficient evidence of each element of the offense to prove its case beyond a reasonable doubt. Further, you should develop your direct examination to also elicit all of the facts you intend to rely upon in addressing the jury. In other words, make sure you elicit facts that are important for setting the scene, background, motive, bias, and the like, which you intend to reference during opening statement or closing argument. If, for example, you want to tell the jury during opening statement or closing argument that the bank robbery occurred on a bright, sunny day, then you will need to make sure that some witness will say it was. This is one reason why it is important to prepare your opening statement and closing argument in tandem with outlines for the direct examination of your witnesses.

B. RULES TO DIRECT EXAMINATION

There are few federal rules governing direct examination in federal criminal cases, but lawyers should be aware of them.

First, only evidence that complies with the Federal Rules of Evidence is admissible. Fundamentally, this means in a very broad sense the evidence must be relevant, reliable, and more probative than prejudicial. This is the goal of the Federal Rules of Evidence, and each individual rule is written to address various types of evidence with this in mind.

Second, the trial judge has considerable discretion to control the mode and order of direct and cross examination to promote the discovery of the truth, to avoid wasting time, and to protect witnesses from harassment or embarrassment. Fed. R. Evid. 611(a).

Third, on direct examination the lawyer should not use leading questions "except as necessary to develop the witness's testimony." Fed. R. Evid. 611(c). A leading question is one that suggests the answer and leaves the witness with the choices only of either confirming or denying the truth of the statement. An example where a leading question might be permitted on direct examination is when covering the witness's background, or in transitioning the witness to a new topic, or in having the witness explain a more complicated matter, like a plea agreement. So, for example, a prosecutor may be permitted to lead a cooperator with preliminary questions about the plea agreement (*e.g.*, "You are here today after pleading guilty?" "You did so pursuant to what's called a cooperation plea agreement?") before asking non-leading questions about the witness's understanding of the plea agreement (*e.g.*, "What do you understanding that plea agreement requires you to do?" "What do you understand is the benefit you could receive as a result of that plea agreement?").

Fourth, upon a party's request, the witnesses may be excluded from the courtroom prior to their testimony. Fed. R. Evid. 615. This does not apply to a criminal defendant or the case agent. The purpose for the rule is to prevent witnesses from tailoring their testimony to what they have heard another witness say on the stand. Some courts have local rules implementing this sequestration requirement, regardless of whether it has been requested by a party. From the government's perspective, it is a preferred practice, even if not requested by the defense, because it is more likely to result in truthful testimony and it also eliminates a basis for cross examination of a government witness.

Finally, witnesses are generally required to testify based on their memories of events. So, a law enforcement officer, for example, may not take his or her reports to the stand and then refer to the reports in response to questions. Reports, or other writings, or anything else can be provided to the witness during the testimony if necessary to refresh the witness's memory. Fed. R. Evid. 612. When an attorney provides a witness with something in writing to refresh the witness's memory, the witness may not read from the writing—rather, the witness can review the writing, then return it to the lawyer before answering the question.

A note regarding admissibility of evidence is appropriate here, although this is not an evidence course. A law enforcement officer's report is not generally admissible as an exhibit. The report is hearsay because it is a prior out of court statement offered for the truth of the matter asserted. Fed. R. Evid. 801(c). Although a police report is written by a public official in the course of his or her duties, a police report is explicitly excluded from the "public records and reports" exception to the hearsay rule. Fed. R. Evid. 803(8). An officer may testify about the matters contained in the report, but the report itself is not admissible evidence unless some other exception to the hearsay rule applies.

C. KEYS TO CLEAR AND MEMORABLE DIRECT EXAMINATIONS

1. PACING AND PLOT DEVELOPMENT

To achieve clarity and memorability, ask questions designed to control and develop the testimony. Narratives, in the form of unfocused diatribes by witnesses, do not achieve this goal. Narratives are often rambling and directionless. Questions designed to control and develop testimony give jurors time assimilate the information. More important, these questions allow you to show the jury the direction of your case and highlight your key points.

2. PREPARE POINTS, NOT QUESTIONS

Prepare your direct examination by writing down points you wish to make, not the questions you will use to make your points. Written questions can cause you to ignore the answers your witness is giving. You must listen to the answers and use them as you develop the testimony. If you know the points you want to make you will be able to form the questions naturally and instinctively. Trust yourself. The exception to this general rule we mentioned before; it may be advisable to write down complete questions when important to lay the proper foundation for the admission of an exhibit. For example, for a document to be admissible under the business record exception to the hearsay rule (Fed. R. Evid. 803(6)), there are certain facts that must be established. To make sure you hit all these facts, it may be helpful to write out each question.

3. QUESTIONING TECHNIQUES

There are several techniques an advocate can use during direct examination that makes the testimony more coherent, memorable and persuasive.

a. Looping

Looping is the method of fitting the last answer into the next question. Looping emphasizes an important point, or a fact that is necessary for the jury to connect with the next part of the testimony in order to fully understand it. For example:

Question: When did you arrive at the apartment?

Answer: About 10:30 that night.

Question: When you arrived at 10:30 that night, who was there?

b.   Transitions

Transitions are statements designed to alert the jury to a shift in the testimony and to bridge the gap between subject matters. Transitions are very effective and should be used frequently. In essence, transitions allow you to begin a new direct and capitalize on primacy. They also help the witness, and more importantly the jury, know where you are going next. It helps the jury fit the testimony in to segments which are more easily remembered and understood. For example, a transitional phrase may sound like this:

Question: Now, directing your attention to the evening of July 15th, where did you go that night?

Or,

Question: I'd like to talk with you now about how you got to the bank; can you explain to the jury how you got from the defendant's house to the bank?

c.   Non-Leading, Leading Questions

There is also a way to ask effectively leading questions during direct examination which are not leading in the legal sense. These types of questions give the witnesses choices. Some questions are better than others because they are more fact-specific and seem to be less suggestive of an answer. This type of question might look like this:

Question: When you arrived at the apartment that night, did you go right in or did you knock and announce that you were police officers?

d.   Repetition

A certain amount of repetition makes testimony memorable. Too much repetition, however, can be boring and distracting. Using the repetition technique, a lawyer may want to first have the witness explain an event in broad strokes, then back up and discuss each part of the event in greater detail. Although the testimony is repetitive in a sense, it is not mere repetition when greater detail is elicited from the witness with each following question. An example of this type of questioning may look like this:

Question: Can you explain to the jury what happened when the man approached your teller station?

Answer: He walked up to me, handed me a note that demanded money, and then pulled a gun from his waist band. He pointed the gun at me and whispered "Don't do anything stupid." Then he handed me a paper bag and I filled it with money.

Question: I'd like to go back over a few things you said and unpack them a little. When the man walked up to your teller station, was he alone?

Answer: Yes.

Question: What was he wearing?

Answer: He was wearing blue jeans, a plaid shirt, a ball cap, and sun glasses.

Question: Did he have any facial hair?

Answer: None that I saw.

Question: You said he handed you a note. What did the note say?

Answer: It said "Put all your money in the bag and don't trigger an alarm or you're dead."

You get the idea. The prosecutor would want to continue through the interaction that the teller summarized in three sentences and develop all the rich detail of the story.

e.   Pacing

If an event or occurrence is very important, the lawyer can emphasize this by slowing down the presentation of evidence to draw greater attention to the particular facts. This is done by asking one-fact questions instead of a general question. For example, let's assume the prosecutor thinks it is important the jury remember that the defendant hid from the police and ran when he was found. Rather than asking the officer "What happened when you arrived at the defendant's apartment," the lawyer can place greater emphasis on the facts by slowing down the pace through asking tighter questions, like this:

Question: When you arrived at the apartment that night, who was present?

Answer: The defendant and his girlfriend.

Question: Was anyone else present other than the defendant and his girlfriend?

Answer: No.

Question: Where were the defendant and his girlfriend located in the apartment?

Answer: They were in the bedroom, hiding in the closet.

Question: When you found the defendant, what happened?

Answer: He bolted out of the closet and tried to jump out the window.

f. Referencing the Jury

It is always important for lawyers to remember throughout the trial that the jurors are the most important persons in the courtroom. The jurors will decide the fate of the case. You want the jurors to know that you know that they are important. You want your witness to look at and have eye contact with the jurors. And, you want the jurors to remain engaged and listening carefully. One very effective way to accomplish all this is to reference the jurors through questions. When a lawyer begins a question with "Can you explain to the jury . . . ," or "Please describe for the jury . . . ," or "Tell the jury . . . ," the jurors comprehend that the lawyer understands how important they are to the outcome of the case. By referencing the jury at the beginning of the question, it tends to cause the witness to turn to the jury and look at the jurors. Finally, just like we all perk up when we hear our name mentioned, when a lawyer references the jury by name, the jurors perk up and pay attention.

4. ILLUSTRATIVE AIDS, DEMONSTRATIONS, AND PHYSICAL EVIDENCE

Jurors have a much greater retention rate when you combine oral testimony with some type of visual communication. This can be accomplished by the introduction of physical evidence through a witness. So, for example, after having a witness testify about the drugs seized from the apartment, you should then hand the drugs to the witness and have the witness identify and describe the drugs. You can also use illustrative aids, such as photographs, charts, summaries or other graphic displays that help explain the point being made through oral testimony. Finally, in some cases courtroom demonstrations are most effective. For example, when a bank teller explains that the bank robber was ten feet away from her when his fired his weapon at her, you might have the witness step down from the witness box and approximate the distance for the jury. Or, if a witness testifies that he pointed the gun at her face for twenty seconds, it may emphasize just how long that is by asking the witness to let twenty seconds go by in silence to replicate the length of time she was facing down the barrel of a gun.

Generally speaking, it is best to use illustrative aids, physical evidence, or demonstrations after broader questions to emphasize the evidence. In other words, these aids should be used in conjunction with the repetition technique mentioned above. While going back over the events in more detail, use the exhibits, charts or other aids to draw out and add detail to the more general testimony. So, in the bank robbery example above, during the repetition portion of questioning the teller about being robbed the prosecutor would want to introduce a copy of the demand note, or a diagram of the bank, or photographs of the interior of the bank, for example.

5.   MAKE A RECORD WHEN NEEDED

It is important for lawyers to summarize or recapitulate testimony by providing descriptions "for the record" when necessary to make a good record for appeal. Trial lawyers sometimes forget that the written transcript is limited to what is verbally stated in the courtroom. The transcript will not reflect what is seen by the jury in the courtroom unless it appears in an exhibit. For example, when a witness explains that the bag of cocaine was "this big," using his hands to show the jury the approximate size of the baggie, you need to translate this demonstration into the written word. Thus, you might then say something like:

> Question: Mr. Witness, when you said the bag was "this big," you were holding up your hands in front of you approximately one-foot apart, is that correct?

Even when an exhibit is used in testimony, and will be part of the record on appeal, a further record may be necessary regarding the witness's testimony about the exhibit. If a witness describes something on an exhibit or diagram, for example, unless the witness marks on the exhibit and those markings become a part of the exhibit, the references will not appear in the record on appeal. For example, a lawyer may clarify a record like this:

> Question: Looking at exhibit 45, a photograph of the bank lobby, can you describe for the jury where you were standing when the robber entered the bank?
>
> Answer: I was standing here, behind the counter.
>
> Question: So, on exhibit 45, you are pointing to the far right of the photograph, to the first teller window next to the wall?
>
> Answer: Yes.

6.   OPEN QUESTIONS AND CLOSED QUESTIONS

An effective and persuasive direct examination often uses a combination of open and closed questions. Open questions allow the witness to give as much information as he or she wants. Dramatic incidents are better presented through open questions. An example of an open question might be: "Please describe for the jury what happened when the defendant entered the bank holding the shotgun."

Closed questions, on the other hand, allow you to control the amount of information, guide the witness's answer, and control the pace of the examination. Critical portions of the examination should be elicited through closed questions. Closed questions are not the same as leading questions; rather, they are simply questions with a very narrow scope to the answer. For example: "When the defendant entered the bank, did he have a gun? What type of gun? How large was it? What color was it? Did he approach the counter? When he came to the counter, did he say anything to you?" None of these questions are leading, but each is a close-ended question.

7. GROUP TESTIMONY AND EVIDENCE TOGETHER

Just as pieces of evidence are sequenced in opening statement, points of proofs can be effectively grouped together in a way to direct the jury to a conclusion. Done well, it allows the lawyer to make an argument during direct examination. Think through the evidence you intend to present with each witness and determine if there is an order to the presentation that is more persuasive in making your point. For example, assume you are trying to show that the defendant knowingly possessed a firearm found in his house. In chronological order, the defendant obtained a gun from a pawn shop, then six months later officers searched his house and found the gun, then the defendant denied knowledge of the gun during a Mirandized statement. You may present the evidence in chronological order and do fine. On the other hand, you may choose to present the evidence of the search first, defendant's denial second, and then the records from the pawn shop third so as to more closely juxtapose the defendant's claimed lack of knowledge of the gun with documentary proof that he lied. This may make your point much more effectively. Remember, evidence does not have to be presented in chronological order and, sometimes, it is more effective if it is not.

8. USE EXHIBITS EFFECTIVELY

In order to present a persuasive direct examination, you should carefully think out how to use the exhibits you intend to introduce into evidence. This preparation encompasses not only thinking about which exhibits to use with which witnesses, but more fundamentally, what is necessary to get the exhibit into evidence. You may need, for example, several witnesses to get a single exhibit into evidence. Organize your case with your evidentiary requirements in mind so that the exhibits enhance, not inhibit, the presentation of your case. Moreover, you should prepare in advance the foundation you will need to lay in order to get each exhibit into evidence. Your credibility and persuasiveness will suffer greatly if you stumble during your presentation because you cannot figure out how to lay the foundation for an exhibit. Finally, use the exhibits; don't quit once you get them into evidence. Have the witness hold the exhibit, explain it, describe it and present it to the jury. If it helps tell the story, use the exhibit with additional witnesses as appropriate after the exhibit has already been admitted into evidence through an earlier witness.

9. ANTICIPATE OBJECTIONS

As you prepare your direct examination, you should do so with an eye to possible objections the opposing party may raise to the questions you are asking. You may find ways to ask the questions that do not raise objections. Or you may prepare a way around an objection if raised. For example, opposing counsel may make a hearsay objection if you ask your witness to repeat what another person said on the telephone. You can move around the hearsay issue by asking the witness what he did after the phone call. Almost always, the witness's conduct after a conversation will reveal the content of the conversation sufficient for the jury to understand the point you were making. Finally, as we mentioned in a prior chapter, review the rules of evidence and case law in advance and incorporate cites in your notes where you anticipate you may receive an objection so that you have the authority immediately available to argue the matter with the court if the need arises.

D. CREDIBILITY

Regardless of how clear and memorable you are able to make your direct examination, your ability to win the case rests upon whether the jury believes your witnesses. Thus, establishing the credibility of your witnesses makes the difference between a clear and memorable direct examination, and a persuasive examination.

As with other parts of effective trial advocacy, preparation is absolutely necessary for success. To conduct an effective direct examination you must prepare the questions you intend to ask in the order you intend to ask them, as discussed above. In addition, however, as we mentioned in the chapter on trial preparation, you must also prepare your witness. Only when your witness is prepared for what they will encounter on the stand will they have the confidence to speak the truth without hesitation.

Preparing a witness to testify requires a recognition of what the witness will face on the stand—not only the questions, but the emotions. Speaking in front of other people is often a very frightful experience for many people. Part of preparing your witness entails familiarizing them with the court, its procedures and the surroundings. You want to minimize the psychological effect testifying in court will have on your witness so that they can concentrate on what they are saying.

You also need to prepare your witness for the questions you will be asking them. This does not mean, however, that you should ever provide a witness with questions and answers. Ethically, you cannot suggest to witnesses what they should say—they should only testify truthfully. Further, your witness will lose all credibility if you provide him with questions and answers because it will become apparent to the jury very quickly that the witness is merely reciting a prepared text. Indeed, in some cases opposing counsel may pick up on such rehearsed testimony and make the preparation itself the focus of cross examination. The last thing you ever want one of your witnesses saying is: "The lawyer told me to say. . . ."

Instead, during preparation you should discuss with your witness the topics you will ask the witness without ever suggesting what the answer should be. Explain to the witness the scope of your direct examination from start to finish so that they are not surprised at trial. This includes reviewing any exhibit you intend to discuss with the witness. During preparation show the witness the actual exhibit, with the exhibit sticker attached, that you intend to introduce at trial. Make sure the witness is still able to testify about the exhibit, understands it, and can testify effectively about it. Likewise, to the extent that you intend to introduce any summaries or demonstrative exhibits through the witness, you should have the witness also review them carefully and change or correct them as necessary to accurately reflect the witness's testimony. If you have a videotape or audiotape, play it for the witness in its entirety so they are completely familiar with the exhibit.

Finally, think carefully about the image of the witness you wish to create before the jury. How you ask questions of the witness can greatly affect the impression the jury has of the witness. For example, you may want to humanize your witness so that the jury can empathize with the witness. For example, a defense attorney may want to ask some questions of her client regarding the defendant's background, education, family situation, job history or the like in order to create a connection between the jurors and the defendant. With other witnesses, you may choose to create an aura of expertise or professionalism, not familiarity. With a forensic pathologist testifying about blood tests performed on the victim of a crime, you will want to spend time asking about the expert's education and professional history, but skip altogether questions that elicit information about her family life. Finally, don't over-commit your witness to unnecessary detail. If it does not matter, for example, exactly what time or date an event occurred, do not ask the witness for the exact time or date. Each unnecessary detail you elicit from the witness creates a potential for the witness to make a mistake and to be impeached by opposing counsel.

E. PREPARE FOR CROSS EXAMINATION

Part of presenting direct examination is preparing for cross examination. As you consider the testimony you intend to elicit from your witness on direct examination, you should endeavor to anticipate the cross examination to which your witness will be subjected by the other side. When you prepare for direct examination in this manner, you begin to counter the cross examination before it begins.

Countering cross examination is possible in several different ways. First, use motions in limine liberally when you recognize, through your preparation, areas of improper examination that the other side may attempt to conduct. Second, you may want to structure your questions in such a way so as to minimize the effect of cross examination. For example, as mentioned above, do not unnecessarily pin your witness down to unimportant details. You may even choose to call two witnesses to testify about an event, even if not necessary, to anticipate an attack on the credibility of your witness.

One of the most important ways to anticipate and blunt cross examination is to deal with your witnesses' weaknesses during direct examination. Use the weaknesses as affirmative aids to your case, not as glitches to be explained away. The question often posed is when, during the direct examination of a witness, should you address the weakness: in the beginning, middle, or end of your examination? Seldom should you deal with a weakness at the beginning of the examination: the rule of primacy suggests that jurors will remember what they first heard about the witness—you don't want that thing to be a negative fact. Often the advice is to "bury" adverse facts in the middle of the examination because it will be less likely to be remembered. You may consider, however, waiting until the end of the examination because, by then, the jurors will hopefully have connected with your witness to a degree that hearing something bad about your witness will not sway them from the opinion they have already formed.

As you conduct the direct examination of your witness, you may hear the witness testify inconsistently with prior testimony or statements the witness has made. You need to make a judgment call whether to bring this to the jury's attention and deal with it during your direct examination, or let the other side attack the witness. The Federal Rules of Evidence permit permit a party to impeach the party's own witness. If the inconsistency is on a minor point, do not concern yourself with it. There will seldom be a person who can recount past events more than once in completely the same way, even though they are telling the truth each time. On the other hand, if you recognize that your witness has just testified inconsistently with a prior statement, and the issue is material and important, it is better for you to confront your witness with the inconsistency rather than wait for the other side to do it. The inconsistency may be nothing more than stage fright or nervousness. Bring out the explanation for the inconsistency as a natural part of the witness's testimony and without flagging the effort by asking pointed questions that will draw objections. In other words, draw the witness's attention to the inconsistency, then just ask why they said something different before. The witness will have some explanation. If cross examined on a prior inconsistent statement, opposing counsel may not give the witness a chance to explain. Although you can elicit an explanation on redirect examination, it is not as effective.

Part of preparing for cross examination is placing the witnesses and the exhibits in an order that protects witnesses from cross-examination. You can order your witnesses and exhibits in many different ways—chronologically, by placing key witnesses first and last to maximize the primacy and recency effect, or by first using the witness who will give the biggest picture of the case, for example. In deciding the order for presenting your evidence, consider the following test: What order of witnesses in relationship to each other will be the most persuasive? The first witness should help you the most, while hurting you the least. Never put a witness on at the beginning of your case who could deal you a substantial wound on cross-examination. The ability of the adversary to successfully cross-examine may depend on what the jury has heard before that witness testifies.

Every case has at least one witness who must be believed for the party to win. That witness needs to be protected on cross-examination. The placement of witnesses must be calculated not only to reduce the adversary's ability to successfully cross-examine that witness, but also to reduce the impact of the cross-examination of that witness upon the entire case. For example, in a drug case, you may want to put on the agent who corroborates the confidential informant before you put on the confidential informant. Further, you need to corroborate details of testimony with documentary evidence.

Also, consider using admissible hearsay to insulate your witnesses from effective cross examination. Such evidence is often invulnerable to cross-examination. For example, use testimony of present sense impression (Fed. R. Evid. 803(1)), excited utterances (Fed. R. Evid. 803(2)), or business records (Fed. R. Evid. 803(6)) exceptions to the hearsay rule.

You must also prepare your witnesses to defend themselves on cross-examination. Teach the witness to resist demands for yes or no answers if such an answer would distort the testimony. However, the witness should not give long narratives, thereby losing the appearance of impartiality. Teach the witness to ask for supporting documents, if necessary. Teach the witness not to hesitate to repudiate a prior inconsistent statement if that prior statement was not accurate or true. Teach them how such impeachment works and what it will sound like so they are ready for it if it happens. Teach the witness to say she doesn't remember if she doesn't remember. In the end, teach them how important it is to tell the truth. Juries are perceptive and so long as the witness is telling the absolute truth, a jury will likely see that, no matter how many other missteps the witness may take.

At the end of cross examination, you will face the decision of whether to conduct a redirect examination. We suggest you avoid conducting a redirect examination unless cross-examination reveals the unexpected or creates an ambiguity that must be clarified, or for some other significant reason. Redirect examination seldom does anything to prove your case, may in fact weaken the testimony already provided, may cloud the issues, and may raise new ones. Better to leave it alone unless major damage has been inflicted by cross examination.

F. OTHER THOUGHTS

Lawyers in federal court should carefully monitor the language they use when examining witnesses. This means not only a prohibition on swear words; it means using effective, persuasive language. Avoid pompous legal jargon. Likewise, avoid "Okay" or "uh-huh." Watch your witness' language, also. Witnesses who uses jargon or uncommon words fail to communicate effectively with juries. Interrupt your witness, if necessary, to get her to use common English that helps the jury understand your case, or to define professional, industrial, business, or other technical jargon. You should also use language that more effectively draws out the testimony. The language of direct examination is different from the language of cross examination. Use "who," "what," "when," "where," and "how" more than "did," "is," or "was." Enrich the witness' testimony with words like: "describe," "explain," or "demonstrate."

Once in a while you will run into problems with witnesses. Some cannot seem to answer questions without launching into a narrative; you must control the runaway witness, if necessary, by interrupting them. Other witnesses may forget important facts you know they know because of your familiarity of the case during preparation. You may need to direct the witness's attention to forgotten facts on those occasions.

CHAPTER 11

CROSS EXAMINATIONS

■ ■ ■

Cross examination is, perhaps, the most frustrating, yet potentially rewarding, part of a trial. It is frustrating because we picture ourselves bringing an adverse witness to his or her knees through our superior skill and intellect, when, as often as not, we sit down at the end of a cross examination merely satisfied that we did not harm our own case. It can be the most rewarding aspect of a trial because, once in a great while, when you have prepared properly, you can significantly damage the other side's case.

Cross examination is an art and it takes practice to do it well. The reality, however, is that federal prosecutors seldom have the opportunity to cross examine witnesses. In the vast majority of federal criminal cases, defendants call few or no witnesses, so the government conducts few or no cross examinations. Occasionally, prosecutors will have an opportunity to cross examine witnesses during suppression hearings or sentencing hearings, but the rules of evidence do not apply in those settings and there is no jury whose perceptions prosecutors must consider. It is often the case, therefore, that criminal defense attorneys perform better at cross examination than do prosecutors.

When the opposing party is putting on her case, she is bound to make some points. The goal of cross examination is not to make points for your case as much as it is to damage the other party's case. Attacking the other party's case requires careful thought and preparation. The opponent's witnesses are not your friends and will, whenever possible, harm your case. Thus, a poorly prepared and executed cross examination can do your case immense harm.

Thus, in many ways cross examination can be dangerous to your case, especially for the government which has the burden of proof and whose case has already been presented to the jury by the time the government's chance for cross examination rolls around. It is dangerous because, first of all, the jury has high expectations—the jurors have seen just as many Perry Mason shows as you and expect to see you bring the witnesses to their knees through brilliant cross examination. When you fail to produce this result, they may be disappointed. Second, as a lawyer you have limited information about the witness to use in cross examination. This is especially so for the government, whose right to discovery is severely limited compared to defendants. Regardless, however, as an advocate you are almost always going to know less about the other party's witnesses than your own. Third, as mentioned above, opposing witnesses are often motivated to injure your case whenever given the opportunity.

So cross examination involves questioning hostile people, without much knowledge, while the jury expects miracles. You can see, then, why cross examination should be approached carefully and with significant preparation.

A. KNOW YOUR ENEMY

There is no substitution for preparation. A good trial attorney knows more about the case than anyone else in the court room. This extends to cross examination. You must carefully prepare for cross examination; do not think that you can simply wait to hear what the witness says and trust your instincts. Preparation for cross examination encompasses two aspects: (1) You must know more about the subject of your cross examination than anyone else; and (2) You must know more about your witness than your opposing counsel knows about her own witness.

Preparing for the subject matter may mean looking at the same evidence from a different point of view. For example, if you are trying a fraud case, you should already have a solid grasp of all the relevant facts. Preparing to cross examine one of the employees of the defendant corporation, however, may require you to look at those same facts from the witness's perspective—to examine the same facts not from the standpoint of what you know now, but what the witness knew then. Such preparation may require you to revisit the scene of a crime and view it all over again from the witness's perspective. You may find, for example, that by visiting a bank and standing in the place where the teller stood, she could not have seen the robber like she has claimed because there was a column or some other object in her line of sight. Without such research, you may never know how to effectively cross examine the witness.

In other cases, preparing for cross examination may require you to develop an expertise in a whole new discipline. For example, if you are prosecuting a doctor for prescribing controlled substances outside the usual course of medical practice, to effectively cross examine the defendant's witnesses you will need to educate yourself about the usual course of the medical practice at issue. Read as much as you can on the subject matter, especially everything the witnesses have written on the subject. Learn as much as possible about how the business, industry, or profession operated, and about its policies, rules, and practices. This will give you the background to effectively cross examine the witness and, more often than not, provide you with ammunition for impeaching the witness.

Preparing for cross examination also requires that you know everything you can about the witness. In federal criminal cases, the defense usually has a great amount of information about government witnesses long before trial, due to discovery obligations by the government. On the other hand, the government often has little information about, or notice of, a defendant's witnesses. Nevertheless, a prosecutor must endeavor to find out as much as possible about them. Prosecutors can call upon the case agent to investigate the witnesses by running their criminal histories and driving records, by accessing public records regarding the witnesses, and by searching social media regarding the witnesses. In short, the agent can use some of the same investigation techniques discussed in the investigation chapter of this book for investigating the underlying criminal conduct. The key is to find the witnesses' vulnerabilities, if possible, and the motivation for their testimony. Sometimes, pointing out the biased motive for a witness's testimony (family relationship, employment, debt, etc.) may be the only point an attorney can make during cross examination.

B. ADAPT TO THE TERRAIN

An effective cross examination requires an attorney to adjust the nature and tone of the cross examination to the case and the witness. Different cases will call for different approaches. Your approach in a complex fraud case should be different from your approach in a violent carjacking case where a child was killed. For example, a lawyer's cross examination in the first case will require him or her to simplify matters for the jury and will probably call for a somewhat respectful tone with most witnesses. In the latter case, though, the jury will easily understand the subject matter and may expect and accept a lawyer's tone to be more confrontational or aggressive.

Likewise, different witnesses require different approaches. For example, your questioning of a Harvard professor should be different from your approach with a high school dropout. Your tone should be different when cross examining the government's case agent than it would be when cross examining a fraud victim. Likewise, your approach in questioning the defendant's mother should be different from the approach you take in questioning the defendant.

There is no single approach or tone that works in every case with every witness. You must learn to adjust your approach and adapt it to the case and witness you are cross examining.

C. SEEK A LIMITED GOAL

Because cross examination can be a minefield, with as much potential to harm your case as help it, you should approach it cautiously and with a limited goal in mind. Consider what goal you hope to achieve in the cross examination and focus your questions toward that goal. If you lose sight of your goal, it is easy to lose sight of the rest of the rules of cross examination and you will tend to expose yourself to harm. The goal you are seeking is different from the points you will try to make during cross examination, much as the theme of your case is different from the elements.

For example, if you are conducting a cross examination of an expert, your goal may be to use her to validate an important part of your case while invalidating the importance of the rest of her testimony (*e.g.*, she will agree that it is outside the usual course of medical practice to prescribe controlled substances to a pregnant woman, but claims that the defendant's medical records don't necessarily indicate the doctor knew his patient was pregnant). Therefore, since this is your goal, you will not want to make her out to be a quack because you want the jury to believe part of her testimony.

On the other hand, if you are conducting a cross examination of the defendant's wife, who will claim that the defendant was with her when the First National Bank was robbed, your goal will be to totally discredit her testimony.

In determining what your goal should be, try to picture what you want to tell the jury about this witness during closing argument.

D. LISTEN TO THE ANSWER

Listen carefully to the witness's answers during both direct examination *and* during your cross examination. This rule seems obvious, but it is one of the easiest mistakes to make in trial. If you have prepared well for cross examination, you will have in your mind a series of questions you intend to ask to make a limited number of points. You will be asking leading questions and, presumably, taking the witnesses through the points you intend to make. It is easy during questioning like this not to pay attention to the answers they are giving.

A witness may surprise you by saying something in your favor that you did not expect. Likewise, you may have a series of questions you intended to ask in order to make a point, but one of the first answers may clue you in that the line of questioning will not work. If you simply ask the questions you planned on asking without listening to the answer, you may play into the other side's case or miss great opportunities to advance your case. The danger here, of course, is that you will be tempted in some cases to ask questions, the answers to which you do not know. Ask at your own risk.

Along these lines, it is important to remember that you should not repeat the direct examination. Many attorneys seem to conduct cross examination by endlessly having the witness reaffirm what they said during direct examination. You want to do this in a limited manner *only* when you are setting up a witness for impeachment.

E. CONDUCT SURGICAL STRIKES

Get in and get out. Cross examination is not the place to put on your case or to conduct a fishing expedition. As a general rule, you should identify a limited number of points, usually no more than three, that you want to make with a witness during cross examination. You should then ask the minimum number of questions necessary to make your points. Then stop. Avoid the temptation to keep going, no matter how well the cross examination has been going up to this point.

Begin with undisputed points and proceed to disputed ones. In other words, when deciding what three points you want to make, begin, if possible, with matters to which the witness will readily agree. If you are prosecuting a drug case and the witness admits that he took trips to Arizona with the defendant, but denies that they brought back any drugs, start by getting him to confirm as many details about those trips as possible to corroborate your other witnesses. Then move onto issues that he will likely deny. Similarly, if, as a defense attorney, you are cross examining a government agent, start by getting the agent to agree, for example, that although she found drugs in the defendant's house, she did not find scales, cash, drug notes or other items consistent with someone allegedly involved in the drug trade.

The points you make through your cross examination should further and be consistent with the goal of cross examining this witness. Remember the goal of your cross examination and choose the three points you wish to make in order to further that goal. For example, if your goal is to show that the witness, the defendant's wife, is a biased liar, then your three points may be: (1) She is the defendant's wife; (2) she has no witnesses to corroborate her claim that the defendant was with her when the bank was robbed; and (3) she was convicted of making a false statement to a law enforcement officer in 1996. Each of these three points furthers your goal of cross examining this witness.

Make your questions short and succinct. Part of making surgical strikes is to keep your questions short and focused. Long, rambling questions are hard for the jury to follow, allow room for the witness to stray, and risk handing over control to the witness. Your questions should be one-fact questions. Do not ask compound questions. Strike from your questions judgmental or value-ladened terms. For example, ask "You took five trips to Vegas last year," not "You took a lot of trips to Vegas last year."

F. DON'T KNOW, DON'T ASK

Never ask a question if you don't know the answer. Rather, carefully craft your questions to box the adverse witness into a position, the significance of which you can later explain to the jury. Never give the witness an opportunity to provide an explanation. Thus, during cross examination, you should structure your leading questions such that the witness is either affirming or denying facts in the manner you want. Accordingly, your question is, in reality, the answer.

Occasionally during direct examination a witness will say something that tempts you to ask a follow up question. This may occur by accident, or it may be the result of intentional sandbagging by the witness. Resist the temptation to ask the follow-up question because, if you don't know the answer, you may damage your case.

G. USE LENDING QUESTIONS

Cross examination should almost always be conducted with leading questions. Leading questions allow you to maintain control of the witness and the direction of the examination. It allows you to keep the questioning focused on the points you are trying to make. Leading questions, when properly asked, turn you into the witness and the witness into your corroboration.

Asking leading questions does not mean, however, that every question should begin with: "Isn't it true that . . .". Juries will quickly tire of such repetition. The art of cross examination is to lead the witness without seeming to lead the witness. Consider various ways of leading a witness by the tone of your voice and by the structure of your questions. You may ask questions such as:

Question: "After work you went to the bar, of course?"

Answer: "Yes."

Question: "You had more than one beer there?"

Answer: "I don't remember."

Question: "As you walked out of the bar you now claim you saw the defendant drive by in his blue car?"

Answer: "I did see him."

Question: "So, of course, then, that's what you told the police that night?"

Answer: "Well, not exactly."

Reserve the "Isn't it true" phrases for witnesses who are being combative. Then these phrases may give you more control and will be more accepted by the jury.

H. WEAVE THEMES INTO CROSS EXAMINATION

You should never lose sight of the theme of your case (if you have one—in simple cases sometimes there really is no basis or need for a theme). This includes cross examination. Do not confuse the theme of your case with the goal you are seeking in cross examining a specific witness, or the points you intend to make in seeking that goal. While all of these should be harmonious, they are not synonymous. Think of them, if you will, in terms of constructing a building. Your theme may be to make a solid house (versus a theme of making a unique house or a beautiful house). Your goal, then, in constructing the walls will be to make them strong. The points you will strive for in constructing the walls, therefore, may be 2 by 6 studs (instead of 2 by 4s), on 12 inch centers (instead of every 16 inches), with triple headers over all doors and windows (versus doubleheaders).

Applying this analogy to your case, the theme of your case may be that a doctor unlawfully prescribed controlled substances to his patients because he wanted their adoration. Your goal in cross examining his secretary may be to have her agree that he fished for compliments from his patients and fixated on his status as a god in his patients' eyes. The points you may want to make with her are that: (1) he invited patients to his house for parties; (2) he got upset when a patient saw another doctor; and (3) his prescriptions for controlled substances increased for patients after they got upset with him or went to another doctor.

Just as it is important to remember your goal in cross examining a specific witness, it is important to remember your theme in cross examining all of the witnesses. For example, while it may be tempting to cross examine the doctor's secretary about how much money he made for each visit, this does not further the theme of your case and may, in fact, confuse the jury regarding your theory of the case. It is important to win the war, not win the battle. In other words, unless cross examination helps the case, it matters little if you effectively destroyed the witness in cross examination. Indeed, some cross examinations may be effective in discrediting the witness, but actually hurt the cross examiner's case. For example, let's assume a male defendant and on direct examination a government's witness says he found ammunition in the top left dresser drawer, but in his report he wrote that he found the ammunition in the top right dresser drawer. A lawyer could effectively cross examine the officer by impeaching the officer with his prior inconsistent statement.

But, if the top left dresser drawer contained women's underwear, and the top right dresser drawer contained men's underwear, pointing out that the firearm might have been in the right, not the left, drawer only hurts the defense case.

I.   CONTROL THE WITNESS

Controlling a recalcitrant or combative witness is much more difficult than it seems and there are many pitfalls in this area. There is a line between controlling a witness and beating them senseless that you do not want to cross, no matter how tempting it might be. Keep the jury in mind at all times—indeed, you should try to watch them when you are having trouble controlling a witness—because the object is to persuade the jury to the justice of your cause, not to win a battle of wits with the witness. Sometimes, for example, you may pick up that the jury hates the witness, in which case you may want to let the witness get out of control. On other occasions, it may work to your advantage to let the jury see how controlling and unresponsive a witness is because it may detract from the witness's credibility.

There are several rules of things to do and not do when seeking to control a witness.

Things to do:

Use leading questions.

Repeat the question, slowly, until it is answered.

Keep your temper and control.

Things not to do:

Do not ask for the judge's help.

Do not instruct the witness to answer "yes" or "no."

Do not belittle the witness.

J.   REMAIN FLEXIBLE

Flexibility is the mark of a good trial attorney. Trials, especially criminal trials, can take on a life of their own. When, during cross examination, the trial takes an unexpected turn, or an opportunity presents itself, you may judge it best to abandon some of these and other guidelines.

There are certain guidelines we discussed above, however, which we do not advise you ever abandon. Thorough preparation allows you to be flexible, for only by knowing your enemy can you make an educated prediction of how he or she will react in a given situation. Part of being flexible, of course, is to adapt your approach to the witness and the nature of the examination. Cross examination should always be limited toward seeking a specific goal with a witness and then quitting. You must always listen to the answers. You should consistently conduct precise questioning directed toward your goal, and get out.

On the other hand, there may be times when it is best to disregard some of the guidelines. There are times when a witness is well within your control, where she appears very predictable during cross examination, and where you know the witness and the case well enough that it is worth the risk of asking a question to which you don't know the answer. This is a rare event, but sometimes wonderfully damaging.

There are time you may want to ask non-leading questions. It is best to ask open-ended questions on non-critical, background matters you have to ask to lay the foundation for the critical questions. Likewise, you may want to ask non-leading questions to change the pace of questioning or to show your reasonableness. Sometimes an opposing witness is not adverse to your case—indeed, may be a reluctant witness—in which case non-leading questions may work best. Use your own judgment.

You may not always be able to weave the theme of your case into cross examination. Returning to the doctor case, if my theme is that the doctor gave out drugs because it made him feel like a god, it would be hard to weave this theme into the cross examination of a pathologist who is testifying about the cause of death of one of the doctor's patients.

Finally, sometimes you may choose not to control a witness. If a witness comes off so obviously rehearsed and you can tell that the jury does not like the witness, it can be fun to give that witness enough rope to hang himself.

K. THE ETHICS OF CROSS EXAMINATION

As lawyers, we have certain ethical obligations in conducting cross examination. These include the following: (1) You must have a factual basis for asking a question; (2) You must have a legal basis for asking a question; (3) You must not ask a question that implies facts not in evidence; (4) You cannot ask questions for the sole purpose of harassing or intimidating a witness (this includes advising a witness of their Fifth Amendment rights); and (5) You should not discredit a truthful witness simply because you can.

L. CROSS EXAMINATION OF EXPERT WITNESSES

1. CROSS EXAMINATION STARTS DURING DIRECT EXAMINATION

Effective cross examination of an expert witness actually begins during direct examination by the opposing party. A lawyer must control the opposing party's expert witness through proper objections. They also must prevent the expert from exceeding the scope of the disclosed expertise and opinion. Finally, lawyers must take careful notes so as to discern shifts in or nuances of the opposing expert's opinion, and to be alert as much as to what the expert fails to say as to what the expert says.

Expert witnesses, especially ones with experience testifying in court, can take over the courtroom in an attempt to dazzle the jury with their expertise. It is important, therefore, that lawyers be fully alert and on the edge of their seats to fully enforce the rules of evidence so as to keep the expert from seizing control of the courtroom. Experts, especially biased ones, are often unresponsive to the direct examiner's questions. Experts will often respond to a question that calls for a "yes" or "no" answer with a long diatribe about why the answer is "yes" or "no." Experts may even take the liberty to explain why the lawyer's question is a poor one, state the question that should have been asked, and then proceed to answer the expert's own question. Lawyers need to shut this down through objections as early and often as necessary to maintain control of an opposing expert. Lawyers should object to such answers as "unresponsive" the second the expert becomes unresponsive, interrupting the expert's answer, if necessary.

Experts will also take over by providing a narrative answer. Some expert's answers have later consumed four or five pages of transcript. In practice, it is sometimes difficult to discern when an answer has evolved from being responsive to becoming a narrative. Nevertheless, lawyers should remain alert and if the expert is testifying for more than 60 seconds without a question, it has likely become narrative.

Experts will often also speculate. Again, this can be a difficult area to formulate appropriate objections because experts are permitted to render opinions. There is a difference, however, between speculating and opining based on superior knowledge and experience. For example, an arson expert who testifies that the defendant must have accidentally dropped his cigarette, causing the fire, is speculating. The defendant may have intentionally dropped his cigarette. The expert can testify about whether the cigarette caused the fire, but there's nothing about the expert's superior education, training, or experience regarding arsons that would allow him to determine whether the cigarette was accidentally or intentionally dropped.

2. CONTROLLING THE ADVERSE EXPERT

It is very important to maintain control of the opposing expert on cross examination. Again, experts are often expert at answering questions. If the lawyer is not careful, the expert will seize control during cross examination, negating any effective cross examination.

Control on cross examination starts with asking leading questions. There will be times when a non-leading question will be appropriate, even with an adverse expert witness. These occasions will be rare, however. Experts will often take any open-ended question as an opportunity to insert adverse statements, even if not responsive to the question. So, generally speaking, use leading questions.

Another way to lose control of an expert witness is to ask compound questions. Experts will take advantage of these questions to expound beyond the point the lawyer is trying to make. Sometimes, the lawyer will have two facts in a question where the expert's answer might be "yes" to one fact, but "no" to another fact. This gives an opening to the opposing expert to expound. The questions should be short, concise, one-fact questions.

Lawyer must be precise in the use of language and terminology. Precision of language is especially important with expert witnesses. An adverse expert witness will take advantage of imprecise language to expand the answer beyond where the lawyer wants to go, and will sometimes use the imprecise language to show off the expert's superior knowledge. For example, an expert will be quick to point out that a "delusion" is a symptom, not a mental disorder. A lawyer who uses the terminology loosely will quickly be told by the expert, who will use the opportunity to elaborate.

The lawyer's questions need to be free from qualitative, judgmental, and value-laden language. In other words, ask only fact questions. If a prosecutor asks: "Isn't it true you have spoken a lot at criminal defense attorney conferences," it allows the expert to take issue with the term "a lot." The expert may legitimately have a different opinion than the prosecutor about what is a lot and what is not. Rather, the question should be precise, based on the research, with back up to impeach the expert should he or she equivocate. For example, it is much better to ask: "Isn't it true that you have spoken at criminal defense attorney conferences nine times in the past five years?" If the expert denies it, or claims a lack of memory, the prosecutor should be prepared to whip out the expert's CV or whatever else the prosecutor found that shows how many times the expert spoke and make the expert confirm each engagement. Again, use short, concise language when doing this—"you spoke on December 2, 2013, at the Iowa Criminal Defense Bar's Annual Meeting in Des Moines, Iowa." Don't ask "When you spoke on December 2, 2013, at the Iowa Criminal Defense Bar's Annual Meeting in Des Moines, that was an instance of speaking for defense attorneys, wasn't it?" A defense expert may respond to this question by stating that he does not speak "for" anyone, but speaks at the invitation of anyone; it's just that the government has not yet invited him.

Attorneys should not hesitate to interrupt and object to the opposing expert's answers if they are unresponsive or the expert starts in on a narrative. Lawyers seldom object to a witness's answers on cross examination when they would quickly do so were the same answer given in response to a question on direct examination. This may be a result of a perception that a lawyer cannot object to his or her own question. It must be remembered that objections may be posed not only to a question, but also to an answer. Interrupting an expert needs to be done politely so jurors do not see the lawyer as rude. A simple "excuse me," repeated until the expert stops, suffices. Then the lawyer may then repeat the question or otherwise direct the expert to answer a different question.

Attorneys should avoid getting into an argument with any witness, including an expert. Attorneys only lose credibility when they squabble with experts. If the expert is unresponsive or evasive, simply keep objecting and move to strike unresponsive answers as necessary, then repeat the question. If necessary, repeat the question many times. If the lawyer has done a good job formulating one-fact, concise questions, the jury will quickly see the expert is being evasive. We do not recommend asking the court to instruct the expert to answer the question. First, the court may refuse to do so. Second, asking the court to help shows the jury the lawyer has lost control of the expert. Repetition of the same simple question will generally suffice as well as, or better than, a court instruction for the expert to answer the question.

3.   STRUCTURE OF CROSS EXAMINATION

Start strong and end strong. No matter which expert a lawyer is facing, there will be something the lawyer has to work with on cross examination. It is important to start strong and end strong because of the primacy and recency effects of memory. If the lawyer flounders and fails to make any points in the middle of cross examination, the jury will likely forget that and remember only how the lawyer started and ended cross examination.

How one starts may depend on the type of expert one is facing. If the lawyer is facing an honest expert, for example, it may be best to start with having the expert admit certain things that are favorable to the government's case. A dishonest expert will refuse to concede anything, and an incompetent expert may simply not know. So, with an honest expert, a lawyer may want to start off with some fundamental, key facts the defense expert will concede which form the basis for the lawyer's own expert's opinion.

If the opposing expert is dishonest, the best way to start the cross examination may be to expose the expert's bias. This could be done by showing that the expert fudged or exaggerated his or her qualifications, or on the work he performed on the case, or the fact the expert always testifies solely for other side (e.g., is always a "defense expert" or always a "government expert"). The goal would be to immediately discredit the expert in the jurors' eyes and to set the tone with the expert that the lawyer recognizes the expert for who he or she is.

If the opposing expert is incompetent, the best way to start the cross examination is to question the expert about his or her qualifications, or lack thereof. Or, if there is a glaring error or oversight in the expert's conclusion, it may be effective to start with that glaring error to set the tone for the rest of the cross examination.

The cross examination should also end strong. In preparation for cross examination, the attorney will accumulate a number of areas of attack. The attorney should examine those areas and determine which are the strongest and the most certain. For example, a lawyer may have a line of questions in mind, but the effectiveness of the questions may depend on how the expert answers them. If answered a particular way, perhaps the questions will be very effective, but may fall flat if answered a different way. This is a poor way to start or finish. Rather, the lawyer should choose an area involving prior sworn testimony or some other area where the proof is definitive. Using these criteria, lawyers should choose the best and most certain ground for cross examination to end on. This need not always involve an attack on the expert's credibility. Rather, it may involve something positive for the lawyer's case which the expert must concede, or be firmly impeached.

4.   USE OF PRIOR INCONSISTENT STATEMENTS

In cross examining experts, it truly is a case of "the bigger they are, the harder they fall." Generally speaking, the more prominent the defense expert, the more often they're hired and the more they testify and write and speak, the more ammunition the lawyer will have for cross examining the expert. Conversely, the truly honest expert who does not testify for a living, and who has seldom stepped out of their daily profession to be a hired expert, can be the most difficult to cross examine because there is little out there in the form of prior statements. In preparing for cross examination, therefore, lawyers will have varying numbers of prior sworn or written statements which can be used to impeach the expert should the expert testify differently at trial.

Knowing how to impeach with prior inconsistent statements is very important in cross examining experts. Remember, these experts are often experts at testifying. They do it enough that they have seen many lawyers' tricks and know how to anticipate being impeached by a prior inconsistent statement. If the lawyer does not execute precisely in this exercise, it will fall flat and the expert will gain the upper hand.

The basics of cross examination with a prior inconsistent statement are:

1) Ask the affirmative statement.

> Q. *"Isn't it true that the best predictor of future behavior is prior behavior."*

> A. *"No, that's not accurate."*

2) Establish the source of the prior inconsistent statement.

> Q. *"You testified in United States v. Smith in April, 2011, didn't you."*

(Here, you would hand the expert witness a copy of his or her transcript from that case.)

> Q. *"You testified under oath in that case, didn't you."*

> Q. *"That's the same oath you took today, isn't it."*

3) Confront the witness with the prior inconsistent statement.

> Q. *"At page 10, line 15, you were asked this question and gave this answer:"* (now read the question and answer where the expert testified that past behavior is the best predictor of future behavior).

> Q. *"That question was asked and that was your answer, wasn't it?"* or

> Q. *"Did I read that correctly, sir?"*

Other variations of these questions can be found in trial advocacy books, like Thomas A. Mauet, TRIAL TECHNIQUES, 280–92 (6th ed. 2002), or Edward J. Imwinkelried, EVIDENTIARY FOUNDATIONS, 198–203 (5th ed. 2002). It is incredibly important that lawyers follow the script precisely when trying to impeach an expert with a prior inconsistent statement. Given any leeway, the expert will evade the impeachment attempt.

Attorneys sometimes err when they mix up impeachment with a prior inconsistent statement with refreshing recollection. The purpose of impeachment is to discredit the witness. The purpose of refreshing recollection is to help the witness. Do not get these mixed up. Do not ask the witness, for example, if the transcript from a prior trial would refresh the witness's recollection. Just give them the prior transcript and impeach the witness. Likewise, after reading the prior testimony, do not ask the expert if it refreshed the expert's recollection. The cross examining lawyer does not care whether it refreshes the expert's recollection. Impeach the expert, then move on to the next question.

In order to do it properly, the attorney's outline for cross examination should be notated with precisely where the expert made the prior statement that, if denied, will constitute the prior inconsistent statement. This will include page and line number. A lawyer's cross examination outline may look something like this:

> *"The best predictor of future behavior   [Smith, p. 10, L. 15]*
> *is past behavior."*

It is important, when impeaching an expert witness with a prior inconsistent statement, to be very accurate in wording the question to match perfectly the prior statement. To be effective, the inconsistency needs to be clear. If the question is slightly different from the prior statement, not only is the impeachment less effective, but it also gives the expert room to differentiate on redirect examination. For example, if the witness previously said that "past behavior *can be a strong predictor* of future behavior," the question needs to be worded the same way. If the lawyer asks "Isn't it true that past behavior *is the best predictor* of future behavior," and then tries to impeach with the prior statement if the expert says "no," it may appear to the jury the lawyer is trying to trick the expert, and the expert legitimately has grounds for insisting that he or she is not being inconsistent.

Organization becomes especially important in cross examining experts with prior inconsistent statements. When impeaching a lay witness with a prior inconsistent statement, a lawyer will likely only have a single transcript and a few statements to work with. With experts, in contrast, lawyers may have a half-dozen or more transcripts or articles to work with, any one or all of which may be needed to impeach the expert with prior inconsistent statements.

Here is how we suggest organizing cross examination with multiple prior statements. First, collect a copy of the transcript/articles for yourself and put them in three-ring binders in alphabetical order by case name or article name or some other manner where you can quickly access them. Make an identical set for opposing counsel. Then have another copy of each transcript/article in the same order in a box. You'll use that copy to hand to the expert on the witness stand when needed. On your set of transcripts, tab the various pages where the statements upon which you are basing your questions appear, and highlight the precise Q&A you are going to read if you need to impeach the expert with the prior inconsistent statement. Then, the first time during cross examination you decide to impeach the expert with the prior inconsistent statement, provide opposing counsel with the defense set of transcripts/articles at the same time you approach the expert with a copy of the single transcript you are referencing at that moment. Then proceed to impeach with the prior inconsistent statement. At that point you can retrieve the transcript from the expert and put it back in the appropriate folder or, if you think you may be impeaching the witness again with the same transcript later, leave it with the witness.

A couple points should be made about our suggested methodology. First, the opposing party is allowed to have a copy of what you are using for impeachment purposes, but not until you impeach. So, you need not provide the opposing lawyer with copies of the transcripts and articles before trial or even before you begin cross examination. Second, you could provide the opposing lawyer with a copy of the pertinent transcript each time you take a copy to the witness. This slows down cross examination and allows the adverse expert time to think. It is also more courteous to opposing counsel to provide them with all of the transcripts at one time. The possible downside is that of the dozen or so transcripts you may have in the binder(s), you may end up using only a few of them to impeach the witness because the witness otherwise admits the statements in the first instance. Thus, the opposing attorney will have copies of transcripts of the expert which you had no obligation to provide. It is unlikely this will hurt your case, but it could better equip the expert in future cases by providing him copies of transcripts from his prior cases. Make sure, of course, that the copies you provide to the opposing attorney are not highlighted or have your notes or comments in the margins.

5.   IMPEACHMENT ON BIAS

Unless the adverse expert is an honest one who will concede his or opinion may be different if all the facts were known, lawyers will likely want to attack the expert's credibility based on bias. Bias here means a prejudiced view of the case which could be unintentional or intentional. In other words, an expert may be biased or prejudiced because he or she is uneducated or uninformed. Conversely, an expert could be biased or prejudiced out of personal choice, meaning it is the result of the expert's values (*e.g.*, anti-death penalty or anti-criminal) or orientation (pro-defense or pro-government).

The attorney's tone during cross examination will be dependent on the nature of the bias. With the uneducated or uninformed, the attorney may want to adopt an approach which almost sounds sympathetic to the expert. The expert's biased view may be, for example, the consequence of being misinformed or inadequately informed by opposing counsel who attempted to manipulate the expert's opinion. Or it could be that the expert has been put in an untenable position by opposing counsel who hired the expert to opine on a matter that was beyond the professional's expertise.

When it is apparent, however, that the expert is biased by choice—that is, the expert is personally antagonistic to the lawyer's party or litigating position (e.g., the expert is morally opposed to the death penalty and is testifying for the defense in a capital case), or has articulated an opinion based more on who hired the expert than on the evidence, then the lawyer may adopt a more accusatory tone. Jurors will understand and permit an attack on an expert's biases if the lawyer establishes up front that the expert purports to claim neutrality or independence, but is not. Most professional organizations to which experts belong have ethical guidelines which address work in forensic settings. These ethical rules generally emphasize the need for the expert to be neutral and not allow his or her opinion to be influenced by the party or personal beliefs. Further, experts often pad their reports or testimony with claims of being retained to conduct an "independent" or "objective" review of the case. Pointing these things out before exposing the expert's underlying bias is important for the cross examination to be effective and for the lawyer's tone to be acceptable to the jury.

Experts can be attacked for bias in a number of ways. For the uneducated or uninformed expert, attorneys will want to impeach the expert's credibility by focusing on what the expert does not know. This relative ignorance could be the product of lack of education or experience. This is where research on the expert's education and background kicks in. Questions focused on the lack of advanced degree (especially compared with the party's own expert), lack of fellowships, post-graduate internships, board certifications or licensure, and/or lack of experience in a particular area are all effective areas of attack.

If the expert is uninformed because the opposing lawyer did not provide the expert with all the relevant background information about the case, then the lawyer will want to emphasize this in questioning. Again, precision of language is key. By the time the expert testifies, the opposing counsel may have remedied this weakness by providing the expert with information previously lacking. This does not help the expert much, however, if the expert rendered an opinion before receipt of the additional information. The cross examining attorney should carefully premise the question with, "before you reached your opinion in this case, you had not seen. . . ." The attorney can later argue to the jury that confirmation bias would obviously make it unlikely the expert would change opinions even after confronted with new information. If an attorney asks "you have never seen . . . ," the expert may correct the attorney by stating that they have seen the document when it was later provided to the expert. When confronting an expert on the lack of information or records reviewed, an attorney should specifically list, in full, all the information the expert did not review prior to reaching an opinion. The longer the list, the greater the impact in calling into question the reliability of the opinion.

When cross examining an expert who is biased by choice, lawyers can point out how the adverse expert has aligned him or herself with the opposing side. This may be shown by consistent testimony for criminal defendants and not the government, or vice versa, for example, or by the tone or nature of the articles written or statements made, or reflected in the expert's history of speaking out against the government on a topic (like the death penalty), or for defense oriented organizations generally. As mentioned above, if the opposing party made the mistake when hiring the expert to disclose the theory of the case, the cross examining lawyer should point out this error by referencing the expert's report where it states the purpose for which the expert was hired.

6.   TAKING ON THE MERITS OF THE OPINION

Cross examining the expert on the merits of the opinion is perhaps the most difficult task. This is where the expert likely has the upper hand because of superior knowledge of and experience in the subject matter. Nevertheless, lawyers generally need to take on the merits of the opinion or it will appear that the lawyer cannot rebut it. Lawyers should rely heavily on the lawyer's own expert in this area to formulate questions that will expose the weaknesses in the opposing expert's opinion and contrast it with the lawyer's own expert's opinion.

If the lawyer mounted an unsuccessful *Daubert* challenge to admission of the opposing expert's testimony, the lawyer should dust off that challenge and raise the same issues on cross examination. For example, if the lawyer challenged admissibility because the expert used a questionable methodology, then the lawyer should cross examine the expert on all the problems previously identified with the methodology. The fact the court ruled against the lawyer and permitted the expert to testify does not mean that the basis for the *Daubert* challenge did not have merit. The court's *Daubert* ruling only addresses admissibility, not the persuasiveness of the opinion.

A prior *Daubert* challenge aside, there may be any number of other weaknesses in the opposing expert's opinion the lawyer may use as the basis for cross examining the expert on the merits of the opinion. This may be an invalid or questionable assumption made by the expert, reliance on erroneous facts, or the failure to consider material information. Additionally, the cross examination could focus on the inherent weakness of the information upon which the expert based the opinion, such as the inherent unreliability of a witness's statements or the limitations of tests or examinations. Alternatively, cross examination may focus on the expert's reliance on the wrong tests, treatise, or theory, or the failure to conduct tests or examinations which could have and perhaps should have been performed.

Generally speaking, avoid asking the "would it change your opinion if you knew . . ." questions. Unless the opposing expert is really an honest, neutral expert, it is unlikely the expert will ever agree that anything would change his or her opinion. Indeed, on redirect examination it is common to ask an expert whether anything brought up on cross examination changed the expert's opinion and for the expert to say "no." A lawyer is better off simply pointing out during cross examination what the expert did wrong and leave the rest to argument.

During cross examination of the opposing expert on the merits of the opinion, it is important to pin the expert down to specifics. Experts often speak in generalities, especially when the basis of the opinion is questionable. It is important when cross examining an expert to insist on precision by the expert. If the lawyer asks imprecise questions, the expert can evade the lawyer's questions with vague or general answers. Do not allow the expert to do this.

If during direct examination it appears the expert has strayed beyond the scope of his or her expertise, it may be effective to cross examine the expert about it. Hopefully, the lawyer objected during direct examination when this happened, but if asleep or overruled, cross examination is the time to bring this out. For example, if the expert is a toxicologist whose real expertise is limited to testifying about what type and quantity of substance was found in the defendant's blood, the expert may be straying beyond his or her expertise when opining about what affect the substance would have on the defendant. Questions focused on the toxicologist's lack of medical degree or psychologist's license, failure to examine the defendant or collateral materials, and the variability of effect based on any number of factors (such as metabolism, weight, etc.), will expose the expert's limitations and speculative nature of his or her opinion. Effective cross examination on this issue may suggest a bias by the expert, showing he or she is willing to overreach to help the side that hired him or her.

The Federal Rules of Evidence permit lawyers to use learned treatises during cross examination of an expert. *See* Fed. R. Evid. 803(18). This can be an effective way to challenge an expert's testimony when the opinion is at odds with other authorities in the field. The method is similar to impeaching a witness with a prior inconsistent statement. First, commit the expert to the position that is contrary to the authority. For example:

> Q. *Dr. Smith, you testified during direct examination that you diagnosed defendant has having a brief psychotic episode lasting several hours on the night of the murders, correct?*

Second, establish the validity of the learned treatise or authority.

> Q. *Dr. Smith, the Diagnostic and Statistical Manual of Mental Disorders, 5th Edition, is an authoritative manual in the practice of psychology, isn't it?*

Third, confront the expert with the inconsistency between the expert's opinion and the authoritative treatise.

Federal Rule of Evidence 803(18) provides that the learned treatise may be read into evidence, but not received as an exhibit.

One final area of cross examination on the merits is to ask questions designed to show the limited scope of the expert's opinion. Generally, the expert will be testifying about only one element of the offense. For example, in a death by heroin case, the expert may testify to whether the heroin caused the victim's death. So, it is helpful to point out that the expert is not providing any opinion about whether the defendant distributed heroin to the victim, whether the defendant did so knowingly, or whether the drug was, in fact, heroin.

7. ADAPTING TO EVOLVING OPINIONS AND FACTS

Lawyers need to be alert to the possibility that the opposing expert's opinion will evolve either as a result of being provided additional information after forming the opinion, or as a result of adjusting to the evidence or questions on direct or cross examination. It is important that lawyers are sufficiently familiar with the expert's report and that they pay sufficient attention to the answers to pick up these changes of opinion. During cross examination it may be effective to point out the changing opinion. It may also be the case, however, that the opinion has shifted in the lawyer's favor, in which case it may not be wise to remind the expert and the jury about the expert's prior, less favorable opinion. Further, lawyers should be alert to whether the change in opinion requires rebuttal evidence that takes advantage of the evolving opinion.

8. RE-CROSS EXAMINATION

Lawyers should generally resist the temptation to conduct re-cross examination of the opposing expert. Lawyers generally have difficulty allowing the other side to ask the last question. Redirect and re-cross examination seldom achieve important results. This is especially so with opposing experts. Presumably, the cross examining lawyer has shot every arrow in the quiver already. It is unlikely the lawyer has anything left that will effectively impeach the expert. Moreover, the opposing expert is an unfriendly witness. Given any opportunity, the opposing expert will seize it to damage the other side's case. Also, asking more questions gives time to the opposing counsel to think of more questions. So, absent some clear need, keep your seat.

CHAPTER 12

CLOSING ARGUMENTS

■ ■ ■

A closing argument is the only time to argue your case in its entirety, directly to the jury, without interruption, free from the rules constraining opening statements. You are finally permitted to argue what the evidence means—to explain why the evidence leads to logical inferences supporting the verdict sought. This is your opportunity to tell the jury why certain facts are important, and more crucially, what conclusion the jury should draw from the facts. A strong case is made stronger and a weak case may, at times, be salvaged by an effective closing argument.

As with all other aspects of trial advocacy, preparation is crucial to effective closing argument. There are, likewise, certain aspects to the presentation itself that makes the difference between a closing argument and a *memorable and persuasive* closing argument. There are also some differences and distinctions between a prosecution closing and a defense closing. Regardless of the party you represent, closing arguments are fraught with the possibility of error. Each of these various aspects of closing argument is discussed more fully below.

A. PREPARATION

Much of the closing argument can and should be outlined *prior* to trial. Pretrial consideration of the important facts for closing argument leads to a more effective presentation of the evidence during trial. Further, thinking ahead about what you intend to say during closing argument helps you focus your case on the important issues, and ensures that you put into evidence the testimony and exhibits you will need during the closing argument to drive home your case. For example, when using a cooperator, a government attorney should carefully outline during his testimony and through other witnesses all the evidence that will later be argued at closing demonstrates the cooperator's credibility. By thinking it through before trial, you will make sure to present all corroborating evidence during trial. Indeed, if a lawyer thinks about closing argument well before trial, there is still an opportunity to develop evidence before trial that will help the lawyer make the argument at trial. A lawyer may decide that to really tell the story and have the jury draw the desired conclusion from the evidence, a picture or chart or diagram would be helpful. Unless the lawyer has presented this as evidence in the trial, it will not be available during closing argument.

Lawyers should also listen carefully to an opponent's opening statement. Make note of promises and key points. During closing argument you can remind the jury of promises not kept or key points left unsupported at the end of trial. It stands to reason that by thinking ahead of your closing argument throughout the trial, you will keep in mind the promises you made the jury during opening statement as well, so that you will not be caught at the end of trial promising more than you could deliver.

To aid in preparation for closing argument, you may consider keeping a folder in which you can place notes of things you may want to address during your closing argument. You can add to this folder before and throughout trial. Or, perhaps, during trial make marginal notes on your legal pad to remind yourself of things you want to mention or points you want to make during closing argument. In long, complex trials, keeping notes like this is critically important, for if you wait until the end of the trial to think about your closing in such a case, you will fail to remember important points. A jury, with twelve people paying attention and taking notes, seldom misses things.

Therefore, preparation for closing argument does not start after the presentation of evidence. It starts before the trial begins and should be on a lawyer's mind throughout the trial. Closing argument may be considered the framework around which you structure the presentation of your case.

B. PRESENTATION

There are some similarities regarding presentation between opening statements and closing arguments. The rules of primacy and recency still apply, for example, so you should start strong and end strong. As with opening statements, you should memorize the opening and ending few minutes of your closing argument because that is what will remain in the jurors' minds the most while deliberating. All the advice about using appropriate, non-legal language during opening statement pertains to closing argument as well.

As with opening statement, you should use exhibits whenever possible and appropriate. Indeed, at closing, you no longer have to worry about whether the other side objects or whether the evidence will be admitted. You may use any exhibit introduced into evidence during trial. You should pick them up, show them to the jury, display them and explain them. Use of exhibits can be overdone, however. Limit yourself to discussing key exhibits. There is no need to employ every exhibit admitted into evidence in your closing argument—to do so would distract the jury's attention from the key exhibits.

Likewise, you may use visual aids, such as time lines or summaries, during closing argument. These need not have been admitted into evidence. So long as the summary or visual aid is supported by the evidence, you may use such aids, like speech, as a way of arguing your case. Again, be careful not to overwhelm the jury with graphs, time lines and summaries—use them when they help you communicate a point.

As with opening statements, you should not rely heavily on notes. You should know the case very well by the end of the trial. Notes should be seen and used only as reminders of points you wish to make, not as a script for your presentation.

Closing arguments are unlike opening statements, however, in important ways. The first way they are different is the existence of jury instructions. In federal criminal cases, the trial court will always provide written and oral instructions to the jury. Whether the court reads the instructions before or after closing argument, courts will invariably permit the attorneys to reference and often even display the jury instructions during closing arguments. Lawyers should use the important and key parts of the jury instructions during closing arguments. Juries rely heavily on jury instructions—they are, after all, instructions for how the jury is to go about doing their job—and a closing argument that helps the jury understand the instructions and how the evidence should be viewed through the instructions can be very persuasive.

Another key difference between opening statement and closing argument is that, in the latter, a lawyer is permitted to argue the case. You are not limited to a cold recitation of the evidence. You may draw inferences and assert conclusions to be garnered from the evidence. The use of persuasive language—the language of argument—is permitted. You may use pacing and movement more dramatically than in opening statement.

During an opening statement you cannot use metaphors or provide analogies. During closing argument you may. Relating analogies and using metaphors can be an effective means of communicating an idea or theme to a jury during closing argument. But be careful, though, for they can easily backfire. The opposing side may be able to twist your analogy upon itself, destroying any persuasive value it may have had. Thus, prosecutors should save them for rebuttal, when the defense no longer has an opportunity to respond.

Closing argument is an opportunity for you to use your language skills, and performance skills, to convert the evidence you presented into a persuasive reason for why the jury should vote in your favor. In federal criminal cases, the presentation of closing arguments takes on slightly different modes than in civil cases because of the burden of proof. That burden allows the government to present its argument first and to provide a rebuttal closing argument. The defendant, of course, cannot provide any rebuttal. Due to the different burdens on the parties, there are some nuances in presenting closing arguments for the government that are different from those for presenting closing arguments for the defense. Thus, we will discuss closing arguments for each side separately.

C. PROSECUTION CLOSING ARGUMENT

At the end of a federal criminal case, jurors await closing arguments with anticipation. They are waiting for the attorneys to explain the case to them, to show them the right way to go, to lead them along, and to answer all the questions that popped into their minds during the trial which they were not allowed to ask. The government attorney is the first to address this waiting body.

It is therefore obvious that the prosecutor's opening should not be wasted. Do NOT explain the purpose of closing argument or thank the jurors for their attention. Get straight to the point. The first five minutes of closing argument, when the jury is fully paying attention and not distracted, is most important part of closing argument for the government. The prosecutor should highlight a critical fact and/or set out the critical issue. If you have developed a theme to your case, this is where you remind the jury of the theme and state succinctly why the evidence supports your theme.

After the introductory part of the prosecutor's closing argument, the prosecutor must turn to a review and analysis of the evidence. There are many different ways to organize this part of the prosecution argument. The best method for a case will be determined by considering the length of the trial and complexity of the issues. For example, a prosecutor may review the evidence in a chronological order. This is especially effective if the trial has been long or complex and there is a risk that the jury will have forgotten certain key facts. Another method is to tell the story of the crime. This may not fit wholly in a chronological format. Likewise, you may review the history in the order in which the government learned of the evidence during the investigation.

In addition to reviewing the evidence, a prosecutor usually needs to set out the elements of the offense or offenses for the jury. While most prosecution closing arguments should include a discussion of the elements, some need not do so if the elements are simple (i.e. simple bank robbery—defendant took money that didn't belong to him from a federally-insured bank). A closing argument can actually be organized around the elements. This can be effective if the offense is of a technical nature (*i.e.*, securities fraud). This is less effective if the offense is more garden variety (*i.e.*, felon in possession of a firearm).

In some cases, the most effective organization is simply to review the evidence in relation to the critical issues in the case. When a case turns on one issue, such as whether defendant did or did not have criminal intent, an effective closing argument can be organized around that issue. A prosecutor can, for example, spend the entire closing argument showing how each piece of circumstantial evidence tie together to reveal the defendant's criminal intent.

Whatever the organizational structure you chose, you will want to explain to the jury how the evidence supports a guilty verdict. Sometimes the evidence is not clear on its face and requires explanation. You may, during closing argument, argue inferences that can be derived from the evidence. Marshall facts supporting the inferences you seek and argue for them.

Every case has weaknesses. The existence of the weakness is probably why the case is proceeding to trial in the first instance. Do not delude yourself that the jury does not see the weaknesses in your case— as a group, jurors are very perceptive. Regardless, you can be sure the defense attorney will point out any weaknesses. You do not want it to appear that you are so dense that you did not see your own weaknesses, or so devious that you really intended to snow the jury. Acknowledge the weaknesses and deal with them. You should deal with them head on. Explain to the jury why the weakness should not dissuade them from returning a guilty verdict.

For the government it may be particularly effective to weave the important instructions into the closing argument. Keeping in mind that the government has the burden of proof, sometimes it is helpful for the jury if the prosecutor explains the elements of the offense instruction, points out that circumstantial evidence is treated the same as so-called direct evidence, and discusses pertinent instructions regarding the criminal intent or knowledge requirement under the statute. The prosecutor should discuss the instructions by relating them back to the evidence in the present case to demonstrate how the evidence has satisfied each of the essential elements.

Finally, a persuasive federal prosecutor will prepare strong concluding sentences, summarizing the argument and seeking a guilty verdict. As with the initial remarks, these final remarks should be memorized so that they are delivered to the jury with full eye contact, meaning and conviction.

Although the defense will invariably present a closing argument, the defendant has no constitutional obligation to do so. A prosecutor should not, therefore, say anything during the initial closing argument specifically addressing what he or she anticipates the defense attorney will say during the defense closing argument. Rather, a prosecutor can build into the closing argument counter arguments to anticipated defense arguments without making a specific reference to the defense argument.

D. DEFENSE CLOSING ARGUMENT

In federal criminal cases, closing argument for the defense in some ways resembles a government closing argument, but in other, significant ways, is quite different.

As for similarities, as with the government a defense attorney's opening remarks should be a memorized, succinct, and persuasive selling point for why the government has failed to meet its burden. Do NOT explain the purpose of closing argument or thank the jurors for their attention. A defense attorney will also want to look to the jury instructions for those instructions which are most important to the defense case (such as a theory of defense instruction, or burden of proof instruction). As with the government, an effective defense closing argument weaves the evidence (or lack thereof) into a discussion of the instructions to show why, based on the instructions from the court, the government has failed to prove its case. In general, leave the elements of the offense to the government. If, however, there is a key technical element you are attacking, explain it and why the government has failed to prove it. Finally, as with the government, a defense closing should end strong, with a memorized summary argument setting forth the very essence of the defense case.

A defense closing, however, will appear very different from the government closing in several respects. First, a defense attorney will probably want to sympathetically portray the defendant or his plight. A defense attorney should spend some time during closing argument emphasizing the human element of the courtroom drama, but must do so without pandering to the jury's emotions. This can be done by focusing on facts about the defendant and his life that arguably demonstrate a lack of motive or intent to commit the crime and weave those facts into the closing argument. In this way, the facts that make the defendant human are emphasized not as a ground for jury nullification but as a ground to find lack of intent or to challenge the motive.

Another defense strategy for closing argument is to highlight key weakness in government's case. Depending on the government's case, consider arguing weaknesses in the following areas: Witness credibility (the government witnesses are all snitches, or inconsistent, etc.); the government's investigation (the government failed to interview witnesses, conduct tests, follow leads); the government's case (the government failed to deliver something promised in opening statement, or is weak on a particular element); knowledge or intent (the government proved the act, but has failed to prove the *mens rea* requirement); or technical elements (government failed to show federal jurisdiction).

The key difference between a government closing and defense closing is the burden of proof. The government must persuade the entire jury that it has proven each element of the offense. The defense has no such obligation; rather, it need only convince the jury that there is a reasonable doubt as to any one of the essential elements. Thus, the government's argument is an affirmative, positive assertion, while the defense is a negative argument. A defense closing argument should always focus on the government's burden to prove its case beyond a reasonable doubt. A defense closing argument should leave no doubt in the jury's mind that there remains a reasonable doubt. The defense closing should emphasize that it is the government that bears the sole burden of proof at trial.

A mistake sometimes made by defense attorneys is to assume a burden of proof the defendant does not have. This occurs when a defendant asserts a theory of defense so strongly that it creates an expectation by the jury that the defendant will prove the alternative theory to the jury. A criminal defendant has no such burden of proof. Let's use a bank robbery example where the defense theory is that the teller misidentified the defendant and the real bank robber was another man who resembles the defendant. This is a fine defense theory, if there are facts that would support the argument, but the danger exists that in asserting this theory of defense the jury will expect the defense to prove the other man was the bank robber. In these circumstances, it is critically important for the defense attorney to point out during closing argument that the defendant has no burden of proof. The defense attorney should emphasize that only the government has the burden of proof. A defense attorney may want to explain to the jury that the defendant did not set out to prove the other man robbed the bank, because it doesn't have the resources of the federal government and was not charged, as the government was, with solving the crime. Rather, the defendant offered the evidence or theory of the other man to show how defective the government's investigation was, how the agents focused on the defendant without considering other possible suspects, and how all this shows reasonable doubt. The defense attorney should remind the jury that the trial is not about whether the other man committed the bank robbery, it is about whether the government proved beyond any reasonable doubt that the defendant committed the bank robbery.

A defense closing argument should end strong, just as it started strong. The defense attorney should memorize the last five minutes of closing argument. Step away from the lectern, if that is permitted in the courtroom, and look the jurors in their eyes. This is the defense opportunity to make a final, impassioned argument for why the evidence fails to prove guilt beyond a reasonable doubt. Don't waste that opportunity.

Finally, a defense attorney should end with telling the jury what he or she wants the jury to do—that is, find the defendant not guilty. Perhaps it seems obvious what the defense attorneys wants in a criminal case and that asking for the obvious is unnecessary. As with sales people, however, deals are closed more often when the pitch ends with a specific request of exactly what it is that the sales person wants the prospect to do. The same is true with closing argument. At the end of a defense closing, the attorney should specifically ask for a verdict of not guilty, and sit down.

E. PROSECUTION REBUTTAL ARGUMENT

The government has an opportunity to present a rebuttal closing argument because it has the burden of proof. The rebuttal closing should be true rebuttal—that is, it should rebut what the defense attorney said during closing argument. Prosecutors should not sandbag defense attorneys and save a significant argument to present only in rebuttal closing argument completely unresponsive to anything the defense attorney said during closing argument.

A federal prosecutor should have prepared responses, however, to anticipated defense arguments. There are certain defense arguments that can be predicted in most cases, such as the emphasis on reasonable doubt and witness credibility. Others may be issues that arise in a particular case that the prosecutor can expect will be part of the defense closing, such as the alleged failure to produce witnesses or an attack on the quality of the investigation. Prosecutors should draft an outline of arguments to be made in rebuttal to the anticipated arguments of defense counsel.

There may be other arguments that defense counsel raised in closing argument that the prosecutor did not anticipated. The prosecutor should take careful notes of the defense argument and make marginal notes where the prosecutor believes something needs to be addressed in rebuttal closing argument. It is not always easy to formulate cogent and coherent rebuttal arguments under these circumstances and prosecutors must think quickly to do this well.

Prosecutors should not attempt to rebut every argument or issue raised by a defense attorney in closing argument. Rather, prosecutors must use judgment and address only those issues that are important to the government's case. A rebuttal closing argument is best when it is short and concisely rebuts the primary arguments made by defense.

If the defense made promises during opening statement that were not kept during the case, the government should point this out during rebuttal closing argument. If pointed out during the government's main closing argument, it provides the defense attorney an opportunity to respond and explain the failure to keep the promise. If the government points out the unkept promise during its rebuttal closing argument, on the other hand, the defense attorney has no opportunity to respond. The rebuttal closing should also address evidence the defense failed to explain or ignored during closing argument. Finally, the rebuttal closing argument should end on a strong note. In other words, the prosecutor should restate the essential evidence which compels a conviction in this case. Then ask for a conviction, and sit down.

F. CLOSING ARGUMENT ERRORS

Closing arguments are often a place for attorneys, especially prosecutors, to cross over the line and create error. During closing arguments attorneys often find themselves overly excited, focused on persuading the jury, and inadequately paying attention to constitutional law, the rules of evidence, and ethical cannons. This is especially true for the government's rebuttal closing argument when the prosecutor has not prepared the argument in advance because it is necessarily a response to the defense closing argument.

There are certain things attorneys should never do during closing arguments. First, attorneys should not express their personal beliefs or opinions. Any statement following the words "I" or "we" is likely to constitute an expression of a personal opinion or belief. These personal pronouns are best omitted from a lawyer's vocabulary during closing argument. This is equally the case if the prosecutor substitutes in the word "the government" before a phrase expressing a belief or opinion.

The prosecution can never comment on the failure of the defendant to testify. This can be more complicated than it first appears. Obviously, the prosecutor cannot argue that the jury should derive any conclusion from the defendant's failure to testify and even the most inexperienced prosecutor would understand this is improper. A prosecutor may be deemed to have commented on a defendant's failure to testify in other more indirect ways, however. For example, if a prosecutor asserts that some point or piece of evidence was "unrebutted" or "uncontested," that may be deemed a comment on the defendant's failure to testify or present a defense if the defendant is the only person who could have rebutted or contested the fact.

The prosecution cannot argue in a way as to shift the burden of proof to the defendant. Again, this can be trickier that it would first appear. Arguments by prosecutors that suggest or imply that a defendant should have presented evidence or called a witness or done something affirmative to counter the government's evidence can constitute an argument that shifts the burden of proof to the defense.

Neither attorney should ever use inflammatory appeals to the jury's passions or emotions. This includes appealing to the conscience of the community, or appealing to the jury's pity for the defendant. Juries should be making decisions based on the facts and the law. To suggest that the jury make a decision on any other ground is asking the jury to ignore the law and the facts.

Likewise, neither attorney should comment on or imply there is other evidence that was not presented in the trial. This can be difficult in some cases where significant or important evidence has been excluded by an order in limine or suppression order. The attorneys know this evidence exists and it sometimes happens that in the heat of closing arguments an attorney may slip up and make reference to such evidence, forgetting for the moment that it was not part of the case submitted to the jury.

Prosecutors and defense attorneys alike are not to misstate or mischaracterize the evidence. The court will often instruct the jury that in closing arguments the lawyers are attempting to summarize the evidence and will not intentionally misstate the evidence, but that the jury's recollection of the evidence should prevail if it is different from what the attorneys recall. Nevertheless, attorneys lose credibility with the jury if they makes erroneous statements about what the evidence was at trial.

Although either attorney may comment on any witnesses' demeanor while on the stand (including the defendant), the government may not make any reference to the defendant's courtroom demeanor while not on the stand. This is the case even if the defendant's demeanor was notable and obvious during the trial. For example, perhaps the defendant acted up during trial, or sat emotionless when a victim testified about some horrible act the defendant committed. Nevertheless, closing arguments are limited to the evidence admitted at trial. The evidence admitted at trial is limited to testimony under oath from the witness box, and tangible objects, documents, photos, or the like admitted as exhibits.

Finally, neither attorney should attack the other attorney, their ethics, their competency, or their motives. Frankly, neither attorney should reference the other attorney at all during closing arguments. Attorneys are simply agents for the party. It is far better to use the phrases "the defendant" or "the government" if necessary to refer to the opposing side or opposing argument. Making derogatory comments about opposing counsel can actually detract from the lawyer's credibility. Moreover, it is important that, as a matter of professionalism, attorneys show respect to each other. Each is performing the important duty of zealously representing his or her client. It is not personal and should not be made personal by attacks on opposing counsel.

In sum, attorneys practicing in federal court, either prosecuting or defending a case, are expected to live up to very high expectations of professionalism. Preparation, and careful thinking, can prevent errors in closing arguments. Although closing arguments should be persuasive and assertive, attorneys must always maintain restraint and not let their emotions overtake their intelligence. Fight hard, but fight fair.

CHAPTER 13

FEDERAL SENTENCING

■ ■ ■

The conviction of a criminal for committing a federal offense is not the end of the case. Sentencing of federal defendants often involves significant litigation and calls for effective advocacy by both sides. It requires lawyers to understand the intricacies of the Federal Sentencing Guidelines, the nuances of the law surrounding the shifting burdens of proof, and comprehension of Title 18, United States Code, Section 3553(a).

Since the advent of the Federal Sentencing Guidelines, the sentencing of defendants found guilty of federal offenses has become one of the most important and difficult aspects of federal criminal trials. Further, the importance of sentencing considerations becomes apparent not just after a defendant is found guilty, but during the investigation itself. Indeed, consideration of possible sentencing ramifications is important at nearly every stage of a federal prosecution. If federal agents conduct an investigation with a view toward finding evidence deemed important for sentencing a federal defendant, it can make a tremendous difference in the strength of the government's bargaining position and the ability of a defendant to mount a meaningful defense. Likewise, a federal defense attorney must conduct his or her investigation and defense with the sentencing guidelines in mind in order to take full advantage of those sections in the guidelines which can, when the appropriate facts are present, reduce a defendant's sentence.

In this section, we will briefly explore the history of sentencing within the federal system, and in particular, the changes that occurred with the adoption of the United States Sentencing Guidelines. Next we discuss the evolution of sentencing law from a system that, with limited exceptions, required sentencing judges to impose the sentence dictated by the guidelines, to a system where the guidelines are advisory. We will then discuss the frame work of the federal sentencing guidelines, including a review of those facts which the United States Sentencing Commission deemed important in arriving at an appropriate sentence. We will explore the interplay between statutory mandatory minimum and maximum sentence on the one hand, and the federal sentencing guidelines on the other. We will also discuss how and why both the government and defendants should and can conduct their investigations

195

and litigation with a view toward the guidelines in order to ensure that individual defendants are sentenced in an appropriate manner. We will explain the sentencing court's obligation to sentence federal criminal defendant's pursuant to the factors set forth at Title 18, United States Code, Section 3553(a). Finally, we will touch upon advocacy in federal criminal sentencing hearings.

A. HISTORY OF SENTENCING IN THE FEDERAL CRIMINAL JUSTICE SYSTEM

Sentencing, in a criminal justice system, encompasses the determination of both the type and extent of punishment imposed on a guilty defendant. Historically, the federal system utilized an indeterminate method of sentencing in which the type and extent of punishment were determined by all three branches of government—the legislative branch, the judicial branch and the executive branch. Under this system Congress first had input into the appropriate sentence by establishing a statutory maximum (and sometimes minimum) sentence that could be imposed for a particular crime. The judicial branch was given essentially unfettered discretion by the legislature to then determine the appropriate sentence in any given case, bound only by the statutory maximum and minimum sentences set forth in the appropriate statute. Finally, the executive branch was allotted limited discretion to release a prisoner on parole from the Federal Bureau of Prisons before the expiration of the term of imprisonment imposed by the sentencing judge.

This system came under significant criticism over time for a number of reasons. First, there was perceived to be great disparity in the sentences imposed by courts. A judge in Milwaukee may sentence a bank robber to seven years' incarceration, for example, while in an almost factually identical case a judge in New York may sentence a similarly situated defendant to one year in prison. Second, there was criticism about the uncertainty of the amount of time defendants would spend in jail. Not only was there a lack of predictability about the sentence that could be imposed by the court, there was uncertainty even when sentenced to a term of years that the defendant would actually serve that amount of time in prison. A defendant may be sentenced to ten years in prison, but be paroled in one. There grew to be a demand for what was called "truth in sentencing."

In the early 1980s Congress began seriously to consider changing the way federal courts conducted sentencing. Congress determined that it was time to reexamine the goals for and methods of imposing a criminal sanction. There are a number of goals in punishing a person, including retribution, rehabilitation, deterrence (specific and general), education and incapacitation. Congress determined that rehabilitation had failed and rejected imprisonment as a means of promoting rehabilitation. Congress also determined that sentences, to be fair, should be similar for people who are similarly situated and commit similar crimes. Finally, Congress determined that parole should be abolished and that the sentence imposed by a judge should, to a great degree, be the sentence actually served in order to promote certainty in sentencing.

In 1984 Congress passed the Sentencing Reform Act (Title II of the Comprehensive Crime Control Act of 1984) which was intended to bring about these changes. In this Act Congress created the United States Sentencing Commission and charged that body with the task of developing a new, reformed sentencing system. The original United States Sentencing Guidelines adopted by the Commission became effective on November 1, 1987. Although the Act, and the Guidelines promulgated pursuant to the Act, came under a barrage of attacks by defendants, courts and others, they withstood constitutional challenges. *See, e.g., Mistretta v. United States*, 488 U.S. 361 (1989).

Since their adoption in 1984, the Guidelines have been changed many times. At first, the changes were frequent and significant. As time passed, however, and some of the kinks were worked out, the changes came far less frequently and were less substantive. The mechanism is still in place, however, for Congress to make additional changes to the Guidelines when and where appropriate.

The guidelines, when first adopted, were deemed mandatory on sentencing courts. If the guidelines called for a sentence within a certain range based on the facts of the case and the defendant's criminal history, then the court was bound to sentence the defendant within that range, absent a ground to depart from the range authorized by the guidelines. That changed at the turn of the century.

B. FROM MANDATORY TO ADVISORY FEDERAL SENTENCING GUIDELINES

In a series of cases decided between 2000 and 2005, the Supreme Court resolved what it concluded was a conflict between the sentencing guidelines and the Sixth Amendment to the United States Constitution. In *Apprendi v. New Jersey*, 530 U.S. 466 (2000), *Ring v. Arizona*, 536 U.S. 584 (2002), *Blakely v. Washington*, 542 U.S. 296 (2004), and *United States v. Booker*, 543 U.S. 220 (2005), the Supreme Court concluded that the Sixth Amendment "proscribes a sentencing scheme that allows a judge to impose a sentence above the statutory maximum based on a fact, other than a prior conviction, not found by a jury or admitted by the defendant." *Cunningham v. California*, 549 U.S. 270, 274 (2007). In *Apprendi*, the Court held that, "[o]ther than the fact of a prior conviction, any fact that increases the penalty for a crime beyond the prescribed statutory maximum must be submitted to a jury, and proved beyond a reasonable doubt." 530 U.S. at 490. In *Ring*, the Court held that a grand jury must find, and the indictment reflect, any alleged fact that could, if found, increase the statutory maximum sentence to which a defendant is exposed. 536 U.S. at 609. In *Blakely*, the Court clarified that "the [relevant] 'statutory maximum' . . . is the maximum sentence a judge may impose solely on the basis of the facts reflected in the jury verdict or admitted by the defendant." 542 U.S. at 303. Finally, in *Booker*, the Court held that the United States Sentencing Guidelines were unconstitutional, to the extent that they were deemed mandatory. 543 U.S. at 245.

With this series of decisions spanning five years (during which, by the way, litigants and lower courts struggled with the consequences of the upheaval), the paradigm of the sentencing system underwent a seismic shift. Nevertheless, although the sentencing guidelines are no longer mandatory, the guidelines still significantly influence sentencing litigation. In *Booker*, the Supreme Court held that the guidelines could serve as just that—guidelines—as opposed to mandatory rules, and still comply with the United States Constitution. Sentencing courts must now consider the advisory guidelines as a starting place for determining the ultimate sentence, but must also consider all the factors set forth at Title 18, United States Code, Section 3553(a) in arriving at the appropriate sentence. Appellate courts are now charged with the responsibility to review sentences to determine if they are reasonable.

In the wake of *Booker*, many commentators, practitioners and judges predicted the federal sentencing guidelines would become largely irrelevant in sentencing federal criminal defendants. The reality has been different. The guidelines, although no longer mandatory, are recognized by the sentencing and appellate courts to be a compelling and persuasive means for achieving fairness and uniformity in sentencing in the federal system. Thus, by in large, sentencing courts follow the general contours of the guidelines, even though they are no longer mandatory. Indeed, the United States Supreme Court held that appellate courts may consider a sentence within the advisory guideline range to be presumptively reasonable. *See Rita v. United States*, 551 U.S. 338, 352 (2007). "Under an advisory Guidelines regime, sentencing judges are only required to find sentence-enhancing facts by a preponderance of the evidence." *United States v. Garcia-Gonon*, 433 F.3d 587, 593 (8th Cir. 2006) (citation omitted).

C. FRAMEWORK OF THE UNITED STATES SENTENCING GUIDELINES

A description of the structure of the United States Sentencing Guidelines, and the competing interests that led to the development of the Guidelines is set forth in great detail in Chapter 1, Part A— Introduction, to the United States Sentencing Guidelines. Rather than repeat what is set forth in that section, you are encouraged to read that ten-page section. Here we will provide a more concise explanation of the guidelines.

There are eight chapters in the United States Sentencing Guidelines Manual. Chapter 1 contains the introduction and, as mentioned above, a description of "General Application Principles." Chapter 2 sets forth "Offense Conduct," which will be explained in more detail below. Chapter 3 is a section that deals with adjustments to the offense conduct calculations for aggravating or mitigating circumstances, such as victim-related factors, role in the offense, obstruction of justice, multiple counts, and acceptance of responsibility. Chapter 4 sets for the guidelines for determining a defendant's criminal history. Chapter 5 provides the direction for determining the appropriate sentence based upon the defendant's offense conduct and his criminal history, and provides grounds for a court to depart from the guidelines. Chapter 6 addresses the impact of plea agreements and provides for sentencing procedures. Chapter 7 indicates what would happen in the event that a defendant, once sentenced, violates the terms of the sentence or supervised release. Finally, Chapter 8 of the Guidelines Manual establishes the guidelines for sentencing organizations, as opposed to individuals.

The United States Sentencing Guidelines are based on some fundamental conceptions. To begin with, the Commission determined that there were two basic factors which should determine a defendant's sentence: (1) his offense conduct and (2) his criminal history. In order to create consistency in sentencing, the Commission established a point system for determining offense conduct and a point system for determining a defendant's criminal history. Then, establishing a grid with offense conduct on the vertical axis and criminal history on the horizontal axis, a defendant's sentence would be determined by plotting the combination of a defendant's offense conduct and criminal history. Starting in the upper left-hand corner of the chart, the points increase for offense conduct as one travels down the vertical axis and likewise increases for criminal history points as one travels to the right on the horizontal axis. The greater the number of points a defendant has in both these categories, the greater a defendant's sentence will be.

Once the offense level is established for a crime and the criminal history points are calculated, the two are plotted on the chart and establish a sentencing range. The range varies from six months for short sentences to years for relatively lengthy sentences. A sentencing judge has essentially unfettered discretion to determine the sentence within the range, so long as the sentence is not based on some unconstitutional reason (such as a defendant's sex, race, etc.). Further, the Guidelines permit the sentencing judge to depart from the sentencing range in certain cases where it can be shown that the individual defendant's characteristics or offense characteristics fall "outside the heartland" of cases contemplated by the Commission in creating the guidelines. 18 U.S.C. § 3553(b). This includes motions by the government to depart in exchange for cooperation by a defendant.

1.   THE OFFENSE LEVEL

The first step in determining a defendant's sentence, under the United States Sentencing Guidelines, is to determine the defendant's offense level (the defendant's location on the vertical axis). The Sentencing Commission established a "base offense level" for each crime. This offense level was determined by looking historically at the sentences imposed in 10,000 cases involving a large number of crimes. Using this historic data, the Commission attempted to assign base offense levels for each crime reflecting, statistically, the relative punishment historically imposed for each type of crime. Thus, for example, historically bank robbery was punished more harshly than bank larceny. Thus, bank robbery has a higher base offense level than bank larceny. Murder, however, was historically punished more harshly than bank robbery, so it has an even higher base offense level. Over time these "base offense levels" have been adjusted in response to new data or for other reasons deemed appropriate by Congress.

Thus, to determine a defendant's base offense level, a prosecutor or defense attorney first consults Appendix A to the United States Sentencing Guidelines. Appendix A contains a reference to almost every federal criminal statute that will direct a lawyer to a specific section in Chapter 2 of the Guidelines. Then a lawyer will turn to the indicated chapter section and there will find a "base offense level" for the offense. For example, if you had a case involving the distribution of controlled substances, a violation of Title 21, United States Code, Section 841(a), you would look in Appendix A for that code section and discover that the offense level for that crime is located at Section 2D1.1 of the Guidelines Manual.

Now, that sounds too simple to be true, and it is. First, there are some federal criminal statutes not included in Appendix A. Second, when you look up some statutes in Appendix A, it refers you to 4, 5, or in some cases up to 15 different sections in Chapter 2 (e.g., Title 21, United States Code, Section 846 (drug conspiracy) directs lawyers to 15 different sections of Chapter 2). The general rule of construction to overcome these and similar difficulties is that the sentencing court is to apply the most appropriate guideline section.

The United States Sentencing Commission recognized that there will be factors present in every case which may justify a sentence which should be higher or lower than in another case for a violation of the same statute. Accordingly, the Sentencing Commission created a system whereby these relevant factors could be taken into account to adjust a defendant's sentence from the base offense level. Generally, these factors fall into two categories: (1) offense characteristics; and (2) aggravating or mitigating factors.

Offense characteristics are specific to the offense in question and are found in the Chapter 2 section for the offense. For example, the base offense level for a defendant who was convicted of being a felon in possession of a firearm may be 14. USSG § 2K2.1(a)(6). Congress decided, however, that if such a defendant possessed many firearms, not just one, then his base offense level should be increased. USSG § 2K2.1(b)(1). Likewise, if he possessed stolen weapons, then he is deemed more criminally culpable than a similar defendant who possessed weapons which were not stolen, such that the former should be punished more harshly than the latter. USSG § 2K2.1(b)(4). On the other hand, if the defendant only possessed the firearms solely for hunting or sporting purposes, then his sentence should be less than that of another felon who possessed the firearms for some unlawful purpose. USSG § 2K2.1(b)(2). Each offense section contains one or more such "offense characteristic" adjustments which may be applied in an appropriate case.

Aggravating and mitigating factors are more general and apply regardless of the offense in question. For example, regardless of the offense, if the defendant is shown to be a leader or organizer of others in the commission of the underlying offense, he should be punished more harshly than someone else. USSG § 3B1.1. On the other hand, if the defendant is shown to have occupied a minimal or minor role in the offense, then he should receive a lighter sentence than the average defendant. USSG § 3B1.2. There is a number of such aggravating or mitigating factors listed in Chapter 3 of the Guidelines, including reductions for acceptance of responsibility, given when a defendant pleads guilty.

2. THE CRIMINAL HISTORY SCORE

Once a defendant's offense level is determined, then the next step is to determine the defendant's criminal history score. This is determined by reference to Chapter 4 of the Guidelines. Congress determined that a person with a criminal history should be punished more harshly than a person without a criminal history. Likewise, a person with a serious criminal history should be punished more harshly than a person with a minor criminal history. Thus, in creating a new sentencing system under the Guidelines, Congress provided for a point system whereby a defendant was given points for each prior conviction. The more points a defendant had, the greater the sentence would be.

The points are awarded for each prior qualifying conviction. The word "qualifying" is used because the Guidelines exclude some prior convictions deemed too minor to be counted (disturbing the peace, for example), regardless of how harshly that crime may have been punished at the time. Further, certain convictions are excluded if they are too old, or for other similar reasons where it was deemed unfair to impose criminal history points.

Generally, the greater the sentence imposed at the time of the prior conviction, the greater the number of criminal history points that will be imposed on the defendant. Essentially the Commission concluded that the length of sentence imposed for a prior offense is the best surrogate for determining the seriousness of the prior offense. For example, if a person was sentenced to more than one year and one month in prison for a prior robbery, the defendant gets three criminal history points. USSG § 4A1.1(a). If the sentence was for more than 60 days, but less than one-year and one-month, then the defendant gets two criminal history points. USSG § 4A1.1(b). The underlying offense may be the same in each case (say, for example, robbery), but the greater sentence in the first case suggests that the offense was presumably more serious than in the second case or else the sentencing judge would not have imposed that sentence. The guidelines provide for many adjustments and nuances in determining the number of criminal history points, taking into account such things as whether the sentence was suspended, and other such matters.

Once the number of points is determined, then the next step is to determine the defendant's Criminal History Category based on the number of points scored. If a defendant has 0 to 1 criminal history points, then he will be placed in Criminal History Category I, the first vertical column on the Guidelines Sentencing Chart. If a defendant has 2 or 3 criminal history points, then he is placed in Criminal History Category II. This system continues up until the last criminal history category (VI), for those with 13 or more criminal history points. Again, the Guidelines provide for an adjustment by allowing the sentencing court to depart upward or downward from the final sentencing range if it is determined that a defendant's criminal history score unfairly over- or under-represents the seriousness of the defendant's criminal history.

The guidelines also provide for scoring certain defendants as career criminals. USSG § 4B1.1. Under this Section, if a defendant is: (1) at least

18 years old; (2) has two or more prior felony convictions for crimes of violence or controlled substances; and (3) the instant offense involves a violent crime or controlled substances, then the defendant is determined to be a career offender. In such cases, the prior calculation of offense level is thrown out the window. In its place, the defendant's offense level is determined by the maximum statutory sentence that could be imposed for the instant offense (*e.g.*, if life, then the offense level is 37; if 25 years or more, then the offense level is 34). USSG § 4B1.1. Further, the defendant is placed in Criminal History Category VI, regardless of how he would otherwise have scored given his number of criminal history points. As the term "Career Criminal" suggests, the belief is such defendants need to be punished more harshly because of their career in crime than the guidelines might otherwise call for with respect to another defendant who had not made a career out of crime.

D. INTERPLAY BETWEEN STATUTES AND GUIDELINES PROVISIONS

The simple rule to remember is: "statutes trump guidelines." In other words, if there is a conflict between a statutory penalty and the penalty called for under the Guidelines, the statutory penalty prevails. For example, if a statute provides for a mandatory minimum sentence of five years for distribution of a controlled substance, yet the guidelines would call for a sentence of four years, the defendant must be sentenced to the statutory mandatory minimum of five years, regardless of what the guidelines would call for. Similarly, if the guidelines would call for a sentence of fifteen years for a defendant, but the statute provides for a maximum sentence of ten years, then the defendant may only be sentenced to ten years, regardless of what the guidelines would call for. While typically the guidelines do not conflict with statutory penalties, there are times when conflicts arise. Just remember—statutes trump guidelines.

If the criminal statute in question has a mandatory minimum sentence, there are only two ways for a court to impose a sentence below the mandatory minimum sentence. The first way is if the defendant qualifies under the so-called safety-valve provision. This is a section of the Guidelines regarding drug offenses which negates the effect of any mandatory minimum sentence if the defendant is essentially shown to be a very minor criminal and truthfully provides information to the government. To qualify, a defendant must meet five criteria, including having no more than one criminal history point, having no involvement with dangerous weapons or violence in the commission of the offense, is not a leader, and provides a full confession of his criminal conduct to the government no later than the time of his sentencing. The only other way for a court to impose a sentence below a mandatory minimum sentence is pursuant to a motion by the government to depart in exchange for the defendant's cooperation. 18 U.S.C. § 3553(e). Absent a defendant qualifying for safety-valve, or getting a motion from the government, there is no way for a sentencing court to impose a sentence below the statutory mandatory minimum sentence.

E. IMPACT OF THE SENTENCING GUIDELINES ON FEDERAL CRIMINAL INVESTIGATIONS

The United States Sentencing Guidelines can significantly impact a federal criminal case from its inception. Government prosecutors and defense attorneys must keep them in mind at all stages of the investigation through the trial. There are several reasons for this emphasis on the Guidelines.

The Guidelines provide each side a great degree of certainty in determining the ultimate sentence, if the necessary facts are known. This greater certainty permits more intelligent and effective plea bargaining by both sides. Whereas before the adoption of the guidelines neither the government nor the defendant could predict with any certainty the sentence that would be imposed if the defendant was found guilty of an offense, now each side is better able to predict the outcome in a given case if they know of all of the relevant offense conduct, aggravating and mitigating factors, and the defendant's criminal history.

The difficulty comes in knowing the necessary facts. Federal agents and defense investigators must be trained to investigate the case with the guidelines in mind. For example, an untrained agent may not realize that there is a sentencing enhancement for a defendant who sells controlled substances to a minor. If she does not know of this sentencing enhancement, she may not obtain admissible evidence to prove that it occurred. Absent the evidence, the defendant will not be sentenced as he should have been.

Knowledge of the guidelines is also important to determine whether and when to enter into a plea. The Guidelines and the impact of any mandatory minimum sentences may be such that a defendant gains nothing simply by pleading guilty. Further, the Guidelines award a greater reduction for pleading guilty early than waiting until shortly before trial to enter a guilty plea. Similarly, the government may discover that a defendant's sentence in a given case will not be worth the investment in time and resources to justify further investigation or prosecution in a given case, or may determine that a defendant can be more effectively prosecuted by the state in a given case.

The criminal sanction imposed upon the defendant is, perhaps, the most important part of any criminal case. Without a thorough knowledge of how the United States Sentencing Guidelines apply in a given case, therefore, a prosecutor or defense attorney would be flying blindly through an investigation without any real idea of where he or she was going to land.

F. TITLE 18, UNITED STATES CODE, SECTION 3553(a)

The appropriate guideline sentence is the first, but not only, thing a sentencing court must consider in determining the appropriate sentence in a federal criminal case. A federal judge is also to impose sentence based on the factors set forth at 18 U.S.C. § 3553(a). As a general matter, the court is to impose a sentence that is "sufficient, but not greater than necessary, to comply with the purposes" of sentencing as set forth in § 3553(a)(2). Title 18, United States Code, Section 3553(a), sets out the following factors to guide a judge's sentence:

(1) The nature and circumstances of the offense and the history and characteristics of the defendant;

(2) The need for the sentence imposed—

(A) To reflect the seriousness of the offense, to promote respect for the law, and to provide just punishment for the offense;

(B) To afford adequate deterrence to criminal conduct;

(C) To protect the public from further crimes of the defendant, and;

(D) To provide the defendant with needed educational or vocational training, medical care, or other correctional treatment in the most effective manner;

(3) The kinds of sentences available;

(4) The kinds of sentence and the sentencing range established for—

(A) The applicable category of offense committed by the applicable category of defendant as set forth in the guidelines. . . .

18 U.S.C. § 3553(a).

Under the current system, the guidelines are only advisory and a sentencing judge is not bound by them. The guidelines are just that—guidelines for a sentencing judge to consider in structuring the appropriate sentence. A sentencing judge may vary from the guidelines and impose any other sentence authorized under the statute (bound by the statutory minimum and maximum penalties). This is so regardless of whether the facts of the case would support a "departure" from the advisory guidelines sentence under the departure provisions of the guidelines. For example, if a bank robber's advisory guidelines sentence calls for a sentence within the range of ten to twelve years, and no facts would support a departure from that guidelines sentence under the departure provisions of the guidelines, a judge may nevertheless sentence the defendant to probation based on the judge's consideration of the history and characteristics of the defendant or based on some other factor listed under § 3553(a). A judge is free to assign whatever weight the judge believes appropriate to the factors set out in § 3553(a). Ultimately, if a judge choses to vary from the advisory guidelines sentence, that decision is provided significant discretion on appeal and will be overturned only if an appellate court finds the sentence imposed to be unreasonable.

In a very real sense, then, the sentencing methodology in federal court has returned to one where federal judges have largely unfettered discretion to impose a sentence the judge deems appropriate, bound only by any mandatory minimum sentence and the maximum sentence imposed by Congress in the statute. The guidelines help structure a sentencing judge's analysis of the appropriate sentence, but otherwise are not binding in any way upon a judge. The concept of "truth in sentencing" remains from the 1984 reform, however, in the sense that there is no parole in the federal system. A defendant must serve the entire sentence imposed, reduced only up to approximately 13% for good time if the defendant behaves while incarcerated.

As a matter of advocacy, both prosecutors and defense attorneys should recognize that federal sentencing provides an opportunity to persuade the court as to the appropriate sentence. Judges have great discretion to determine the sentence, so lawyers must view the sentencing hearing as an opportunity to bring advocacy skills to bear on the sentencing court to push for the sentence the lawyer thinks is most important. Lawyers should present arguments and offer evidence that directly address the factors set forth at 18 U.S.C. § 3553(a). Sentencing is the last opportunity, before the appellate process, for lawyers to use advocacy to affect the outcome of a federal criminal case.

G. ADVOCACY IN FEDERAL SENTENCING

Lawyers who practice federal criminal law, either as prosecutors or defense attorneys, need to realize that sentencing hearings require advocacy just as much as any other stage of a federal criminal case. The guidelines and the factors at 18 U.S.C. § 3553(a) provide a basis for each side to argue why the law, facts of the crime, and history and characteristics of the defendant should call for a stiffer or more lenient sentence.

Sentencing advocacy starts prior to the actual sentencing hearing. Prior to the sentencing hearing the United States Probation Office will generate a Presentence Investigation Report ("PSR"). The PSR sets out a factual summary of the offense conduct, calculates the defendant's offense level under the guidelines, determines the defendant's criminal history score, and contains a summary of the defendant's personal history, including family, education, employment, and physical and mental health history. The parties have an opportunity to lodge objections to the PSR, including any objections to the facts in the PSR or the probation office's determination of the guidelines provisions.

Also in advance of the sentencing hearing, the parties will often submit lengthy sentencing briefs. The briefs will typically outline the facts deemed relevant to the sentencing issues, and point out any factual disputes that remain. The sentencing briefs also analyze the legal issues at play regarding application of the guidelines, departures from the guidelines, or variances from the advisory guidelines sentence pursuant to the factors at 18 U.S.C. § 3553(a).

In federal criminal practice, sentencing hearings can be litigated as much or more than a trial on the merits of the case. In some instances, sentencing hearings can last days with the parties calling scores of witnesses. The parties may call expert witnesses to testify about the defendant's mental or physical health. Because a sentencing judge may sentence a defendant based on relevant criminal conduct, even if not the conduct that resulted in a conviction, evidence of other crimes may also be presented during a sentencing hearing. Parties should prepare for a sentencing hearing much as they prepare for trial. This includes identifying witnesses and exhibits, creating an outline of questions, meeting with and preparing witnesses for their testimony, and structuring the presentation in a manner that is compelling and persuasive.

The federal rules of evidence do not apply at a federal sentencing hearing. Therefore, for example, hearsay is admissible. Sentencing judges retain substantial discretion, however, to control the admissibility of evidence and are free to give whatever weight they deem appropriate to the evidence. Although the rules of evidence do not apply, a defendant's Sixth Amendment right of confrontation remains. Therefore, the government must produce witnesses so the defendant can cross examine the witness.

As with other hearings, such as preliminary hearings or detention hearings, the judge is the fact finder. Lawyers are wise to adjust their advocacy with this in mind. Federal judges will typically have spent considerable time reviewing the PSR and the parties briefs and will by very familiar with the law regarding sentencing issues. It is still important to present a case that is persuasive, but advocates should make the presentation as efficient and cogent as possible, trusting that the judge will be able to comprehend and follow the evidence and the law.

INDEX

References are to Pages